Celebrating the Jewish Year

The Spring and Summer Holidays

Celebrating the Jewish Year

The Spring and Summer Holidays

Passover ▲ The Omer ▲ Shavuot ▲ Tisha b'Av

Paul Steinberg

Edited by Janet Greenstein Potter

JPS
Nourishing Mind and Spirit
2009 • 5769
Philadelphia

JPSis a nonprofit educational association and the oldest and foremost publisher of Judaica in English in North America. The mission of JPS is to enhance Jewish culture by promoting the dissemination of religious and secular works, in the United States and abroad, to all individuals and institutions interested in past and contemporary Jewish life.

The Jewish Publication Society
2100 Arch Street, 2nd floor
Philadelphia, PA 19103
www.jewishpub.org

Design and Composition by Masters Group Design

Interior artwork by Adam Rhine, with permission frm the artist, www.HebrewArt.com

Cover artwork by Adam Rhine, with permission from Sounds True, 413 S. Arthur Avenue, Louisville, CO 80027

Manufactured in the United States of America

10 9 8 7 6 5 4 3

ISBN: 978-0-8276-0876-9 (volume 1)
ISBN: 978-0-8276-0849-8 (volume 2)
ISBN: 978-0-8276-0850-4 (volume 3)

Library of Congress Cataloging-in-Publication Data

Steinberg, Paul.
  Celebrating the Jewish year / Paul Steinberg ; Janet Greenstein Potter, editor. — 1st ed.
  v. cm.
  Includes bibliographical references and index.
  Contents: v. 1. The fall holidays: Rosh Hashanah, Yom Kippur, Sukkot
  ISBN 978-0-8276-0842-9 (alk. paper)
  1. Fasts and feasts—Judaism. 2. Calendar, Jewish. I. Potter, Janet Greenstein. II. Title.
  BM690.S72 2007
  296.4'3—dc22
  2007010805

Publisher's Note:
With few exceptions, the essays taken from other sources are as they appear in their original. As a result, there are variations in spelling and language from piece to piece.

JPS books are available at discounts for bulk purchases for reading groups, special sales, and fundraising purchases. Custom editions, including personalized covers, can be created in larger quantities for special needs. For more information, please contact us at marketing@jewishpub.org or at this address:
2100 Arch Street, Philadelphia, PA 19103.

To my teachers

There is one who ascends with all these songs in unison—
the song of the soul, the song of the nation, the song of humanity,
the song of the cosmos—resounding together, blending in harmony,
circulating the sap of life, the sound of holy joy.

—Abraham Isaac Kook

Contents

Part 3: The Omer

Part 4: Shavuot

Acknowledgments

This book has undergone several transformations. It began as one thing, and only because of the grace and guidance of Janet Greenstein Potter, the developmental editor, does it arrive in its current form. I am indebted to her undying persistence in pursuit of excellence and her careful reading of the manuscript. If there are any errors, they are indeed my own.

I must also acknowledge all of my teachers who have helped and supported me in my learning from the American Jewish University and from the Ziegler School of Rabbinic Studies. The Ziegler School is a unique place of study, one that embodies the essence of both academic integrity and the true spirit of Torah learning. I am especially grateful to two of my rabbis there: Bradley Shavit Artson and Elliott Dorff. Thank you for being my models of *hokhmah, yirat Shamayim,* and *hesed.*

Furthermore, I am thankful to those who generously contributed original pieces for this volume, namely rabbis Alan Abrams, Bradley Shavit Artson, Michael Berenbaum, Daniel Cotzin Burg, Pinchas Giller, Arthur Green, Reuven Hammer, Adam Naftalin-Kelman, Marc Soloway, and David Wolpe.

Finally and most of all, I thank my wife, Maureen, and our children, Rina and Nili, for your patience and support. You are my greatest teachers of all.

I would also like to extend my gratitude for permission to use material from the following sources:

"Thoughts on Cleaning for Pesach" by Haviva Ner-David in *The Women's Passover Companion,* ed. Sharon Cohen Anisfeld, Tara Mohr, and Catherine Spector (Woodstock, Vt.: Jewish Lights Publishing, 2003), 49–53.

"The Debate on Machine-Made Matzot" by Philip Goodman in *The Passover Anthology* (Philadelphia: The Jewish Publication Society, 1961), 90–92.

"Welcoming Strangers to Your Seder" by Mark I. Rosen. First appeared on www.jewishfamily.com, a Web site copyrighted by Jewish Family and Life!/JFLmedia, Boston and Washington, D.C.

Arnold M. Eisen, *Taking Hold of Torah: Jewish Community and Commitment in America* (Bloomington: Indiana University Press, 1997), 40–46.

Irving Greenberg, *The Jewish Way: Living the Holidays* (New York: Touchstone Books, 1988), 73–75.

Alan Lew, *This Is Real and You Are Completely Unprepared: The Days of Awe as a Journey of Transformation* (New York: Little, Brown & Company, 2003), 52–63.

◀━━━━━━━━━━━━━━━●━━━━━━━━━━━━━━━▶

The book epigraph is from *Orot Ha-Kodesh* 2:444–45 by Rabbi Avraham Isaac Kook, translated by Daniel C. Matt in *The Essential Kabbalah* (New York: Quality Paperback Book Club, 1995), 154.

Introduction

Spring and Summer and the Holidays of Promise

Spring is the season of life. Its days are fertile, ripe with potential. Bees buzz and flowers bloom, while greens and yellows warm us and light up the day. Contrasted to the spiritual accounting and deep reflection that occur during the holidays of fall—Rosh Hashanah, Yom Kippur, and Sukkot—the holidays of spring are more forward looking. Rather than focusing on accumulation and preparation for winter, spring is about planting. We look out at the green pastures and the budding of the physical world, and we are filled with the excitement of possibility. No wonder Nisan, the quintessential spring month, is the appropriate time for Passover, the festival that reunites us with our Jewish identity. Celebrated with foods that help us relive the Israelites' escape from Egypt and their subsequent wandering in the desert, Passover is a festive, optimistic time of spiritual spring-cleaning. The liturgy that harmonizes Jewish voices worldwide—the Passover haggadah—sings a truly Jewish love song, encouraging us to dip into our unforgotten, salty past and toast our undying dreams for the future. Spring is the season of victory and hope.

The enthusiasm of spring, however, winds down during the Omer, as we count each day of these seven weeks to the holiday of Shavuot, for we are aware that beyond the heights of the spring mountain lays the parched summer valley. With the sliding of spring into summer comes a spiritual paradox, in which we try to balance the exuberance of the passing season with the fatigue of the one ahead. Shavuot, commemorating the giving of the Torah, becomes the spiritual turning point. The simple enthusiasm found in the youthful months of the year grows into the turmoil of summer adolescence. Praying for strength as we enter summer, we dedicate the first fruits of the spring harvest to God; and we are given God's first fruit, the Torah, to see us through our struggles. Inevitably, the destruction and spiritual crisis of Tisha b'Av arrive, and we fast in commemoration of five great tragedies.

The summer presses onward. Yet, once beyond the rock-bottom of Tisha b'Av, the autumn light of the new year—Rosh Hashanah—beckons to us and will renew our vigor. The romance is rekindled between heaven and earth, as the olives in Israel begin to ripen, filling with the nourishing juices of life and growing plump with oil before the fall harvest. The prophetic songs of comfort ease our spirits, as the weeks turn back to the starting point, back to the spark that caused the world to come into being.

Framework of This Book

THE JEWISH TRADITIONS ARE ROOTED in certain assumptions about the meaning of human existence and the world in which we live. Such assumptions play out in Jewish holiday observance and ideology. The first part of the book explores those foundational beliefs, particularly focusing on how the holidays provide a space in our lives for connection with spirituality. Then each of the four holiday sections includes a discussion of the holiday's biblical and historical origins, followed by several explorations of its special ideology and customs. Although synagogue ritual is touched upon, the primary focus of the book is on personal, communal, and home customs and their rationale. These are often the clearest expression of the encounter between the spirit and the world.

Another one of the most significant forms of spiritual expression in Judaism is found in the study of texts. As Rabbi Louis Finkelstein of the Jewish Theological Seminary has said, "When I pray I talk to God, but when I study, God talks to me." To help us experience the diversity of viewpoints held and traditions practiced throughout time, each holiday section also includes four groups of writings. In the first group, "Pathways Through the Sources," we look at writings from some of the greatest Jewish thinkers in history, each of which reflects an ideological aspect of the holiday. The richness of these sources invites your own analysis to discover the many treasures each text possesses.

The Jewish tradition teaches that we learn sacred texts on different levels of understanding. Thus in the second group of selections, "Interpretations of Sacred Texts," are passages that I examine at three levels, the first two of which follow traditional patterns of commentary. The first level is *peshat*, the literal, most obvious meaning of the text. The second is *derash*, an interpretation that incorporates explanations of the text given over thousands of years of rabbinical and historical inquiry. The third is "Making It Personal," my own interpretation, which addresses new ways by which we today may identify with this sacred text and apply it to our lives. I hope that by following these three levels of interpretation you will be enabled to grow cognitively along with the development of ideas in the text. If you ease the integration of the text into your personal life, ultimately it may become a part of your self-knowledge. These three levels—two that are traditional and one that is more modern—reflect the ways we converse and build relationships with the voices of the past, and how those voices live on through us.

The third group of selections, "Significance of the Holiday," comprises contributions, original to this book, from renowned scholars and rabbis of our time. These essays discuss the historical development of the holiday in that section, as well as its theological, ethical, agricultural, and seasonal meanings. Also provided are additional essays on important themes and practices unique to particular holidays.

Judaism has always recognized that the truth can be understood only in a multiplicity of voices and manners. The fourth group of selections for each holiday section is "Alternative Meditations." These include essays, stories, and anecdotes that add profound expression to a holiday in a nonclassical, innovative manner. The volume is rounded out in part 6, "Guidance along the Way," which includes sketches of many traditional sources and scholars—guideposts on our spiritual journey through the holidays.

PART I

Spirituality in Time and Place

*Happy are Israel! They are honored to hold this pledge of the Ruler on High.
Because, even though they are in exile, every new moon and Sabbath
and festival the Holy One blessed be He comes to watch over them,
gazing at His pledge that is with them, His treasure.*

— Zohar 3:114

From the Desert to the Heart

WHAT DO WE DO IN OUR LIVES that we would describe as "spiritual"? Surely this question evokes different or multiple responses from each of us. For some, spending time with our family or children might be our definition of spiritual. For others, lighting Shabbat (Sabbath) candles or engaging in traditional prayer and study may satisfy our conception of spiritual. For many, watching the sun rise is the quintessence of spiritual. Whatever our notions of spiritual may be or include, they share with each other something important about the human experience: They capture a flicker within the soul, a moment when the walls separating heaven and earth collapse. The spiritual moment is a pure one, during which the present alone exists. Mind, being, and spirit are no longer independent but clearly in harmony with the universe. In this encounter, we perceive ourselves as wholly alive.

Is any one place more conducive to such a spiritual experience than another? The answer from many Jews would be Israel, because Jews have always understood the Land of Israel to be imbued with pervasive spirituality. As a holy land, Israel can bring forth the spiritual potential in a person and nurture it. In fact, Jerusalem—especially the Western Wall of the Temple Mount—is the most universally accepted site of spiritual association for Jews. The city is deeply connected to the Bible, in particular the Torah (the Five Books of Moses) as the place where many revelatory moments occur.[1] One might say that the following words of the psalmist are branded on our hearts: "If I forget you, O Jerusalem, let my right hand wither" (Ps. 137:5).

Jerusalem, although hilly, is part of the southern desert region of Israel; for that reason, its spiritual significance can be seen in even broader terms of place. In the Jewish tradition, the desert or wilderness (*midbar* in Hebrew) is generally understood to be a site of profound spiritual connection. It is in a desert that Moses encounters God in the burning bush;[2] it is in a desert that the Israelites spend 40 years of wandering after fleeing the slavery of Egypt; and it is in a desert, at Mount Sinai, that God reveals God's self, when giving the Torah to the entire Jewish people.

The Rabbinic sages noted the apparent association between revelation, prophecy, and the desert. They interpreted the desert to be a place of inherent symbolism and thereby extracted meaning and lessons about life from the desert's role in the Bible. In midrash (a body of work that includes theological, homiletical, and ethical lore) the Rabbis say:

> Why was the Torah given in the desert? It is to teach us that anyone who does not make one's self as empty and un-entitled as the desert cannot acquire wisdom or Torah—and that is why the Torah was given at Sinai.[3]

The point of connection between the desert and the giving of the Torah for the Rabbis is the "empty and un-entitled" character of the desert landscape and the personality of the one who receives Torah. That is, the fact that the Torah was given in the desert, an unassuming and modest region, teaches us that to receive Torah we, too, should be unassuming and modest. The Talmud (the central and most important body of Rabbinic literature) reinforces this connection, as it says, "One should be as open as the desert to receive the Torah."[4]

Thus the Rabbis interpret the physical makeup of the desert as a metaphor for our own spiritual disposition. They see humility in the sparse and arid conditions of the uninhabited desert, which represents humility of spirit. In this way, the terrain mirrors the soul.

Yet, despite the open, quiet humility of the desert, there is latent power, intrinsically contained by the natural boundaries of brown pebbles and silent heat. In the absence of water, the desert contracts into its extreme dryness and conceals its intrinsic force. This potential vigor is long withheld until, suddenly, thunder and lightning bring forth a torrent of rain. Fertilized by the heavens above, the desert finally blooms, erupting in beauty. And then it hides again, secluded and waiting to be found. This eternal cycle of renewal integrates the many components of nature and unites heaven and earth. Is it any wonder that our ancient ancestors discovered monotheism in the desert? The desert, we learn, is a place from which God speaks, as the prophet Isaiah once proclaimed:

> A voice rings out:
> "Clear in the desert
> A road for the LORD!"
> —Isaiah 40:3

Spirituality happens naturally in a place like the desert precisely because it is empty and unsettled. The prophets of the Jewish tradition discovered God in the emptiness, outside of culture and settlements, where life remains unknown and passes slowly. In this unknown there is an element of humility, as the harmony of nature reigns. There, away from both the world of the mundane and the noise, they could listen to what they did not hear before—the still, small voice—and see things in their natural settings. From these desert borderlands, the prophets would then return to the settlements as people spiritually sated and inspired to teach and preach what they had learned.

Today, we seem to be unceasingly plugged into days filled with commonplace concerns and rapid-fire information. Loyally attached to our cell phones and portable Internet access, we find ourselves neglecting the gradual, deliberate wisdom of experiencing nature and history. Yet in our hearts, we are struggling to leave the plodding confines of modern society and reclaim the spirit of the desert.

In Judaism, there is a way to break from the intellectual irons of civilization and taste the spiritual nourishment of arid land. We can do so by celebrating the Jewish holidays, the bricks that make up the Jewish path of celebration and joy. They bring us together with our families to share meals; they inject us into the greater community of Jews where we learn, pray, and sing together; and they infuse us with an appreciation of the rhythms of nature and the seasons, helping us to see the universe through God's eyes. The holidays provide a way to step out of our daily life and participate in something much bigger, something eternal. Built around the cycle of the year, they offer both variety and depth of expression that help us satisfy our inherent yearning for spirituality. They touch our hearts, nourish our minds, and rouse our spirits. Judaism offers us these beautiful holidays, which bring the openness, humility, and renewal of the desert into our lives.

PART 2

Passover

When, in time to come, your children ask you, "What mean the decrees, laws, and rules that the LORD our God has enjoined upon you?" You shall say to your children, "We were slaves to Pharaoh in Egypt and the LORD freed us from Egypt with a mighty hand. The LORD wrought before our eyes marvelous and destructive signs and portents in Egypt, against Pharaoh and all his household; and us He freed from there, that He might take us and give us the land that He had promised on oath to our fathers. Then the LORD commanded us to observe all these laws, to revere the LORD our God, for our lasting good and for our survival, as is now the case. It will be therefore to our merit before the LORD our God to observe faithfully this whole Instruction, as He has commanded us."

—Deuteronomy 6:20–25

Freedom and Responsibility

ASSOVER CAN BE READILY defined by its unique, highly detailed laws and customs observed for eight days during the early spring month of Nisan. But if we look more expansively, behind and beyond our understanding of the religious practices and family customs, we see that Passover, of all the Jewish holidays, most clearly defines what it means to be a Jew. It is the biblical Passover story—the flight of the Israelites from Egypt—that provides the spiritual force of the celebration. The saga of the Exodus points to the core principles that underlie every Jewish value and inform the purpose of Jewish existence. We touch upon this story in our daily liturgy, at our weekly Sabbath dinner table, and when observing each festival throughout the year. During the Passover holiday itself, we recount and relive the story in its entirety.

It begins with the world before the Jewish nation was formed, at a time when the descendants of "Israel," the name God gave to the patriarch Jacob, arrived in Egypt. After living and thriving there for centuries, the Israelites are enslaved by a new Pharaoh who proclaims, "… the Israelite people are much too numerous for us" (Exod. 1:9). Despite ruthless treatment, the Israelites—with their distinctive spiritual ancestry—retain a special relationship with God. An unlikely and reluctant leader named Moses emerges from their midst; and with the help of his brother, Aaron, and his sister, Miriam, acts as an instrument of God's will. Through events that can be understood only as miraculous, the Israelites are able to escape servitude and become free. The story conveys to us that freedom was afforded to this new nation not for the sake of freedom alone but for the promise that each person would take responsibility for himself or herself and, moreover, for anyone who suffers. As we are reminded:

A Day of Many Names

The Hebrew word for the Passover festival is Pesach (PAY-sakh), which comes from the Hebrew three-letter root *peh.samekh.chet.*, likely meaning to pass through, to pass over, to exempt, or to spare. During the last of the 10 plagues, just before the Exodus, God "passed over" the houses of the Jews and killed only the firstborn of the Egyptians. The word *pesach* also refers to the animal (according to the Bible, a yearling sheep or goat) that was sacrificed at Passover in the Holy Temple in Jerusalem. As with most other Jewish holidays, Passover has additional descriptive names: *Hag Ha-Aviv* (The Festival, or Feast, of Spring), *Hag Ha-Matzot* (The Festival, or Feast, of Unleavened Breads), and *Zeman Herutenu* (Season of Our Liberation).

For the LORD your God is God supreme and LORD supreme, the great, the mighty and the awesome God, who shows no favor and takes no bribe, but upholds the cause of the fatherless and the widow, and befriends the stranger, providing him with food and clothing.—You too must befriend the stranger, for you were strangers in the land of Egypt.

—Deuteronomy 10:17–21

The Rabbis instruct us that in celebrating Passover, we are to see ourselves as having been individually and personally brought out of Egypt. Thus we know the experience of being raised up out of the depths of despair, on eagle's wings, to reach the peaks of hope, passion, and faithfulness. From such a vantage point, we are infused with gratitude and indebtedness to God. Humbled, we remember to always stand with and give assistance to the needy and downtrodden, to fight against intimidation, and to work unceasingly for justice.

SETTING THE STAGE

Although Passover officially begins on the 15th of the Hebrew month of Nisan (corresponding to March–April), our preparation begins weeks earlier. By the start of the eight-day holiday, we have made our homes "kosher for Passover," which means that any room in the house where food has been eaten must receive an extremely thorough cleaning. We remove from the house all foods that contain leavening, such as baked goods, cereal, bread, and grain alcohol, which the Torah forbids eating during Passover.[1] Such foods are called *hametz* (literally, "leaven"). Once the holiday arrives, we will eat matzah—bread that has not been allowed to rise—and thus is unleavened.

These days (for many people, weeks) of preparation intensify our eagerness for the arrival of the first night. All Jewish holidays begin at sundown and usually do so with a meal. In this case, the meal is a seder (literally, "order"), a ceremonial experience that involves a prescribed order of traditions and practices, including prayer, study, song, and the eating of symbolic foods. A communal reading aloud of a small book, the haggadah (literally, "telling")—a compilation of biblical passages, prayers, hymns, and rabbinical literature—guides participants through all parts of the meal, as it recounts and elaborates upon the story of the Exodus. The seder is expressly intended to be an active forum, encouraging discussion of elements in the haggadah by both children and adults.

As instructed in the Bible, Passover spans seven days. The first and final ones have greater significance than the intermediary days, *hol ha-mo'ed* (literally, "the mundane of the festival"). They include restrictions from work and the directive to perform certain rituals, such as holding a seder on the first day; and they include customs, such as the recitation of *Yizkor*, the memorial prayer, on the last day. In the Diaspora (Jewish communities that are outside of Israel), a tradition developed of holding a seder on each of the first two nights of Passover. This practice began in the time before a fixed calendar existed, when messengers were sent from Israel to the Diaspora to announce the start of a holiday. Because of the inherent unreliability of this long-distance communication, Jews in the Diaspora began to keep two "first" days of the festival, thus ensuring that the important first day was not missed. To this day, Jews in Israel keep one first day of Passover and thus hold only one seder, and they observe one holy day at the end. Many Jews in the Diaspora keep two first days[2] and hold two seders. They also add a second holy day at the end of Passover, making their holiday a total of eight days long.

Clear Direction

"This day shall be to you one of remembrance; you shall celebrate it as a festival to the LORD throughout the ages … as an institution for all time. Seven days you shall eat unleavened bread; on the very first day you shall remove leaven from your houses, for whoever eats leavened bread from the first day to the seventh day, that person shall be cut off from Israel. … [F]or on this very day I brought your ranks out of the land of Egypt."
—Exodus 12:14–15,17

Passover in the Bible

Passover is a holiday with many connections to the Bible. For example, the injunction to "remember the day you left Egypt" is alluded to, in some form or other, more than 50 times in a wide variety of places.[3] More particularly, the Passover story dominates the most significant chapters of the Book of Exodus; and, one might argue, the story is the centerpiece of the entire Torah (the Five Books of Moses). Culminating with the Revelation at Mount Sinai in Exodus chapter 20, the story includes many well-known biblical events: the Egyptian enslavement of the Israelites, the growth of Moses as a leader, the beginnings of prophecy, the disclosure of God's actual name to Moses at the burning bush, the inflicting of the 10 plagues, the giving of the first commandments from God to the entire nation of Israel, the giving of the first paschal offering, the splitting and crossing of the Red Sea, and the receiving of manna in the wilderness. Although these elements of the Exodus story are only a small portion of the entire Torah, they are prominent as hallmarks of Jewish identity.

PASSING OVER

Three times a year—on the Feast of Unleavened Bread [Passover], on the Feast of Weeks [Shavuot], and the Feast of Booths [Sukkot]—all your males shall appear before the LORD your God in the place that He will choose. They shall not appear before the LORD empty-handed, but each with his own gift, according to the blessing that the LORD your God has bestowed upon you.

—Deuteronomy 16:16–17

In the Bible, the holiday is never referred to as Pesach. Any use of that word is restricted to "the *pesach*"—the designated animal that was sacrificed on the 14th day and eaten on the 15th day of the month we now call Nisan. The Torah's names for the holiday are principally agricultural. We see this first in reference to the period of time when the festival falls. The Torah does not tell us to celebrate in the month of Nisan; it states that Passover must occur in *Aviv*,[4] which is also the season of spring. This designation emphasizes the seasonal and thereby the agricultural association that Passover has. For this reason, postbiblical literature sometimes refers to the holiday as *Hag Ha-Aviv*, The Festival, or Feast, of Spring.

Most often, the Torah uses the name *Hag Ha-Matzot*, The Festival, or Feast, of Unleavened Bread, for example, in Leviticus 23:6 and in Deuteronomy 16:16. This "bread" name touches upon the relationship that Passover has to agriculture when we connect it to the wheat used for baking matzah (plural, matzot). The resultant unleavened bread is the purest example of the relationship between the farmer and God. Unlike fruits and vegetables that need only ripening and harvesting to become fit for consumption, matzah requires an additional step of human ingenuity to become the simple foodstuff that provides basic nourishment. Moreover, the grain used to bake matzah is from the prior year's wheat harvest. We find ourselves focusing on matzah and the old wheat, precisely when the earth is undergoing the renewal of springtime.

The Torah makes another agricultural connection when it links Passover to the Omer (literally, "Sheaf," approximately two quarts of barley), which was brought to the Temple as a communal offering on the second day of Passover. We formally acknowledge this agricultural relationship in two ways. One is by performing the symbolic "Counting of the Omer" from Passover to Shavuot. The other is by inserting a request for dew into the *Amidah* (literally, "Standing"), the central prayer of the Jewish tradition. This extra phrase, added only by those living in Israel and by certain religious communities in the Diaspora, is recited from Passover through the fall holiday of Sukkot.[5]

The Rabbis of the talmudic era were the first to use the term Pesach for the festival itself. They did not, however, derive the name from the the offering made at Passover, but from the Hebrew verb root *peh.samekh.chet.*, the meaning of which has not been conclusively determined. However, a word taken from that root is *u'fasachti*,[6] used in Exodus (12:13) when describing God's implementation of the 10th plague, the killing of the firstborn. In the following example, the 2nd-century rabbi Yoshiyah employs a "midrashic move"—an interpretive device by which a rabbi can extract deeper meaning from a word, phrase, or verse—to develop the phrase into a now-familiar configuration related to "passing over":

U'fasachti aleikhem—*Rabbi Yoshiyah*[7] *says, "In the place of* u'fasachti *read* ufasati, *shall step, for the Holy One, Blessed Be He, leapt over the houses of the Children of Israel in Egypt, as it is said, 'Hark! My Beloved! There he comes, Leaping over mountains' (Songs 2:8)." Rabbi Yonatan says "*u'fasachti aleikhem *means, On you I shall have pity, but I shall not have pity on the Egyptians. If an Egyptian was in the house of one of Israel, we might think that the Egyptian would be saved* [*because God leapt over the houses of Israel*]*. But the verse says* 'u'fasachti aleikhem—*On you I shall have pity, but not on the Egyptians.'"*[8]

The weight of the Jewish tradition agrees with Rabbi Yoshiyah. For example, the 1985 translation of the Bible by the Jewish Publication Society reads, "And the blood on the houses where you are staying shall be a sign for you: when I see the blood I will pass over you [*u'fasachti aleikhem*], so that no plague will destroy you when I strike the land of Egypt" (Exod. 12:13).

NEVI'IM AND KETHUVIM

The Torah is the first of the three-part Hebrew Bible. The second and third parts are Nevi'im (The Prophets) and Kethuvim (The Writings). In these sections, references to Passover celebrations appear at times when there is an expression of reaffirmation of Jewish identity; the original birth story of the Jewish nation is told and the nation is spiritually reborn. Through such tellings, we are able to appreciate the central role of the Passover story in defining the historical and national identity of the Jewish people.

At the end of Deuteronomy, the final book of the Torah, Moses dies while the Jews are still wandering in the desert. The mantle of leadership passes to one of his close attendants, Joshua. The Book of Joshua (the first in Nevi'im) relates that Joshua conquers the city of Jericho, crosses the Jordan River, and takes the Jewish people into the Land of Israel. He then orders them to perform a "second circumcision"[9] and to celebrate Passover.

The conditions and actions described in the Book of Joshua encourage us to see that Joshua is a leader as righteous and dependable as Moses and that his story of entrance into the Land of Israel recalls the story of the Exodus from Egypt. The account in Joshua does so in several ways, among them:

- When the Israelites cross the Jordan River into the Land of Israel, God dries up the waters. This event hearkens back to the miraculous splitting of *Yam Suf,* the Sea of Reeds (the more precise name of the Red Sea) in Exodus 15. The waters of the Jordan are described as being "cut off" from their normal flow (Josh. 3:13).

- The Israelites "came up from the Jordan on the tenth day of the first month [Nisan]" (Josh. 4:19) and "offered the passover sacrifice on the fourteenth day of the month, toward evening" (5:10). On the next day, they ate "unleavened bread" (5:11). These events parallel those that preceded the Israelites' departure from Egypt in Exodus chapter 12, in which they were required to take their paschal lamb on the 10th of Nisan, sacrifice it at twilight on the 14th, and eat unleavened bread during the week that followed.

- Before the sacrifice takes place, Joshua ensures that the Israelite males are circumcised (Josh. 5:2–9), as directed by God. This account parallels the end of Exodus chapter 12, verses 43–50, when God tells Moses and his brother, Aaron, that no uncircumcised male may eat of the paschal offering.

The celebration of Passover also plays a significant role in the Book of Ezra, which is found in the third part of the Bible, Kethuvim. The First Temple in Jerusalem was destroyed in 586 B.C.E. About 50 years later, some of the exiled Jews return from Babylonian captivity. Under the guidance of prophets Ezra and Nehemiah, the celebration of Passover is the first formal assembly to take place.[10] Ezra's account of this Passover celebration parallels descriptions in the earlier Books of Exodus and Joshua. Once again, Passover is used to mark the occasion of a monumental event involving Jewish freedom and spiritual identity and to revisit the birth of the Jewish nation.

The final book of the Hebrew Bible, 2 Chronicles, discusses three key instances in history when the celebration of Passover marked reaffirmation of the Jews' spiritual identity. The first occurred after King Solomon had completed the construction of the First Temple. We are told that he observed all three pilgrimage festivals: Passover, Shavuot, and Sukkot (2 Chron. 8:12–13). The second took place during the time of religious reforms made by King Josiah (35:1–19).[13] He is credited with being the king who returned Jewish practice to its proper place, because he rid Judah, the southern kingdom in the Land of Israel, from the evil and idolatrous ways of King Manasseh, his grandfather. Passover is described as the celebration marking the culmination of those reforms. The third happened under the reign of another religious reformer, King Hezekiah. Besides restoring religious practices to the Temple, he played a role in trying to intensify national unity[14] when he invited the remaining inhabitants of the northern "Kingdom of Israel,"[15] which had just been conquered by Assyria, to come to Jerusalem for Passover (30:1–5,13–27).

From Sacrifice to Prayer

Historically, Passover was a pilgrimage festival, as were Shavuot in the summer and Sukkot in the fall. These festivals drew together Jews from all over the Land of Israel and the Diaspora. The pilgrims met in one national and spiritual center, the Temple in Jerusalem. The obligation of a pilgrim was to bring an *olat re'iyah* (pilgrimage sacrifice) and to make it in the proper spirit and in accordance with *halakhah* (Jewish law).[11] After the Second Temple was destroyed in 70 C.E., Jews continued to make pilgrimages to Israel, often at great personal risk. But there was no spiritual home in which to make sacrifices, and Jewish ritual shifted from offering sacrifices to offering prayers, an act that can take place with or without a formal building. In addition, as was taught by Rabbi Yochanan ben Zakkai (a leading sage in the early post-Temple era), acts of *hesed* (lovingkindess) are an effective substitute for sacrifices.[12]

Through this progression of connections to Passover in the Bible, we see an evolution in the significance of the holiday. The Torah describes it in agricultural terms, but because the festival is directly connected to the story of the Exodus, Passover becomes much more than a springtime harvest celebration. It becomes the symbolic expression of the religious and national identity of the Jewish people. The successive references to its observance, especially coming at such pivotal moments in the Bible, underscore its high-level ritual status as the embodiment of our collective story. Passover is the primary reaffirmation of the spiritual and historical aspects of the Jewish nation.

Traditions in the Month of Nisan

This month shall mark for you the beginning of the months; it shall be the first of the months of the year for you. —Exodus 12:2

We Begin with Nisan

In the Torah, a month will often not be described by a proper name, but rather be referred to by its ordinal, for example, "the third month." The Jewish New Year (Rosh Hashanah, when the universe was created) actually falls in the seventh month[16] (later designated as Tishrei[17]), while Passover falls in the first month of the Hebrew calendar (later designated as Nisan). As stated in the commentary of medieval Jewish philosopher Nachmanides, "The children of Israel should mark this month [Nisan] as the first, and should count months in relation to this one; … This is to ensure we remember the great miracle [of the Exodus],"[18] the birth of the Jewish nation.

The Jewish tradition deems Nisan, the first month of the Hebrew calendar, as particularly holy, because it is the month during which the Jews' miraculous salvation from the Egyptians occurred. It begins a transitional phase in the Jewish year, heralding the renewal of nature and the grand holiday of Passover. We reclaim the portion of our spiritual vitality that was hibernating during the winter months, and we begin our preparations for the festival. To build a sense of joy and celebration during this month, the liturgy directs us to omit from our daily prayers those of supplication, such as the sorrowful *Tachanum* and *Tzidkatkha*.[19]

We also prepare for Passover with two particularly significant Sabbaths. In the talmudic era, the Rabbis designated the Sabbath that falls either before or upon the first of Nisan (depending on the calendar for that year) as *Shabbat Parashat Ha-Hodesh* (literally, "the Sabbath of the Parsashah of [this] Month"). On this Shabbat, the *maftir* (additional Torah reading) comprises God's instructions to the Israelites on preparing to leave Egypt and on making the first paschal sacrifice.[20] The haftarah (a readiing from The Prophets) describes the festival sacrifices made at the Temple and specifically mentions Passover.[21]

Then in the early medieval era, the Sabbath directly preceding the holiday received added importance, making it perhaps the most distinctive one of the Jewish year. It is known as *Shabbat Ha-Gadol*, The Great Sabbath.[22] Scholars have proposed various reasons for its prestige. One idea is drawn from the haftarah read on that Sabbath, which speaks of the time when the Messiah will appear—a time described with the word *gadol* (Hebrew for "great or awesome")—as "the awesome, fearful day of the LORD" (Mal. 3:23). A second comes from the day the Israelites' executed God's orders to have each Jewish household select a lamb (an animal worshiped by the Egyptians) to be used in the sacrifice. This decision was the Israelites first initiative as a liberated people. Rabbis later determined that the day had been the 10th of Nisan, which would have fallen on the seventh day of the week[23]—lending extra importance thereafter to the Shabbat before Passover. A third possible reason contrasts Shabbat with Passover. Shabbat acknowledges God's universal power and relationship with the world. Passover acknowledges the particular relationship between God and the Jewish people. The existence of those two concepts in such close, time-bound proximity may be why the Shabbat that precedes Passover is called "Great."[24] The final suggestion, a rather straightforward one, comes from a historical tradition that continues to this day. In many communities on Shabbat Ha-Gadol, the rabbi gives a lengthy sermon, perhaps the grandest of the year, to discuss the many laws and practices of the holiday. Over time, this tradition came to include the individual practice of spending Shabbat afternoon reading through the haggadah, as a way of educating oneself about the laws of Passover and preparing for the seder.[25]

WHEAT AND WINE

Copious amounts of wine are required for each Passover seder and enough matzah to last the entire multiday festival. The Talmud (the central body of Rabbinic literature) teaches us of a 3rd-century custom in which people gave wheat to the poor for baking matzah.[26] The financially able were required to pay a special Passover tax in wheat, and the recipients of the grain were expected to grind their own flour and do the baking at home, as was the custom. By the medieval period, many people were going to the newly prevalent communal ovens to have their dough baked into matzah. Rather than levying a wheat tax, it was more sensible to collect funds and give money to the poor, who could then buy the grain themselves and pay to have their matzah dough baked at a bakery.[27] And so the custom came to be called *ma'ot hittin*, "money for wheat." The Talmud also tells us of another obligatory charitable act. During the seder, we drink wine to feel joyfully liberated, to help us properly reexperience the miracle of the Exodus.[28] We must be sure that every household has sufficient wine for each person to have the requisite four cups.

Judaism continues to emphasize this practice of giving food and charity around the time of Passover. The spirit of *ma'ot hittin* manifests itself in community food drives, deliveries of food baskets, and requests to contribute funds. Such initiatives reinforce the concept of Judaism as a religion of responsibility—for ourselves and for those around us. *Ma'ot hittin* reminds us that as we prepare for our own celebration of the festival, we must not forget those who are equally enthusiastic but lack the means, physically or financially, to prepare for the holiday. As the words of the haggadah instruct: "Let all who are hungry come and eat; let all who are in need come and share in the Passover meal."

Understanding Matzah and Hametz

Those who celebrate and observe Passover often find it difficult to remain on a steady diet of matzah and to abstain from eating *hametz* (the rather large category of forbidden foods containing leaven) over the course of the week. This situation is especially a challenge in the Diaspora, where, unlike in Israel, most grocery stores have a limited variety of Passover supplies, and many kosher restaurants close down during the holiday rather than changing over to be kosher for Passover. Nonetheless, there are advantages in these restrictions. In the midst of the uncertainty and decision making about what to eat, we discover our lack of knowledge about the components that make up our daily sustenance. The physical discomfort is a path to the spiritual goal of denying *hametz* for the entire week. As Maimonides points out in his *Guide of the Perplexed*, "If, however, the eating of unleavened bread would only last for one day, we would not take notice of it and its meaning would not be made clear."[29] Since abstaining from *hametz* is so central to the holiday, we ask what exactly Maimonides means when he refers to *hametz*.

By definition, *hametz* is food that is made from any of five grains—wheat, barley, oats, spelt, or rye—and has been allowed to rise. The prohibited foods include items such as pasta, cereal, and beer, because they contain by-products or derivatives of the principal forms of *hametz*. According to Jewish law, we must not only refrain from consuming *hametz*, but also remove it from our homes, as spelled out in a phrase from Exodus: "and no leaven shall be found in your houses" (12:19).[30] It is also forbidden to own *hametz* or, as Maimonides and others say, to "derive benefit" from it.[31] We can interpret this prohibition to include, for example, making money in a *hametz*-related business venture or enjoying *hametz* in a social activity with non-Jews.

There is also a separate, specific prohibition about the rising agent itself. The Torah commands us not to own *se'or*, typically translated as "leaven," during Passover (Exod. 12:19). Some of us mistakenly think this concept of *se'or* refers to cultured yeast, but *se'or* is actually connected to the natural fermentation process that can occur with any of the five grains and water. The prohibition is understood as follows. Yeast is a one-celled microorganism that lives in the air and produces energy by converting carbohydrates into carbon dioxide or ethanol alcohol. This process causes the flour in dough, once it is wet with water, to puff and rise, which would happen whether or not we added yeast. But bakers prefer to add yeast directly, as an ingredient to speed up the process. Traditionally, yeast was obtained by making some batter or dough and letting it slowly expand, triggered solely by the intrusion of yeast in the air. The dough would develop a tangy or sour taste (from which the term *sourdough* is derived); the next day, bakers would add a piece of it, now saturated with yeast, to that day's dough to speed the rising of the bread. According to Jewish law, a grain that is in contact with water for 18 minutes is *hametz*[32] because by that time, the *se'or* has begun doing its work. And thus what the Torah specifically prohibits is being in possession of *se'or*, the fermented ball of yeast that is created by this process. By extension, of course, one would not own anything to which leavening has been added.

THE SPIRITUAL DIVIDING LINE

Only a narrow margin separates *hametz*, which is forbidden, from matzah, which is not merely permitted but in fact obligatory as decreed by God, "eating unleavened bread for seven days as I have commanded you" (Exod. 34:18). The difference is created not by an ingredient; the difference is a result of our time and effort. A grain must be carefully monitored and prevented from soaking in water beyond the prescribed 18 minutes because, if that time has passed, the dough will spontaneously become leaven and cannot be baked as matzah.

The 20th-century scholar and rabbi Eliyahu Ki Tov points out that this small difference of effort is revealed in the Hebrew characters for the words matzah and *hametz*. The words have the exact same letters save one: matzah has a *heh* and *hametz* has a *het*.[33] And these two letters are themselves identical except for one small connective line, which, according to the teaching of Ki Tov, represents that tiny bit of effort people make to distinguish what is permitted from what is forbidden and what is sacred from what is impure.

Since very early in Jewish history, *hametz* has carried considerable spiritual and psychological weight. The Hellenistic Jewish philosopher Philo, who lived in 1st-century Alexandria, Egypt, offers one of the earliest interpretations of the difference between *hametz* and matzah. He argues that *hametz* is forbidden because it "puffs up," which makes it symbolic of human arrogance, when, instead, we should be approaching life and our Maker with modesty.[34] This concept provides one of the reasons we abstain from *hametz:* to diminish egotism.

The Talmud implies support for Philo's conception of *hametz* when it states that one must "nullify *hametz* in his heart."[35] In other words, *hametz* is symbolic of something negative that we find within our hearts and minds. The Zohar (literally, "Illumination," a Jewish mystical commentary on the Bible) furthers explains the negative nature of *hametz* by comparing its consumption on Passover to idolatry, one of Judaism's cardinal sins.[36] Rabbinic texts include discussion of the *yetzer ha-ra*, the so-called evil inclination, which is the natural drive toward pleasure, property, and security. If left unchecked, it can lead to doing evil. According to the Zohar, *hametz* must be eradicated on Passover because it is a metaphor for the *yetzer ha-ra*.[37] The medieval Italian mystic Rabbi Moses Chayyim Luzzatto elucidates this interpretation in his treatise on Jewish beliefs, *The Way of God:*

> *Leaven is a natural element of bread, making it more digestible and flavorous* [sic]. *This is also a result of man's appropriate nature, since humans must have an evil urge* (yetzer ha-ra) *and an inclination towards the physical. At a particular determined time, however, Israel was required to abstain from leaven, and be nourished by matzah. This reduced the strength of the individual's evil urge toward the physical, thus enhancing his closeness to the spiritual."*[38]

The 19th-century rabbi Naftali Tzevi Judah Berlin (known also by abbreviation as "the Natziv") suggests that *hametz* represents the inherent evil that is humankind's desire to control and alter God's natural state of the universe. In *Ha-Emek Davar* (The Depth of the Word), his commentary on the Torah, he says: "Matzah takes no advantage of the human technological ingenuity and creativity which allow man to raise the dough more than simple flour and water which are created by God. *Hametz* is the epitome of human involvement in nature. Thus, 'non-leaven' is the symbol of the survival and ongoing existence of the Jewish people as they survive solely through the spirit of God."[39]

We can see that Jewish scholars have long interpreted *hametz* from their personal, spiritual perspectives. They have equated it with the tendencies of people to be haughty, to worship their material possessions, to give in to the evil inclination, and to selfishly dominate nature. These human characteristics are profoundly important and interrelated, as they all are contrary to the quality of humility, which is the most elevated state of spirituality. Humility allows us to be aware and accepting of our imperfections. When we can truly see ourselves, including these flaws, we are better able to express a kindly tolerance for other people and to experience our relationship with a compassionate God. It is when we are "puffed up"—filled to the brim with ourselves and our own needs—that we are most likely to be negligent in our duties to others and in our commitment to our Maker. *Hametz*, as an agent for "filling and puffing," becomes symbolic of excessive pride and even of idolatry (for example, valuing a life of material luxury over spiritual development), conditions in which we elevate ourselves to the status of a deity. Passover is therefore more than the festival of national freedom from servitude under the Egyptians, who thought themselves to be gods; it signifies our ongoing spiritual quest for freedom from the tyranny of our personal selfishness and egotism.

GEBROKTS OR NOT?

Some Ashkenazim (Jews with long-ago ancestors from Germany or France), particularly members of Hasidic groups, will not run the risk of eating *gebrokts* (literally, "broken" in Yiddish, as in broken into pieces or ground up)—any matzah that comes in contact with water after it has been baked. They are concerned that minute amounts of unkneaded flour may remain in the dough and could still become *hametz*. No matzah or any derivative, such as matzah meal, goes into any recipe (potato starch may be used as a substitute) because of its potential to interact with liquid ingredients. Care is taken to keep certain beverages, soups, or damp foods away from the matzah on the table; washed greens used during the seder are meticulously dried beforehand. The Hebrew term for *gebrokts* is *matzah sheruyah* (soaked).

Although there is no textual basis for this stringency in traditional literature, it gained acceptance around the end of the 18th century and is, by now, an "old" custom among its practitioners. On the eighth day of Passover—an added day, not one mandated by the Torah—Jews living outside of Israel who follow this non-*gebrokts* custom do something surprising. They deliberately eat foods made with matzah. They lift the stringency on this one day for a very special purpose: to show unity among different groups of Jews. The adherents to the non-*gebrokts* custom want to demonstrate that they do not regard the *gebrokts*-eating Jews as having consumed *hametz* during the seven mandated days. In addition, by the end of Passover the level of personal spirituality has been increased. The fear of *gebrokts* is lessened and eating it becomes an obligatory part of the joyous celebration.

WHO EATS *KITNIYOT?*

Kitniyot, from the Hebrew adjective *katan* ("little"), refers to rice, corn, millet, and legumes—beans, peas, lentils, seeds, and peanuts—and all their derivatives. Generally speaking, Ashkenazim add this entire group to the list of foods already prohibited on Passover, which are the five grains of wheat, barley, spelt, rye, and oats and all their derivatives. Sephardim (Jews who trace their history back to Spain before the 1492 expulsion) do not adhere to this prohibition. The Ashkenazic injunction concerns the act of consumption only—not the owning of *kitniyot*. Because *kitniyot* is not *hametz*, there is no obligation to destroy or sell it.

The medieval ban against eating *kitniyot* was likely created as an extra protective measure, an effort to make sure people would not accidentally cross the line from non-*hametz* into *hametz*. Three issues may have been the concern. Foods in the *kitniyot* category contain elements that can be ground into flour and turned into products resembling or reminding us of leavened bread, for example, corn bread. Another possibility was that *kitniyot* items could be stored in sacks sometimes used for the five grains, and the *kitniyot* might thereby become contaminated with the *hametz*. It was also possible that crop rotations would result in small amounts of the *hametz* category of grains growing in with the *kitniyot*, and the forbidden grains would then be harvested with the *kitniyot*.

▲   ▲   ▲   ▲   ▲   ▲   ▲   ◄►   ▲   ▲   ▲   ▲   ▲   ▲   ▲

Evolution of the Stringency

The first prohibitions against *kitniyot* are not directly discussed until the 12th and 13th centuries, but the seed for the idea can be found in a statement recorded in the Talmud. It refers to the position taken by 2nd-century sage Yochanan ben Nuri.

> *Our Mishnah disagrees with Rabbi Yochanan ben Nuri, who said* [*in another, but contemporary, source*] *that rice is a species of grain, and one is culpable for it in a leavened state. For it was taught: Rabbi Yochanan ben Nuri prohibits rice and millet, because it is close to leaven* [*can rise even more quickly than wheat*].*"*[40]

The Talmud thus negates the opinion of Yochanan ben Nuri, who says that rice is *hametz*. They do so because his statement is not in conformance with the Mishnah (literally, "Teaching," the foundational text for the Talmud), which lists the five grains that can become *hametz* (wheat, barley, spelt, rye, and oats), and rice is not one of them. In addition, later in the same volume we find a description of the custom of talmudists Rava[41] and Rav Huna[42] (3rd–4th centuries, Babylonia), which is to place rice on the ceremonial seder plate itself. In response to this discussion about whom to follow, Rav Ashi[43] (4th–5th centuries, Babylonia) declares, "We do not pay attention to the opinion of Rabbi Yochanan b. Nuri."[44]

This talmudic consent to eat *kitniyot* remained unchallenged for centuries. This was certainly the case throughout the Sephardic communities. Maimonides, who lived in Spain and Egypt from the mid-12th to early 13th centuries, goes so far as to say: "Even if one kneads rice flour or the like with boiling water and covers it with fabric until it rises like leavened dough, it is permitted to be eaten."[45]

By contrast, in the 13th-century Ashkenazic community of Corbeil, France, we find the earliest known reference to a prohibition against *kitniyot*. The scholar Yitzchak ben Yosef, in his book *Sefer Mitzvot Katan* (literally, "Small Book of Mitzvot"), argues that *kitniyot* share many things in common with the five species of grain, including the ways we harvest and cook them, and we could easily be confused.

> *Concerning* kitniyot *such as beans, rice, lentils and the like ... which Rabbi Yochanan ben Nuri considers a species of grain with respect to leavening, the*

Talmud states that there is no one who takes this opinion .... However, it is difficult to permit a thing which people have treated as a prohibition from the days of the early sages; ... the reason for the prohibition is a precautionary decree; for since kitniyot *are used to make cooked dishes and grain is likewise used to make cooked dishes; and since* kitniyot *are harvested in a way similar to harvesting and piling up of grain ... and also there are places where people are in the habit of making bread from* kitniyot *as from the five kinds of grain—therefore those who are not well versed in Torah could come to confuse the two; and they are not similar to the vegetables [i.e., those things eaten as leaves, stems, roots, or fruit rather than seeds] ... and it is a proper custom to refrain from all species of* kitniyot *.... Despite the fact that the Talmud permits rice [on Passover], that was only permitted in those days, when all were expert in the laws of forbidden and permitted things; but now in these latter generations it is certainly necessary to enact a precautionary decree ... and it should be forbidden even to put them into water which is already boiling, lest people draw the conclusion that cold water is also permitted."*[46]

Sefer Mitzvot Katan admits that the general Rabbinic opinion, including that of the talmudists, permits *kitniyot*, but it claims that the Jews living in his time and place do not have the expertise of those in the talmudic era. They are therefore unable to determine what is permissible and what is prohibited. Moreover, the author suggests that there is an inherent value in the continuance of this prohibition, which, by the time of his writing, had been followed for generations.

The greatest supporters of the position found in *Sefer Mitzvot Katan* were the author's contemporaries: his brother-in-law Mordechai ben Hillel, author of *Sefer Mordechai*[47](literally, "Book of Mordechai"), and Ben Hillel's brother-in-law, Meir Ha-Kohen of Rothenburg, author of *Haggahot Maimoniyot*,[48] (literally, "Maimonidian Elucidations"). Gradually, the Ashkenazim came to an overall acceptance of the *kitniyot* prohibition. In the 16th century, Sephardic legal authority Joseph Karo (Spain, Turkey, and Israel) and Ashkenazic rabbinical decisor Moses Isserles (Poland) each published a milestone work on Jewish law, and the custom was acknowledged by both renowned scholars. In his *Beit Yosef* (literally, "School of Joseph"), Karo cites both *Sefer Mitzvot Katan* and *Haggahot Maimoniyot* in reference to the prohibition against *kitniyot*, but adds, "There are none who take this opinion into account, except for Ashkenazic Jews."[49] Isserles, for his part, notes that the "Ashkenazic Jews adhere to the stringent custom, and one should not deviate from the custom."[50]

Rabbis who favored eating *kitniyot* were not shy in making their comments. Asher ben Yechiel (known by the acronym Rosh) lived in Germany and Spain around the turn of the 14th century. He called the prohibition against eating *kitniyot* an "outlandish thing" of which "no one ever decreed."[51] Another 14th-century legal authority, Yerucham ben Meshullam of Provence, wrote of the prohibition, "It is a foolish custom, and I don't know why they are so stringent."[52] In the 18th century, the notable Ashkenazic talmudist Yaakov Emden called the *kitniyot* prohibition an "inferior custom" resulting in people having to bake even more matzah, which may cause them to become lax in the laws of baking matzah.[53]

This one small area of Jewish life and observance represents an intense expression of Jewish plurality that has lasted for nearly a millennium and cuts across all the dimensions that make up Jewish differences, including geography, ancestry, ethnic customs, and even observance levels. In modern Israel, which has a noteworthy blend of both Sephardic and Ashkenazic Jews, there has certainly been contention over the *kitniyot* issue, especially when considering the cost to the population of purchasing specially processed Passover foods. Furthermore, the majority of Israelis are Sephardic (in contrast, for example, to the predominantly Ashkenazic United States), and the society in general follows Sephardic customs. In this financial and cultural setting, which includes an extensive number of friendships and marriages between Sephardim and Ashkenazim, many of the latter are trending toward abandonment of the "no *kitniyot*" tradition.[54]

Modern scholar David Golinkin is a leader in the Masorti (Israeli Conservative) movement. In 1989, he published a responsum[55] about *kitniyot* that was unanimously accepted by the movement's *va'ad halakhah* (law committee). He cites more than 50 rabbinical authorities living between 1250 and 1500 in various countries, and he concludes that the prohibition against *kitniyot* should not be observed because it does the following:

- detracts from the joy of the holiday by limiting the number of permitted foods;

- causes exorbitant price rises, which result in "major financial loss" and, as is well known, "the Torah takes pity on the People of Israel's money" [i.e., high prices for limited-quantity, high-demand Passover foods cause unnecessary financial hardship];

- distracts from the mitzvah by focusing too much on the insignificant (legumes) and by failing to emphasize the significant (hametz, which is forbidden from the five kinds of grain);

- causes people to scoff at the commandments in general and at the prohibition of hametz in particular—if this custom has no purpose and yet is observed, then there is no reason to observe other commandments;

- causes unnecessary divisions among Israel's different ethnic groups.

In the United States, Askhenazim traditionally do not eat kitniyot during Passover. And yet, some Ashkenazim today, based partly on the arguments above, have begun to accept the consumption of peanuts and their derivatives.[56] For most others, even with plenty of rational support, it is not easy or necessarily desirable to end a 700-year-old custom, especially with the foremost authorities on Ashkenazic customs, for example, Moses Isserles, demanding that no one deviate from the stringency.

On the one hand, we may be uncomfortable to see such a small matter cause such a big commotion. On the other, in this katan ("tiny") piece of Judaism, we witness the unfolding and evolution of the more rigorous customs. Ultimately, each of us can strive to make our chosen tradition into an opportunity for enriched meaning and deeper sanctity, while we remain willing to learn about and consider the practices of others.

Preparing Our Homes and Hearts for Passover

The rituals we perform can be troubling if we give credence only to the intellectual. For example, if we consider the final ritual for disposing of hametz—traditionally done using a feather and a wooden spoon by candlelight—words such as "archaic" or "sorcery" or "incantation" may come to mind. Yet our rituals are seen from a different perspective when we note what the poetic 20th-century philosopher Abraham Joshua Heschel said: "A Jew is asked to take a 'leap of action' rather than a 'leap of thought.'"[59] Although we are encouraged to think freely—to think as much as we please—in the end, we are asked to "do," whether we agree with the action or not. Judaism emphasizes "doing" because it understands that we will not necessarily think clearly or be wholly rational, and we will not be entirely moral or entirely spiritually pure. No human was, is, or ever will be these things. But we can "do" clearly, rationally, morally, and purely. The Jewish tradition guides us as we learn how to "do"; and, with God's help, just maybe, we will all align our thoughts with our hearts. We will think and believe purely and in harmony with our deeds.

CLEAN, SEARCH, NULLIFY, AND DESTROY

In the weeks leading up to Passover, people gradually, painstakingly, and thoroughly clean their houses and get rid of *hametz*. Their efforts include the following: eating up or giving away the *hametz*; locking away the dishes, silverware, and cookware used during the rest of the year; clearing the refrigerator of any non-Passover foods and cleaning its shelves; scrubbing cabinets where *hametz* has been stored; scrupulously wiping down countertops and possibly covering them with a material such as foil; cleaning the stovetop and oven and then using the prescribed method[60] for burning off any *hametz* that may have been missed. After those tasks are completed comes the pleasure of getting out the used-only-for-Passover cooking vessels and dishes, glasses, flatware, and linens.

These efforts become more intense and formalized beginning at sunset on the 14th of Nisan—the evening before the first seder. This moment ushers in

Kitniyot for Vegetarians

During Passover, people discuss and share recipes, often because they wish to accommodate the rules of kashrut (Jewish dietary laws) and the Passover abstentions from *hametz* and *kitniyot*. If a person is a vegetarian, or cooking for one, a perplexing, additional layer of restriction is added to the holiday menu. Does a solution exist for this puzzle? Historically, some Ashkenazic authorities permitted the eating of *kitniyot* in a time of scarcity, such as an agricultural calamity. Yisrael Meir Ha-Kohen[57] (b. 1838–d. 1933, Poland), author of the *Mishnah Berurah* (literally, "Clarified Teaching"), focuses on the difference between *hametz* and *kitniyot* to say that a sick person may eat *kitniyot* even if the circumstances are not immediately life threatening.[58] Some modern rabbis have interpreted this opinion as being consent for vegetarians to eat *kitniyot*, with the objective of maintaining a healthy and satisfying Passover diet. Thus many Ashkenazic vegetarians, taking into consideration their lifestyle, spirituality, and commitment to tradition, find they are comfortable with the idea of eating *kitniyot*.

the period called Erev[61] Passover, which lasts until the following sunset, when Passover begins. The first formal procedure is *bedikat hametz*, the search for *hametz*,[62] which is performed systematically to make sure that no *hametz* is left in the house. (If the first night of Passover falls on Saturday night, *bedikat hametz* is performed on Thursday night).[63] After darkness falls, the family gathers together to begin the search. Many people still follow the description in the Mishnah and do the search in the traditional way by candlelight,[64] although most contemporary authorities do permit using a flashlight. People also may abide by the custom of using a feather to sweep out the smallest crevices and a wooden spoon to collect the crumbs.[65]

Fast of the Firstborn

A portion of the 14th of Nisan is traditionally a fasting period for every firstborn male. In some circles, the fast includes firstborn females. It commemorates the 10th plague, in which all the first-born of the Egyptians were killed, while the firstborn of the Israelites were saved.[69] The fast begins at dawn. To avoid the complications of fasting until nightfall when there is a seder, one prevalent custom shortens the time by holding a special learning session called a *siyum bekhorim* ("concluding study period for firstborn") on the morning of Erev Passover.[70] Upon the completion of an entire text or course of study, we are required to partake of a festive meal. Thus if we hold a concluding lesson for that morning and eat refreshments, that act effectively overrides the requirement to continue the fast.

Before the search begins, to mark the moment a blessing is said. It ends with *al bi'ur hametz*, which means "upon the destruction of *hametz*." In the Middle Ages, this blessing began to trouble some Rabbinic authorities. Because the house has already been thoroughly cleaned, the chances of finding any *hametz* would be slim at best. As a statement about God, a blessing embodies tremendous meaning; if we subsequently do not find any *hametz*, the blessing may have been recited in vain.[66] Therefore, as a measure to ensure that the blessing is fulfilled, a custom evolved to have the head of the household preposition 10 pieces of *hametz* around the home, in places that will be readily accessible to the searchers.[67] The use of the number 10 originated in the 16th century with Isaac Luria, the renowned teacher of Kabbalah, Jewish mysticism. According to Kabbalah, there are 10 spiritual levels to which an angel can ascend in merit, as well as 10 levels to which an angel can descend in disgrace. By searching for *hametz*, a symbol of the evil inclination, we show our desire—as human beings, of course—to ascend to ever-higher levels of spirituality and to conquer any downward-spiraling temptations.[68]

Once we have completed the search for *hametz*, we recite the following Aramaic words: *Kol hamira ve-chami'ah de-ika virshuti de-la hamiteih u'de-la bi'arteih u'de-la yedana leih libatel ve-lehevei hefker ke-afra de-ara.*[71] ("All *hametz* in my possession that I have not seen and have not removed shall be nullified and be ownerless as the dust of the earth"). With this declaration, we renounce our ownership of *hametz* both physically and mentally. In other words, we know that despite our cleaning efforts, there still may be some small amount of *hametz* "unseen" in our possession. Therefore, true freedom from *hametz* (or from anything) requires more than physical freedom. It also demands surrendering any sort of mental or intentional claim to the *hametz* and removing the category from our hearts.

The following morning, we perform a ceremony pertaining to the *hametz* found the previous evening.[72] The procedure is called *bi'ur hametz* ("destruction of *hametz*"). We take the *hametz* outside, burn it, and then recite an Aramaic statement of nullification, similar to the one that was said after the search.[73] From this point on, one may not eat any *hametz*, nor, until the seder, any matzah (only unleavened food other than matzah). This stage in our preparation for Passover is critical in helping us to relive the original Exodus from Egypt by focusing on the importance and centrality of matzah. If we were permitted to eat matzah so close to the time of the seder, its appeal and novelty at the seder, when eating it is required, would be diminished. In fact, some rabbis have compared the isolation from matzah during the day and the consumption of matzah at the seder to the Jewish custom of a bride and groom remaining separated before a wedding.[74] Just as they anticipate their first intimate encounter as husband and wife, so do we anticipate (and appreciate) our first taste of matzah at the seder.

THE SALE OF *HAMETZ*

Many years ago, when people kept less food in their houses than we do today, getting rid of *hametz* in advance of Passover was in some ways less of a challenge than it is for us. Now, even after we have tried to eat up and clean out, we seem to find ourselves with full bags and boxes and jars and bottles of staples and exotic foods that we would like to use after Passover has ended. These items should be stored away in one place, and the cupboard should be sealed with a lock or at least noted by having a tape across it. In addition, we must ask ourselves some questions. Could there be stray *hametz* in the house that can never be found or removed? Maybe one of the kids hid a cookie behind the radiator and has forgotten all about it. Maybe we also own a vacation home that is certainly not *hametz*-free. Would we then be transgressing the prohibition of owning *hametz*?[75] Or, what if we owned a business, for example, a distillery with an inventory of liquor made from fermented grain, and disposing of all of the *hametz* would create a financial crisis? To answer in particular the last question, the rabbis of the Middle Ages established the practice of *mechirat hametz* (sale of *hametz*) to a non-Jewish friend, which would be legally binding, but, at the same time, could be reversed after Passover. The basis for such a sale comes from the following scenario described in the Tosefta, a collection of teachings from the sages of the Rabbinic era:

> *If a Jew and non-Jew are traveling on a ship, and the Jew has* hametz *in his possession, he may sell it to the non-Jew or give it as a gift, and then acquire it back from him after Passover, but only if he had given it to the non-Jew unconditionally [a* matanah gemurah, *which literally means a "full or complete gift"].*[76]

Arrangements for the transaction are made well in advance of Passover, but the contract is not executed until Erev Passover, right before the time when owning *hametz* is no longer allowed (and adjusted to the time zone where the seller will be that morning). To guarantee that this sale is legitimate and that neither party is wronged, a legal contract is drawn up, usually with only a token payment exchanged. In the past, people were represented by a rabbi or they might execute their own contract; but nowadays, granting a "delegation of power" to a rabbi is the typical procedure. The *hametz* is not actually handed over but locked out of our sight with the non-Jew having complete access (for example, possessing a key). These conditions fulfill the technical requirements of a sale and therefore fulfill our obligation not to "own" *hametz*.[77] Shortly after Passover ends, the *hametz* is in effect repurchased according to various rules. In one example, the Jewish emissary meets in person with the non-Jew and buys back the *hametz*, at full value plus profit for the period the *hametz* was under the non-Jew's control. In another example, the non-Jew has made a down payment before Passover toward the sale. Through a stipulation in the contract, at the end of Passover, the ownership of the *hametz* will revert to the seller if the buyer has not paid the balance owed. The agreement states that the buyer's failure to come up with full payment will not retroactively invalidate the sale.[78]

THE SPIRITUAL DISPOSAL OF *HAMETZ*

As we perform each of these detailed, almost obsessive rites regarding *hametz,* we experience two related stages of spirituality. One is a feeling of accomplishment. We have cleaned our home with a level of fastidiousness that we see only from one Passover to the next. This cleaning experience, unlike most others, is artful because of the overarching purpose and clarity of vision that accompanies it. As we wipe each shelf and sweep up each speck of *hametz,* our feeling of accomplishment is akin to victory, a sort of spiritual liberation. For weeks, we anticipate the moment when the house is spotlessly clean and prepared for Passover. We bask in the glimmer of the kitchen tiles and the glow of the countertops. This feeling is not one to be overlooked, however mundane it may seem on the surface.

The second stage of spirituality is a realization that this sense of satisfaction is temporary. We know from the instant we finish cleaning the house that it will not remain clean, and we become aware that we are facing a spiritual window of opportunity.[80] Many of the moments in our lives are spent in preparation for yet another moment in time: studying for the exam, training for the performance, packing for the trip. Because we know these events are windows of opportunity, we invest in preparation. But if after preparing, we then fail to open that window, life will likely remain the same; or, quite possibly, it may go in a direction that is not desired or is even extremely upsetting. The ancient Israelites experienced such a moment in Egypt. They had been asked to collect their belongings, mark their doorposts, and ready themselves for escape—their window of opportunity. They had to decide whether to take this opportunity or not. At the seder, we will describe and relive the Israelites' flight from the Egyptians, and we will reflect upon our own existence. The spirituality of the celebration begins in earnest with cleaning and readying for such a journey.

Hametz and Travel Plans

People who are traveling and will return just before or during Passover must do their *hametz* removal before the trip. But what do people do who will be away for the entire holiday? The answer depends on timing. If they plan to leave 30 days or less before the start of Passover and will not return until after Passover ends, they clean the house, arrange for the sale of *hametz,* and do the formal search. They do not say the nullifying blessing until Erev Passover (from wherever they are), and the burning of hametz is not done at all. No other acts are necessary, assuming no one will be eating in the house during Passover. If people leave more than 30 days before the start of Passover and plan to be away for its entirety, they need do nothing beyond arranging with a rabbi to sell all their *hametz.*[79]

The Seder

The atmosphere at a Passover seder is different from that of other occasions. Although the table is lavishly set,[81] the seder is not meant to be overly formal or stuffy. We are supposed to act like free people, and thus we recline comfortably, as a required aspect of the celebration.[82]

And Now for the Entertainment

The practice of reclining was virtually universal throughout the Greco-Roman world as the marker for a significant, formal banquet. Such a banquet had two main courses. The first was the dinner (in Greek, *deipnon*). The second course was the symposium (in Greek, *symposion* from *sympotein*, "to drink together"). An elaborate ritual marked the division between the two, which included removing the tables, sweeping the floor, and mixing the wine, which was cut with water to allow the attendees to stay alert and awake for a long, lingering evening. A "symposiarch" was chosen from among the guests to direct the festivities and entertainment. He offered a libation to the deity and thus began the symposium.[83]

The original seder, as devised in the talmudic era, was based upon the Roman version of a Greek symposium, a tightly choreographed party, where aristocratic men, reclining on couches, drank wine, ate, and conversed.[84] Today, because the seder is long, some families enjoy holding it on the living room floor with pillows strewn about for everyone's comfort. In this arrangement, true reclining is possible, and small children can move about.

The leader of the seder, according to the most traditional Ashkenazic custom, wears a *kitel*, a long white robe donned at special times of the year and at certain life-cycle events, such as one's wedding. Some scholars contend that the *kitel* worn at the seder evokes the white garments that the ancient priests and Levites wore during the time of the Temple.[85] The medieval Rabbinic authorities who mention the custom suggest that the *kitel* is worn specifically because of its similarity to a burial shroud.[86] Through association, we are likely to take the evening more seriously and not be tempted in the direction of being overly casual.

Based on the prescribed order contained in the haggadah, participants in the seder recall the ceremonial eating of the paschal lamb and the story of the Exodus. Thus the seder fulfills the biblical commandment "And you shall explain to your son on that day, 'It is because of what the LORD did for me when I went free from Egypt'" (Exod. 13:8). The table is typically set with one large seder plate (in Hebrew, *ke'arat ha-seder*) containing symbolic foods, a stack of three ceremonial matzot, bowls of saltwater, and, before each person, a wine cup. About halfway through the seder, a substantial meal is served. The evening concludes with folk songs and with age-old melodies in praise of God.

The Ceremonial Matzot

Traditionally, the three matzot represent the three ritual classes of Jews: the *Kohanim* (priests); the Levites (descendants of the tribe of Levi who were given special religious and political responsibilities); and the Yisra'elim (Jews who trace their heritage to the Israelites, but who are neither *Kohanim* nor Levites). The matzot are prepositioned on the table in front of the person who is leading the seder, usually on a large plate covered with a cloth or inside a traditional, ornamented "matzah cover." Early in the ceremony, the leader breaks the middle matzah into two pieces. The smaller piece is placed back between the whole pieces, all of which will be used to make the blessing over matzah and to begin the meal. The leader hides the larger piece as the *afikoman* (derived from the Greek for either "dessert" or "after-dinner entertainment") somewhere in the house. At the end of the meal, the children hunt for the *afikoman* and a reward is given. (In some families, the children hide the *afikoman* and later demand a ransom from their parents to reveal the location.) The children each receive a prize (often something extra-special for the lucky one who discovered it). Ideally, the prizes are appropriate to the occasion, such as a Jewish book, game, or toy or, perhaps, the promise of money to be given once the initial days of the festival are over. Many families ask that children donate 10 percent of any prize money to *tzedakah* (charity). The activity surrounding the *afikoman* appeals greatly to the interest of fun-loving children and even teenagers.

Shopping for Matzah

A box of matzah should be marked "kosher for Passover," a guarantee the bread has not come in contact with any moisture from the time the wheat was ground into flour. Some people go a step further and purchase the more expensive *sh'murah* (literally, "guarded") matzah for use at a seder. *Sh'murah* means authorities have supervised the product from the moment the grain was harvested, to be sure it does not ferment. For those who are allergic to wheat, oat and spelt matzah with kosher certification are available.[87] The matzot in other categories, such as "egg" (usually made with fruit juice instead of water, but not necessarily with eggs), onion, and even chocolate covered, can be a great for snacks but should not be used at the seder; they do not represent the "bread of affliction" that matzah is meant to symbolize.

This part of the seder is called *tzafun* (literally, "hidden") because everyone eats a small piece of the once hidden, now found, *afikoman*, an act that signals the end of the meal but not the seder. The *afikoman* is the last solid item we are permitted to consume at the seder because matzah should be the final, lingering flavor. Another explanation is rooted in the idea that the *afikoman* symbolizes the paschal lamb eaten by the Israelites with bitter herbs and matzah before they left Egypt. This lamb was eaten as an offering to God, rather than as a meal to satisfy hunger. Later, during Passover ceremonies in the Temple, two sacrifices were made. The first lamb was the "festival" offering, a sacrifice performed at every festival. The second was the paschal offering, to recall the sacrificial lamb the Israelites consumed before leaving Egypt. When we hold a seder today, we remember the sacrifices in the same order: first, the festival sacrifice, by way of the symbolic egg and the meal; and then second, the paschal sacrifice, by way of eating the *afikoman.*

These explanations aside, the term *afikoman* has puzzled sages and scholars for centuries because it is a unique term found in the foundational text of Jewish law, the Mishnah. When describing the order of the seder, the Mishnah says: "We may not add an *afikoman* after the paschal lamb."[88] The Rabbis of the Talmud tried to understand what is meant here by the word *afikoman*.[89] One opinion is that we "should not uproot ourselves from one eating group and join another" in its revelry. From this interpretation, the Rabbis inferred that the word *afikoman* is derived from the Greek phrase *apiku manaikhu* ("take out your utensils"). A different talmudic explanation says that if *afikoman* itself means "dessert," then we should not follow it with other desserts. Therefore, medieval Jewish codes permit us nothing after eating the *afikoman* other than water and the ritually required wine.[90]

Modern scholars again see remnants of the Greek symposium in this expression of *afikoman*. They believe that the word is from the Greek term *epikoman*, which refers to the climax of the symposium when participants would leave the house and enter another to extend the evening.[91] Although the Greek meaning of *afikoman* and the use of the word in a seder are significantly different, they share the concept that this is the symbolic conclusion of the meal.

THE SEDER PLATE

Center stage on the holiday table is the seder plate, which is often an artistic object unto itself. Its function is to hold a collection of ritual food items that invite questioning. Each item is referred to in the haggadah with an explanation of its symbolism and its significance to the celebration; and each, except for the shank bone, will be consumed at a particular point in the seder. The participants receive individual portions to use in the rituals; the foods are typically taken from serving dishes, not from the seder plate itself. However, some families prepare, in addition to the large seder plate, a small, individual seder plate for each participant. Especially with a large group, this practice puts these curious ritual foods in visual proximity to everyone and thereby helps stimulate interest.

- *karpas* Derived from the Greek word *karpos* ("fruit of the soil"), this is the spring vegetable, often parsley, celery, or a potato that we dip in the saltwater and eat after reciting the blessing over vegetables. Dipping may reflect the customs of the Greco-Roman era, when dipping foods in liquids was a common practice; yet it also represents the vitality and rebirth of nature in the spring and, in Jewish hands, the symbol of a newly born nation—the Jews at the time of the Exodus. Some scholars say the *karpas* reminds us of an aromatic herb called *ezob* in the Torah, which is perhaps the plant hyssop. The Israelites used it as a brush for marking their doorways with blood during the final plague upon the Egyptians (the killing of the firstborn) to warn the angel of death that these houses should be passed over.[92]

- *zeroa* Most commonly, a roasted bone with some meat attached, it symbolizes the paschal sacrifice made during the era of the Temple. People often roast the shank bone of a lamb, although some deliberately use a dissimilar bone, such as a chicken neck, to acknowledge that the Temple is gone. The *zeroa* should be scorched to appear as much like a sacrifice as possible. Vegetarians choose a non-bone item for the *zeroa*. The usual one is a roasted beet, which has a "bloody" look and is also appropriate because it relates to the Rabbis of the Talmud, who ate it as part of their seder meal.[93] Some people say they like to use a "paschal yam," simply for the ring of it. Others choose to put a sculpted or toy lamb on the plate.

- *maror* These are the bitter herbs mentioned in the Torah, which says the Israelites "shall eat the flesh . . . roasted over the fire, with unleavened bread and with bitter herbs" (Exod. 12:8). The herbs symbolize the bitterness of slavery experienced by the Israelites. Historically, people used lettuce (*hazeret*), in effect a "bitter" vegetable—a practice many still follow today

The Literal Ritual

The only contemporary practitioners of the ancient paschal sacrifice are the Samaritans of Nablus (the biblical city of Shechem). This very small ethnic group, which broke away from Judaism thousands of years ago—before the advent of the Talmud—sacrifices dozens of sheep each year on the day before Passover. Each family eats its lamb with matzah and bitter herbs.[94]

with romaine lettuce. When Diaspora Jews moved eastward into the cold climates of Germany and Poland, lettuce was not available. Jews began to substitute *chrein* (Yiddish for "horseradish"). Jewish law obligates us to eat a minimum amount of *maror*, that being the size of an olive.[95] For some people, filling the requirement is much more difficult when fresh horseradish is used. We eat the bitter herbs a minimum of two times during the seder: once dipped in *haroset* (see below) that is shaken off and a second time, layered with *haroset* and placed on a piece of matzah. This creation is known as the "Hillel sandwich" (*korekh*) because the great sage Hillel the Elder started a similar custom. He lived at the time of the Second Temple, and thus the original sandwich consisted of matzah, bitter herbs, and the Passover lamb. The custom derives from a question about the precise meaning of a phrase in Numbers 9:11, which instructs people to eat the paschal offering *"al matzot u'marorim."* Although this phrase is usually translated as "with matzahs and bitter herbs," the Hebrew word *al* literally means "on top of." Rabbi Hillel thought that the paschal lamb should be eaten as a sort of open-faced sandwich, with the meat and bitter herbs stacked on top of some matzah. Since there is no longer a Temple in Jerusalem at which to make an offering, we substitute *haroset* for the lamb.

- *haroset* A mixture of chopped nuts (often walnuts or pistachios) and fruits (apples, dates, or figs), wine, and spices. Ingredients vary by ancestral tradition. The Mishnah indicates that *haroset* was a dish served at other times of the year and made with flour;[96] the Passover version is grain free. At the seder, *haroset* is symbolically eaten in combination with *maror*. It represents the clay the Israelite slaves used in making bricks for the Egyptians as well as the mortar used to hold the bricks in place.

• *beitzah* A roasted egg (may be baked or hard-boiled) still in the shell, it symbolizes the festival sacrifice that each Jew was to offer when making a pilgrimage to the Temple in Jerusalem. (The festival sacrifice differs from the additional sacrifice that was made at Passover, the paschal lamb.) Many people choose to use a brown egg to accentuate the scorched look of the sacrifice. Because of its association with the Temple, the egg is also a symbol of mourning, particularly for the Temple itself. And, as one might expect, the egg is a symbol of spring and rebirth. Typically this symbolic egg is not consumed (the haggadah does not contain a directive to eat an egg); however, many hosts have the custom to serve each person an egg that is eaten later, at the start of the meal.

• *matzot* Three pieces of matzah are used in various rituals by the leader of the seder. They are prepositioned on the table and may be wrapped in a cloth and placed on the seder plate, directly on top of the *maror* in the center.[97] Some people use a special stand that holds the matzot above the seder plate, or they may place the matzot inside a special cloth cover with a separate opening for each matzah.

The Sixth Spot

Some seder plates, by custom, have six rather than five spaces. In that case, *hazeret* (bitter lettuce, as interpreted by most scholars) goes in the sixth space rather than in the *maror* space, and something else bitter, such as horseradish, goes in the *maror* space. Why such confusion? It all started with the Talmud, which refers to what we understand to be *maror* as "*hazeret*." Later on, when people tried to understand what specific items they should use on the seder plate, some of them attempted to solve the puzzle by putting not one but two bitter items on the dish. Fortunately, the distinction between having a six-space plate or one with five grows no more complicated, because the haggadah never directs us to "eat *hazeret*," and the blessing for *maror* covers the items in both the *maror* and the *hazeret* spaces.

Mystical Dimensions of the Seder

Kabbalah expresses the mystical significance of many aspects of the Jewish tradition. In this seven-part illustration,* which stylistically resembles a seder plate or a Star of David, the ritual foods of the seder correspond to the 10 *sefirot* on the Tree of Life.

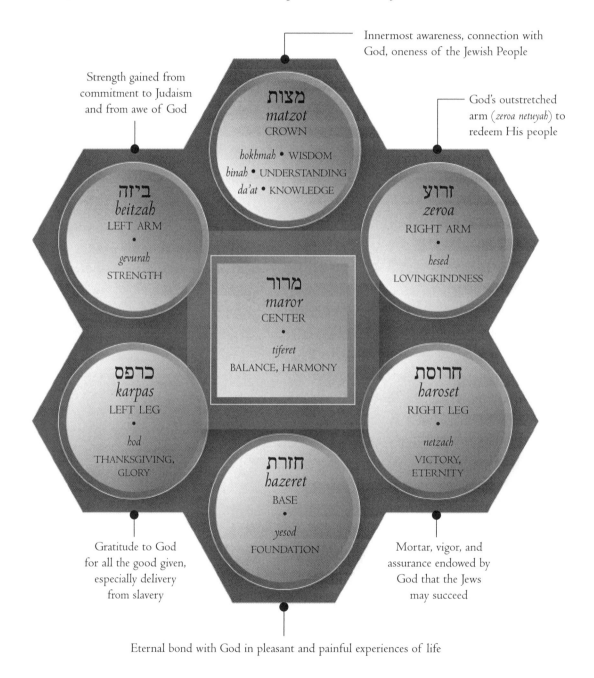

Innermost awareness, connection with God, oneness of the Jewish People

Strength gained from commitment to Judaism and from awe of God

God's outstretched arm (*zeroa netuyah*) to redeem His people

מצות
matzot
CROWN

ḥokhmah • WISDOM
binah • UNDERSTANDING
da'at • KNOWLEDGE

ביזה
beitzah
LEFT ARM
•
gevurah
STRENGTH

זרוע
zeroa
RIGHT ARM
•
ḥesed
LOVINGKINDNESS

מרור
maror
CENTER
•
tiferet
BALANCE, HARMONY

כרפס
karpas
LEFT LEG
•
hod
THANKSGIVING, GLORY

חרוסת
ḥaroset
RIGHT LEG
•
netzach
VICTORY, ETERNITY

חזרת
ḥazeret
BASE
•
yesod
FOUNDATION

Gratitude to God for all the good given, especially delivery from slavery

Mortar, vigor, and assurance endowed by God that the Jews may succeed

Eternal bond with God in pleasant and painful experiences of life

* Shira Goldberg developed the initial concept for the design of this chart.

HAGGADOT

Passover is likely the most universally celebrated and beloved of all Jewish holidays, with its principal religious service conducted at home, the symbolism and meaning found in reliving the story of liberation, the involvement of all age groups, the youngest child (often very small indeed) chanting the Four Questions, the much-anticipated meal, and the singing of songs familiar since childhood. This interactive and joyful learning experience has brought forth, over the past several decades, a surge of renewed interest in the seder and, with it, the publication of many new *haggadot* (plural of haggadah). Beyond having variations in translation and commentary and a profusion of lush illustrations, *haggadot* have been created for special interests and themes, such as study *haggadot* (with commentary from classical or modern scholars and perhaps questions for students), feminist *haggadot*, social justice *haggadot*, secular Israeli *haggadot* (often with a focus on the land, the nation, or the pluralistic society), and even comic-book *haggadot*. Jews of all backgrounds, and non-Jewish guests as well can all connect to this core expression of the Jewish tradition.

The first haggadah was probably assembled during the early post-biblical times in the Land of Israel. The Mishnah and the Tosefta, works of the talmudic sages, are the primary sources for the material in a traditional haggadah. The earliest extant version appeared in Babylonia, in a 10th-century C.E. prayer book; and the earliest extant printed version is one thought to have been published in Guadalajara about 1482, a decade before the Jews were expelled from Spain. The illustrated *Prague Haggadah* of 1526 is the earliest to have survived in its entirety and was used as a prototype for European *haggadot* that followed. For centuries, the text and illustrations (largely scenes from the Bible and from rabbinical legends) of *haggadot* were relatively fixed. Today, besides the variations that reflect contemporary Jewish agendas and events, we see the works of modern Jewish artists such as Arthur Szyk, Ben Shahn, and Yaacov Agam.[98]

Whatever haggadah a family uses, there is much to learn during a seder. The haggadah itself, especially one with additional commentary, explains many of the symbols

When Do We Eat?

In the earliest Passover seders, the meal came first and was followed by extemporaneous questions (meant to prompt discussion), an informal rabbinical recounting of the Exodus, and a recitation of the Ten Plagues. By the year 200 C.E., the meal had been postponed until the end of the liturgy, as it is today, and set questions had replaced the use of ones that were unrehearsed and changeable. Over time, the haggadah, as the narrative portion of the seder, grew larger and more varied.[99]

and customs of Passover. Its 15 sections or steps gracefully guide families and guests through the telling of the story; and they particularly engage the children, who anticipate the annual customs and question-and-answer portions. Upon completion of these stages of learning, praying, drinking, dipping, eating, and singing, participants will have encountered Judaism's premier celebratory class about the spirituality and joy of freedom.

Expanding the Traditional *Karpas*

When hosting a seder, some families choose to enlarge the ritual of *karpas*. They offer more than one vegetable, with plentiful servings of each; and the dips go well beyond saltwater. Some examples are carrots in ranch dressing, artichokes in garlic-spiced mayonnaise, and jicama in guacamole. To hold the interest of children,[100] *karpas* may be expanded beyond the realm of raw vegetables to include potato chips or slices of baked potatoes dipped in ketchup.[101] Thoughtful reasons underlie this practice. Many people have unfortunate childhood memories of attending very boring and exhausting seders, during which the main question on their minds was "When are we going to eat?" With a bountiful *karpas*, the participants can stop waiting to hear only the words *Shulchan orekh*, "The meal is served," and instead can relax, be attentive, and appreciate the readings and conversation. People are less likely to feel the urge to rush through the haggadah.

The enlarged *karpas* serves also as a break for the host family, who may be somewhat exhausted and overwhelmed from preparing for the seder. While the guests are occupied with their veggies and dips, the hosts may have some time to sit down, take a breath, and get into the spirit of the evening.

A Minor Appeasement

"We dip now before the meal, because we cannot wait so long without eating anything. In fact, people generally dip before a meal in order to manage their appetites, though they should not fill their stomachs."[102]
—Rabbi Joel Sirkes[103]
(b. circa 1561–d. 1640, Poland)

Why Four Cups?

For the Rabbis of the Talmud, the purpose of wine is straightforward: to enable the participants to be happy on this festive day of liberation.[104] (Grape juice is a perfectly acceptable substitute for children or for people uncomfortable with wine.[105]) Almost all kosher wines are marked as being acceptable for Passover; and they come in many varieties, from the conventional ultrasweet to the more recent outpouring of gourmet choices from Israel and California. The required amount is four cups of about 3.5 ounces for each person. Why four? The Rabbis explain that the four cups correspond to the four expressions God used in assuring the Israelites of their future redemption: "I will free you … deliver you … redeem you …. And I will take you …" (Exod. 6:6–7).[107] Another commonly expressed reason focuses on the idea that the story of the Exodus truly begins in the Book of Genesis. Before Joseph becomes the viceroy of Egypt, he spends years in prison. While there, he interprets the dream of a fellow prisoner, the Pharaoh's wine steward. Joseph's interpretation refers four times to Pharaoh's cup.[108] Eventually Joseph is released from jail and becomes viceroy, but this high point slides downward into slavery. That slavery leads ultimately to freedom, and we celebrate with four cups to remind us that it all began with Joseph and to ensure our own redemption.[109]

Rabbis in the 14th to 16th centuries offer various other explanations. Among them are suggestions that the four cups correspond to:

- the number of matriarchs (Sarah, Rebecca, Rachel, and Leah), while the three symbols— *pesach* (the roasted bone for the paschal sacrifice), matzah, and *maror*—represent the three patriarchs (Abraham, Isaac, and Jacob);

- the four redemptions of the Jewish people—namely, when God chose Abraham, when God delivered the Israelites from Egypt, when God sustained the Jews through exiles and many prolonged sufferings (right into modern times), and when God will redeem the Jews in the future;

- the four virtues the Israelites retained while in Egypt—they did not change their Hebrew names, they did not change their Hebrew language, they had high moral standards, and they had no informers among them.[110]

Wholeness of the Number Four

In Judaism the number four symbolizes completeness and sufficiency, which unfolds through many aspects of the tradition. Among them are the four corners of the earth from which God will ingather all the Jewish people, the four mothers of the Jewish people, the four rivers in the Garden of Eden, the four levels of Torah interpretation, the four worlds according to Kabbalah, and the four letters in the Inefffable Name of God.[106] For Passover, we have the Four Questions, the four cups of wine, and the Four Children. On a practical level, this number helps us remember important signposts of the seder. On a symbolic level, the number four enriches our understanding of the holiday of freedom. Its use suggests that we rely upon our whole selves, our whole family, our whole community, and our whole relationship with God to accomplish a complete spiritual liberation.

ELIJAH

During the latter half of the seder, just after we drink our third cup of wine, we pour wine into a single, special cup to honor the Prophet Elijah. At the same time, we open an exterior door to welcome Elijah, a ritual symbolizing that we are waiting for our redemption.[113] According to the most common understanding in the Talmud, Elijah's cup represents an additional, fifth expression of biblical assurance that God will redeem the Israelites from the Egyptians: "I will bring you into the land" (Exod. 6:8). The Talmud nonetheless ponders how we can account for a fifth cup, considering that the ritual in the haggadah explicitly says only the number "four." The tradition holds that the arrival of Elijah will herald the coming of the Messiah; in addition, to prepare for an orderly day of judgment, Elijah will clarify issues that have gone unanswered.[114] For that reason, the Talmud says we will wait for Elijah himself to explain the fifth cup and whether it relates to the fifth expression of redemption.

The leader stands to recite a reading from the haggadah that calls upon God to destroy other nations for the pain they have caused the Jews. The components are taken from the Bible.

Pour out Your fury on the nations that do not know You, upon the kingdoms that do not invoke your name, for they have devoured Jacob and desolated his home (Ps. 79:6–7).

Pour out Your wrath on them; may your blazing anger overtake them (Ps. 69:25).

Oh, pursue them in wrath and destroy them from under the heavens of the LORD! (Lam. 3:66).

The Same or Different?

In 1957, Siegfried Stein, then a professor at the Institute of Jewish Studies, University College London, wrote an essay describing what he saw as foundational similarities between the seder and the Greek symposium. He cited, for example, the 4th-century B.C.E. writer Antiphanes, who said that to honor the gods, one must drink a specific number of cups of wine at the symposium.[111] Other scholars have argued that the seder was expressly designed to be different from the symposium. They emphasize that the cups of wine at Passover do not have any pagan ritual as a precedent. Yet, as Joshua Kulp, a founder of The Conservative Yeshiva in Jerusalem, observed in a 2005 article on the seder's origins, "We should note that the need to create signposts to distinguish the Jewish ritual from Greek pagan ritual only emphasizes how close the two may have seemed to actual participants."[112]

This reading has become controversial. Some people question whether, in today's world, it is appropriate to make a statement pressing God with a desire for retaliation against our persecutors. Do we truly believe in vengeance or do we believe in tolerance and peace? The Shalom Hartman Institute in Jerusalem publishes a haggadah that offers an alternative reading. It begins with the phrase "Pour out Your love."[116] Unfortunately, we have yet to see a time when Jews could safely say that as a people they were free from being hated and persecuted—the circumstance that would render the traditional passage undeniably obsolete.

MIRIAM'S CUP

In the late 20th century, some people began the practice of placing on the seder table a special cup that is meant to represent the role of women in the Exodus story. Filled with water, it symbolzes Miriam's well, the water source that legend tells us sustained the Israelites for 40 years in the desert. The Rabbis of the Talmud noticed that in the Book of Numbers a statement concerning the death of the prophetess Miriam (sister of Moses) is immediately followed by a statement about a lack of water. They deduced that during Miriam's life, because of her great merit, a miraculous source of water had moved with the Jewish people throughout their wanderings. This legend is also derived from the talmudic statement, "If it wasn't for the righteousness of women of that generation, we would not have been redeemed from Egypt" (B. Talmud, *Sotah* 11b). Today, the people who perform the ritual of Miriam's cup incorporate it into the seder in various ways.[117] Most commonly, the leader raises it along with Elijah's cup toward the close of the seder, with the declaration, *Zot kos Miriyam, kos mayim chayyim; zekher l'tzi'at Mitzrayim.* "This is the cup of Miriam, the cup of living waters; a memorial to the Exodus from Egypt."

Pouring for Redemption

Rabbi Naftali Tzvi Horowitz (1760–1827, Poland) introduced a particularly beautiful custom. Elijah's cup is filled by having each participant pour in some wine from his or her cup. This custom reminds us that the redemption will occur only when every person has contributed to bringing it about. They will do so by following the mitzvot (literally, "commandments"): religious obligations detailed in the Torah that pertain to our relationships with God and to our relationships with each other. This custom symbolically stresses that commitment, sacrifice, and action are necessary to bring us closer to redemption. In some households, as people add their wine to Elijah's cup, they express (privately or aloud) resolutions to pour their souls into making the next year a better one.[115]

MESSIANISM IN A NUTSHELL

A significant portion of Passover is devoted to thinking about Redemption—the Redemption of the past and the Redemption expected in the future. During the seder, the Prophet Elijah is the bridge between the two eras, because he is a figure from the biblical past while at the same time he will be the heralder of the Messiah. The Hebrew word for messiah is *mashi'ach*, meaning "smeared with oil," in other words "anointed," as were the Israelite kings. When Judaism refers to a messiah, traditionally speaking, the understanding is that a human being descended from King David will arrive in Jerusalem and bring peace on earth. (The liberal streams of Judaism argue that this peace will come in a Messianic Era, brought about by circumstances or groups of people rather than by the arrival of an individual.) In the Talmud, the Rabbis offer several ideas about the conditions under which the Messiah will come. They say Elijah will usher in the Messiah on a day other than the Shabbat.[118] More specifically, many Rabbis suggest that the Messiah will arrive on Erev Passover, because the festival serves as our model of Redemption.[119] In the period before this day comes, the Rabbis say, there will be unprecedented hardship and suffering ("birth pangs of the Messiah"), a world blanketed by war and corruption.[120]

For millennia, people have intensely disputed what the world will be like once the hardship and suffering are gone, once the Messiah has arrived. The Jewish tradition allows for freedom of belief and, consequently, holds a variety of ideas about this time. The Rabbis of the Talmud say that the dead will be resurrected from their graves and that the Davidic kingship will be restored. Others maintain that the Jews will no longer be in exile and hold that this condition is the primary difference between our current world and the Messianic Era.[121] Whatever the concept regarding the Messiah, Judaism maintains a fundamental assertion: If we invest in living our lives with hope, faith, and action, we can look forward to a better world. As a nation and in partnership with God, we have both the responsibility and the power to bring forth a time of the Messiah in which there is universal peace and prosperity.

The Passover Love Song

On the Shabbat that falls during *hol ha-mo'ed* (the intermediary days between the beginning and ending days of Passover), it is customary for the leader of the service or an honored congregant to chant Shir Ha-Shirim (The Song of Songs) before the Torah reading.[122] This book is one of the five megillot (scrolls) in the third part of the Bible, Kethuvim (The Writings), each of which is assigned to be read communally at a different time during the year.[123] The Song of Songs is traditionally ascribed to King Solomon, although modern scholars debate its exact origin. Many are inclined to believe that several authors composed it over time, because such a variety of poetic devices is employed.

Completely allegorical, The Song of Songs describes a loving, intimate relationship between a male lover, in effect God, and a female lover, in effect the People of Israel. Because of this passionate portrayal (and despite some erotic images), Rabbi Akiva, the great scholar of the Mishnah, who lived in 1st- to 2nd-century Israel, deemed it the holiest book in Kethuvim. His assessment seems to be the sole reason it was canonized, which scholars believe occurred about the 2nd century C.E.[124] Rabbis in subsequent generations inferred from the title a further reason for the book's importance. Because the title is The Song (singular) of Songs (plural), the seven-chapter poem is thought to be a summary account of all the "songs"—the moments when God spoke to Israel, for example, at the splitting of the Red Sea and at Mount Sinai.[125] In other words, this one song includes all the other songs. Jewish mysticism, which holds The Song of Songs in a particular place of importance, considers the book to be one that rings out from the heavens at the most holy and joyous moments in history.[126]

Truth be told, many scholars understand the book to be quite profane.[127] The images may appear tame to the casual modern reader, but they can be interpreted as being rather sexually graphic and were perhaps explicitly so for the ancient audience. The Rabbinic tradition, however, sustained its position that the poem is about God and Israel, despite the fact that God is not mentioned; and Shir Ha-Shirim firmly took its place in the biblical canon. Throughout the centuries that have followed, Jewish artists have used it in art related to marriage. More recently, Zionists have found the poem to be a source of inspiration because of its extraordinary, poetic depictions of nature and the Land of Israel.

It may seem odd that during Passover we read a scroll that is not about the Exodus and has no specific mention of God. But without question, the motif of love is appropriate for the festival. The importance of our love, both for others and for God, penetrates each and every dimension of the Jewish religion. Our philosophers and mystics have given a number of explanations, all originating from the first paragraph of the *Shema*, the core statement that defines the relationship between the Jewish people and God: "You shall love the LORD your God with all your heart and with all your soul and with all your might" (Deut. 6:5).

Maimonides articulates the classic view of love for God, which blends rational and mystical concepts:

> *What is the path to love and awe of God? When a person contemplates God's wondrous and great deeds and creations and appreciates His infinite wisdom that surpasses all comparison, he will immediately love, praise, and glorify, yearning with tremendous desire to know God's great name . . . . One who serves God out of love occupies himself in the Torah and mitzvot and walks the path of wisdom for no ulterior motive: not because of fear that evil will occur, nor in order to acquire benefit. Rather he does what is true because it is true, and ultimately, good will come because of it . . . . A person should love God with a very great and exceeding love until his soul is bound up in the love of God. Thus, he will always be obsessed with this love as if he is lovesick . . . . This concept was implied by Solomon [in The Song of Songs 2:5] when he stated as a metaphor: "I'm faint with love." Indeed the totality of Shir Ha-Shirim is a parable describing this love.*[128]

We may relate to the concept of loving God either through the intellectual desire to "know" God or through the intuitive and mystical yearning to cling to God. Both ways can be characterized as spiritual love. Spiritual love is not lustful or related to the corporeal in any way. Spiritual love is the utmost expression of unity—unity created by shared experiences and feelings. These include shared anguish as well as shared good fortune. Spiritual love embodies empathy and compassion, the qualities that require us to eliminate the ego and truly see ourselves as a part of another's being. When we recite the *Shema*, expressing our faith that God is One and affirming that we love God, we realize and marvel at the notion that we are a part of God's oneness. This kind of love is the impetus for the most wondrous and awe-inspiring of human qualities, such as loyalty, persistence, and hope.

▲ ▲ ▲ ▲ ▲ ▲ ▲   ▲   ▲ ▲ ▲ ▲ ▲ ▲ ▲

When God took us out of Egypt and rescued us from the suffering and torture, it was because God heard our cries—heard us and shared in our experience. God saved us because God loves us; and, in return, we made a covenant of love, using the Torah as our guide to keeping that covenant. Since the Exodus, we have been in this loving relationship with God; and because we value the relationship, we follow the mitzvot, seek wisdom and truth, and aspire to live an ethical life. In other words, we do these things as Jews, not for ourselves alone, but out of love and in recognition that we are part of a relationship existent from the moment Moses exclaimed in God's name, "Let My people go" (Exod. 10:3). This relationship calls for our attention and for us to inject into it our devotion and most heartfelt effort. Within this place, we have the essence of what being a Jew means; and Shir Ha-Shirim does not offer us the typical biblical style of expressing our relationship with God—it sings about it.

·✦· Passover ·✦·
Pathways Through the Sources

Midrash
Against All Odds

The hero of the greatest Jewish story was physically flawed. Although Moses was not born with a defect, God willed, through the agency of an angel, that he be deprived of eloquent speech—the typical asset of a powerful leader. This popular piece of Rabbinic lore not only gives us insight into the special spirit and character of Moses but also resonates with the theme of hope found in the Exodus story. If this one man can overcome his personal obstacles and contribute to the welfare of the community, then so can all of us.

Midrash is a large body of work that combines the theological, homiletical, and ethical lore of the Rabbis in the Land of Israel from the 3rd through 10th centuries. It comprises various collections, among them *Midrash Rabbah*, a series of books that expounds upon and further illustrates each book of the Torah.[129]

> Pharaoh's daughter used to kiss and hug Moses, loved him as if he were her own son and would not allow him out of the royal palace. Because he was so handsome everyone was eager to see him, and whoever saw him could not tear himself away from him. Pharaoh also used to kiss and hug him, and he used to take the crown of Pharaoh and place it on his own head.
>
> The magicians of Egypt sat there and said, "We are afraid of him who is taking off your crown and placing it upon his own head, lest he be the one of whom we prophesy that he will take the kingdom from thee." Some of them counseled to slay him and others to burn him, but Jethro was present among them and he said to them, "This boy has no sense. However, test him by placing before him a gold vessel and a live coal; if he stretches forth his hand for the gold, then he has sense and you can slay him, but if he makes for the live coal then he has no sense and there can be no sentence of death upon him." So they brought these thing before him, and Moses was about to reach forth for the gold when Gabriel [the angel] came and thrust his hand aside so that it seized the coal, and he thrust his hand with the live coal into his mouth, so that his tongue was burnt, with the result that he became slow of speech and of tongue.
>
> —*Midrash Rabbah* (*Exodus Rabbah* 1:26)

Midrash

The Divine in the Most Unlikely Places

Nothing in the Torah is without profound meaning—the events, the descriptions, the instructions, and the minute details. Even the crowns atop the letters themselves act as conduits through which God transmits awe-inspiring messages. With this understanding, the Rabbinic sages paid great attention to a miraculous event centered around an object—a thorn bush—from which God chose to communicate and reveal His presence to Moses: "An angel of the LORD appeared to him [Moses] in a blazing fire out of a bush. He gazed, and there was a bush all aflame, yet the bush was not consumed" (Exod. 3:2).

The five Rabbis referenced in this midrash lived in the Land of Israel or in Babylonia in times ranging from the 1st to 3rd centuries. Although they disagree about the exact message in the bush, their various spiritual insights inspire the discovery of meaning all around us.

> A heathen once asked Rabbi Joshua ben Karchah, "Why did God choose a thorn bush from which to speak to Moses?" He replied, "If it were a carob tree or a sycamore tree, you would have asked the same question; but to dismiss you without any reply is not right, so I will tell you why: To teach you that no place is devoid of God's presence, not even a thorn bush …."

> Rabbi Eliezer said: "Just as the thorn bush is the lowliest of all trees in the world, so Israel was lowly and humble in Egypt. It is for this reason that God revealed himself to them and ultimately redeemed them."

> Rabbi Yossi said, "Just as the thorn bush is the prickliest of all the trees and any bird that goes into it does not come out untouched, so too was the slavery in Egypt more grievous before God than all of the other slaveries in the world …."

> Rabbi Yochanan said, "Just as one makes of thorns a fence for a garden, so too Israel is a protective fence to the world. Furthermore, just as the thorn bush grows near any water, so too Israel grew only in virtue of the Torah, which is also called 'water' …. Also, just as the thorn bush produces both thorns and roses, so among Israel there are both righteous and wicked. …"

Rabbi Nachman[130] ... said, "Some trees produce one single leaf, some two or three. The myrtle, for example, produces three because it is called a thick tree (Lev. 23:40), but the thorn bush has five leaves. God said to Moses, 'Israel will be redeemed for the sake of Abraham, Isaac, and Jacob and for your sake and for Aaron.'"
—*Midrash Rabbah* (*Exodus Rabbah* 2:5)

Babylonian Talmud

The Downfall of Our Enemy

The Talmud, the most significant collection of laws, stories, and thought in all Rabbinic literature, appears in two bodies: the Jerusalem Talmud (5th century) and the Babylonian Talmud (c. 6th century). It serves as the primary source for all later codes of Jewish law. In Judaism there is a proper manner of behavior for each and every circumstance. The Passover story teaches us the Jewish response to suffering: we must never lose hope. It also teaches us the Jewish response to victory: we do not taunt the defeated, or exaggerate or brag about the story of our success, or even delight in the pain or loss of others, even if they are a wicked enemy.

The Holy One, blessed be He, does not rejoice in the downfall of the wicked. Rabbi Yochanan said, "What is the meaning of the verse, *one could not come near the other all through the night* (Exod. 14:20), referring to Pharaoh and the Israelites at the sea? The ministering angels wanted to chant hymns, but the Holy One, blessed be He, said, 'The work of my hands is being drowned in the sea, and shall you chant hymns!'"
—B. Talmud, *Megillah* 10b

Babylonian Talmud

A Spirited Seder

The Passover seder is an occasion of intense celebration; and in Judaism, a celebration is not at its highest unless everyone is involved and engaged. This selection from the Talmud, with its descriptions of men, women, children, and post-Temple ideology, is rich with material that can be examined historically. Yet it conveys the joyous atmosphere of the seder, which includes learning, fun, and group participation.

Pesachim is a tractate of the Talmud that is dedicated to the laws, customs, and expositions on Passover that are contained in the Torah. The Talmud draws upon the teachings and opinions of different generations and lays them out here in a manner that seeks to find the truth and to provide the best way to envision what happened and its significance.

It was related of Rabbi Akiva[131] that he used to distribute parched ears of corn and nuts to children on the eve of Passover, so that they might not fall asleep but ask questions.

Our Rabbis taught: A man is duty bound to make his children and his household rejoice on a festival, for it is said, *You shall rejoice in your festival* (Deut. 16:14). With what does he make them rejoice? With wine. Rabbi Yehudah[132] said, "Men with what is suitable for them, and women with what is suitable for them. With what is suitable for men: with wine. And with what for women?" Rabbi Yosef[133] replied, "In Babylonia, with colored garments; in the Land of Israel, with ironed linen garments."

It was taught, Rabbi Yehudah ben Bateirah[134] said, "When the Temple was in existence there could be no rejoicing unless it was over a meat meal, as it is said: *and you shall sacrifice there offerings of well-being and eat them, rejoicing before the LORD your God* (Deut. 27:7). But now that the Temple is no longer in existence, there is no rejoicing unless it is with wine, as it is said: *wine that cheers the hearts of men* (Ps. 104:15)."
—B. Talmud, *Pesachim* 109a

The Zohar
As Below, So Above

In Jewish mysticism, there are two realms: one on earth (the lower one) and one where God's angelic court abides and God's presence is more pronounced (the higher one). What we do here on earth directly affects the heavenly realm. During Passover, our practices and spirituality, including our abstention from eating *hametz* and the joy we experience performing the seder, are a celebration of our relationship with the Divine.

The Zohar is the primary book of Jewish mysticism. The following text comes from one of its treatises, *Raya Mehemna* (The Faithful Shepherd), a kabbalistic exposition of the commandments and prohibitions found in the Torah.

And they baked unleavened cakes of dough that they had taken out of Egypt, for it was not leavened (Exod. 12:39). On the strength of this is founded the precept that the leaven should be burned on the Passover eve. "Leavened" and "unleavened" symbolize the evil and the good inclinations in man.

It is obligatory for every Israelite to relate the story of the Exodus on the Passover night. He who does so fervently and joyously, telling the tale with a high heart, shall be found worthy to rejoice in the *Shekhinah* [the presence of God] in the world to come, for rejoicing brings forth rejoicing; and the joy of Israel causes the Holy One Himself to be glad, so that He calls together all the Family above and says to them "Come ye and hearken unto the praises which My children bring unto Me! Behold how they rejoice in My Redemption!" Then all the angels and supernal beings gather round and observe Israel, how she sings and rejoices because of her LORD's own Redemption—and seeing the rejoicings below, the supernal beings also break into jubilation for that the Holy One possesses on earth a people so holy, whose joy in the Redemption of their LORD is so great and so powerful. For all that terrestrial rejoicing increases the power of the LORD and His hosts in the regions above, just as an earthly king gains strength from the praises of his subjects, the fame of his glory being this spread throughout the world.
—Zohar, *Bo* 40b

Maimonides
The Nature of the Festival

We often take for granted the timing and observances of Passover—two things that have been established for millennia—without noting the inherent rightness of the celebration. If, however, we consider the season of the holiday, spring, which symbolizes rebirth, and the duration of the observance, a week, which influences our perceptions, we can recognize the wisdom and beauty of the Jewish tradition.

Maimonides (Rabbi Moses ben Maimon), a renowned medieval Jewish thinker, provides a novel and pragmatic rationale for the observance of the festivals in this highly acclaimed philosophical exposition.

The festivals are all for rejoicings and pleasurable gatherings, which in most cases are indispensable for man; they are also useful in the establishment of friendship, which must exist among people living in political societies. There is a particular reason for every one of these days.

The account of Passover is generally known. It lasts for seven days, for the period of seven days is a mean between the natural day and the lunar month. You know already that this period plays a great role in natural matters. It does so likewise pertaining to the Law [Torah]. For the Law always tends to assimilate itself to nature, perfecting the natural matters in a certain respect. For nature is not endowed with thought and understanding, whereas the Law is the determining ruling and the governance of the deity, who grants intellect to all its possessors ....

The [Festival of] Weeks [i.e., Shavuot] is the day of the giving of the Torah ....This great gathering lasted only one day; accordingly it is commemorated every year during one day only. If, however, the eating of unleavened bread would last for only one day, we would not take notice of it and its meaning would not be made clear. For man often eats one kind of food for two or three days. Accordingly the meaning of [the eating of unleavened bread] only becomes clear and the account with which it is connected only becomes gradually known through its being eaten for a complete period.
—*Guide of the Perplexed* 3:43[135]

Don Yitzchak Abarbanel

Growing Up into Leadership

At Passover, the Jewish tradition emphasizes that the true hero of the story is God. In fact, the text of the haggadah never explicitly mentions Moses, the greatest prophet in Judaism, a man of most valiant and heroic accomplishments. In other sources, the tradition spends considerable time examining his character and development, thus letting his attributes convey what it takes to become a great leader.

Don Yitzchak Abarbanel was one of the great Bible commentators and Jewish philosophers. He served as an influential participant in the royal houses of Portugal and of Spain, but was not able to prevent the Inquisition. Here he describes the way in which the Torah presents Moses' background and shows us the stages of his spiritual growth.

These three stories were juxtaposed: (1) the murder of the Egyptian; (2) the two Hebrews who were fighting; and (3) the daughters in Midian (and the shepherds). They follow the story of Moses "growing up" in the house of Pharaoh, not because they follow it [i.e., this "growing up"] consecutively, in terms of timely order, but to inform us of Moses's virtues.

He first "grew up" in Pharaoh's royal house, in order to learn royal behaviors and demeanor. The three subsequent stories indicate that Moses "grew up" in another manner—that of his heart and spirit. This transformed him in that he reached a point where he could not tolerate to witness oppression. Through this transformation he also developed the courage to stand up against oppression.

We learn from this that Moses had the characteristics of a righteous, upright, broad-minded, and big-hearted person, and these are the traits appropriate for a prophet.[136]
—Don Yitzchak Abarbanel

Kli Yakar
Stages of Spiritual Redemption

Our physical state of being undoubtedly influences our spiritual state. Thus when God saved the Israelites from physical bondage, the redemption was spiritual as well.

Rabbi Shlomo Efraim of Luntchitz was known by the name of his most popular work, *Kli Yakar* (literally, "The Precious Vessel"). He was the leader of the Jewish community in Prague until his death in 1619. As a commentator, Kli Yakar is known for deriving psychological insights and explanations from his readings of the Torah. Here he suggests that spiritual redemption should begin with whatever stage is most difficult and end with "marriage" to God, echoing the loving relationship between Israel and God expressed in the biblical book The Song of Songs. The order of the stages is based upon the four verbs God uses in Exodus to express how God will redeem the people. These are the same four verbs that are associated with each of the four cups of wine we drink during the seder.

"I will free you … deliver you … redeem you … and I will take you" (Exod. 6:6–7). [These four expressions of redemption] correspond to the four stages [the Jewish people] went through [in Egyptian exile] ….

When He delivered [the Jewish people], God saw fit to liberate them gradually, little by little. First, He delivered them from the most dangerous aspect—the affliction ….Then He delivered them from their servitude …. And then He delivered them from the easiest of all [the four stages]—their being strangers ….

Since the remoteness of the Divine Presence stems from being strangers, [the Torah] was obliged to juxtapose [the phrase that refers to] their being strangers with the phrase "in a land not theirs" (Gen. 15:13), which implies remoteness of the Divine Presence. Corresponding to this, it says here that when they would no longer be strangers, they would merit cleaving to the Divine Presence …. [This] refers to a marriage [between God and the Jewish people] in the manner of a man with a young woman.

Based on this connection [between God and Israel, the verse continues] "And you shall know that I, the LORD, am your God who freed you from the labors of the Egyptians" (Exod. 6:7)—the worst of the four evils. And then He clarified this "marriage" by saying "I will bring you into the land" (Exod. 6:8) [in the same manner that a groom brings a bride into his home].[137]
—Rabbi Shlomo Efraim of Lunshitz

Nehama Leibowitz with Rashi

Freed to Be Jews

We are meant to learn a special lesson from the Book of Exodus. The attainment of "freedom to …" rather than the experience merely of "freedom from …" is the distinction and the object. God's supreme role in the Passover story is important because we must understand that the freedom we gained has a sole purpose—to enable us to freely dedicate ourselves to God's will, to live a life of virtue and responsibility. Without freedom, we cannot truly be responsible.

Renowned Bible scholar Nehama Leibowitz (b. 1905–d. 1997, Livonia and Israel) makes this point unequivocally by elucidating the Torah commentary of the great Rashi, the acronymn of Rabbi Shlomo ben Yitzchak (b. 1040–d. 1105, France). As evidenced here, Leibowitz, although a university professor, was known simply as Nehama to her students and preferred being addressed simply as "Teacher."

> Rashi [commenting on Exodus 3:12]: Regarding your [Moses's] question: what has Israel done to deserve being brought out from Egypt? I [God] have a matter of great importance connected with that bringing out: they are destined to receive the Torah on this mount, three months after they leave Egypt.

> Nehama: Not a privilege but a responsibility awaited them. Not so much as a reward for past good behavior but as a prelude to their future destiny. This release from slavery, this bringing forth was inspired by a purpose and goal rather than a motivating cause. The text contains a profound message well brought out by the Rashi we have cited. The Exodus from Egypt, the liberation from an alien yoke, independence, freedom, and the like are not ends in themselves. The return to the homeland, the transformation from dependence to sovereignty, slavery to freedom are but instruments, the means for achieving the ultimate goal—specified in our text: the service of God ("you shall worship God"). In other words, the Almighty did not release Israel from the burden of persecution in order to set them free from all burden or responsibility. He wished them to become free to accept another burden—that of the Kingdom of Heaven—of Torah and Mitzvot.[138]

Neil Gillman

Accompanied into Bondage

The Jewish people have suffered immensely throughout history, and philosophers and rabbis have struggled to understand the reason. The faithful are faced with a painful question: How could God let so much sustained suffering take place? Neil Gillman, contemporary Jewish theologian and professor of philosophy, addresses this issue. He suggests an approach akin to that found in Jewish mysticism, which reconciles God's goodness with the role of God during the centuries of exile the Israelites underwent in Egypt (and perhaps, during every instance of injustice).

Why the slavery? Why the suffering in the first place? Why 430 years in Egypt (Exod. 12:40)? This is the question that in one form or another haunts the life experience of every believer ....

There is no biblical justification for this suffering. But the midrash offers, if not a justification, then at least hint of consolation. It notes that the text uses different forms of the same word—the Hebrew term *levanah*—to characterize both the bricks that the Israelites were forced to make in Egypt and the pavement that lay under the feet of God when Moses, Aaron, Nadab, and Abihu, and the seventy elders of Israel "saw the God of Israel" at the climax of the Sinai event (Exod. 24:9–11).

The use of the same word suggests that God created God's own domain out of the bricks that the Israelites were forced to make in slavery. This is a statement of God's identification with the suffering of the people of Israel. God too, then, accompanied the Israelites into bondage, as God accompanied our people into exile and throughout our wanderings, and even into the Holocaust.

God suffers with our suffering. Beyond this, we are constantly reminded that we are to remember our experience of slavery and thus to strive to create a social structure that will not tolerate any form of oppression. Suffering provided the indispensable educational experience for a people who, like its God, is commanded to care deeply about people and their fate.[139]

✦ Passover ✦
Interpretations of Sacred Texts

The texts in these pages, each studied at multiple levels, are from the Book of Exodus and from the Passover haggadah. Exodus, the second book of the Torah, is called *Shemot* (Names) in the original Hebrew; an early Greek translation retitled it Exodus because the first 17 chapters tell of the Israelites "going out" from Egypt. The haggadah, the book that guides the seder, includes the Four Children, a reading that may be revealing four aspects of one child, or of ourselves, or of the Jewish people. The *Maggid* (literally, "Telling"), the entire narrative of the haggadah, recounts aspects of the Exodus story, largely by using passages from the Talmud.

THE THREE LEVELS
Peshat: simple, literal meaning
Derash: historical, rabbinical inquiry
Making It Personal: contemporary analysis and application

The Spiritual Journey from Exile to Freedom

Then Moses returned to the LORD and said, "O LORD, why did You bring harm upon this people? . . .

God spoke to Moses and said to him, "I am the LORD. . . . I have now heard the moaning of the Israelites because the Egyptians are holding them in bondage, and I have remembered My covenant. Say, therefore, to the Israelite people: I am the LORD. I will free you from the labors of the Egyptians and deliver you from their bondage. I will redeem you with an outstretched arm and through extraordinary chastisements. And I will take you to be My people, and I will be your God. . . ." But when Moses told this to the Israelites, they would not listen to Moses, their spirits crushed by cruel bondage.

—Exodus 5:22–23, 6:2–9

Peshat

In one of the pivotal moments in the Exodus story, Moses candidly asks God why the Israelites have to endure the pain and suffering of Egyptian bondage. God tells Moses to explain to the Israelites that God will surely save them and that their reward will be possession of the land promised to their forefathers. God's response does not directly address Moses' question. When Moses relays the message, the Israelites are unmoved, as their spirits have been crushed by the torment they have been experiencing.

Derash

God's response to Moses does not offer a reason why the Israelites were enslaved. Instead, God makes several promises of freedom. These provide the textual basis for the tradition of drinking four cups of wine at the seder. The wine is intended to gladden our spirits and rouse us into a state of feeling liberated (not inebriated).

Could it be, however, that freedom is the reason why the Israelites were enslaved in the first place? Perhaps they were enslaved and they suffered, precisely so they could be freed. Of course, this explanation is not an encouraging one for those who do the suffering—witness that the Israelites "would not listen to Moses." Yet there may be some spiritual value to going through the process of moving from bondage to freedom. Did God want the Israelites (and us) to learn a spiritual lesson when being forced to endure hardship before enjoying prosperity?

Samson Raphael Hirsch (b. 1808–d. 1888, Germany) was the founder of contemporary Orthodox Judaism. As he interpreted in his commentary on the Torah, the Israelites could only and truly become God's people if they appreciated what it means to be free and have rights. That appreciation comes from the contrasting experience of having been enslaved. For this reason, the Torah later expects the freed Israelites to be kind to the downtrodden.

Making It Personal

Part of being human is to endure some form of suffering. We do not all encounter poverty or physical hardships, but we all face psychological and emotional suffering. No one escapes exposure to evil, loss, and despair.

In his commentary on chapter 23, verse 22 of the Book of Numbers, Rabbi Chaim ben Attar (known as Or Ha-Chaim), suggests that the Exodus from Egypt is an ongoing phenomenon. He claims that at each Passover seder, we relive the process of being unshackled from the fetters of evil, symbolized by the Egyptian exile, and being released by the sacred sparks of God's grace. Accordingly, the liberation that the Israelites experienced and their subsequent redemption serves as a metaphor for the scope of human spiritual experience.

We all experience the evils of spiritual exile and bondage, and, at the same time, we are all given windows opening onto moments of hope and freedom. Our lesson is to avoid the path of our ancestors who were not "listening" to the opportunity of redemptive promise because of their anguish. While we acknowledge the pain in our lives, we must also allow ourselves to accept redemption when it presents itself. We grow stronger, not from the suffering itself, but from the conscious experience of progressing from suffering toward contentment.

THE THREE LEVELS
Peshat: simple, literal meaning
Derash: historical, rabbinical inquiry
Making It Personal: contemporary analysis and application

What Makes a Jewish Child Wicked?

What does the wicked child say?

"What do you mean by this rite?" (Exod. 12:26).

The child says "you," thereby excluding "himself"! Because the child excludes himself from the community and denies a basic principle of faith, you should set that child's teeth on edge, saying: "It is because of what the LORD did for me when I went free from Egypt" (Exod. 13:8). "Me" and not "him"! If he were there, he would not have been redeemed.

—Haggadah, the Four Children

Peshat

In the haggadah, in the section called the Four Children, we read about the child (traditionally, "the son") who is a *rasha*, translated as a "wicked," "rebellious," or "evil" person. This child is compared to the wise child, simple child, and the one who does not know how to ask.

According to the haggadah, this child is wicked because he excludes himself from the practice of the group. More specifically, he excludes himself from the seder, a core and definitive tradition of the Jewish people. The haggadah is therefore defining a Jewish child as being wicked when he chooses to distance himself from the central rites and ideology of Judaism.

And yet the wicked child's question is not so different from that of the wise child, who asks: "What mean the decrees, laws, and rules that the LORD our God has enjoined upon you?" (Deut. 6:20). Both children seem to exclude themselves from the service, because they use the word "you." This verbal distinction causes us to examine the difference between their questions and to identify what leads to categorizing one child as wicked.

Derash

Both the wise and the wicked child direct their questions toward "you," seemingly excluding themselves. Why then is one child in particular regarded as wicked? Generally speaking, the distinction between the two children is based upon the presentation of their questions: the wise child's question is more detailed and nuanced than that of the wicked child and thus shows that he seeks the true essence of the tradition. Moreover, medieval commentators suggest, the wicked child is distinguished from the wise child by his intention when asking the question. They contend that the wicked child means to embarrass his parents with his accusatory question or to ridicule all of the participants in the seder by using a tone of arrogance. Judaism values *derekh eretz* (common decency), which includes the tenet that we should not exclude ourselves from the community. Accordingly, this question, with its tone of indignation, would sever the bonds of trust and commitment that link him to the rest of the participants at the seder and to the Jewish community at large.

Making It Personal

The Jewish tradition has long acknowledged the presence of "self-hating Jews," categorized as *malshinim* (informers); heretics; and *chaver ra* (literally, "evil friend" and loosely in the plural, "corrupt companions"). They seek to malign the Jewish people. The wicked Jewish child is depicted in this light, as a Jew who looks down upon the Jewish tradition by mocking and sneering at its values. In fact, many of the artistic representations of the Four Children portray the wicked child as snobbish, duplicitous, or completely assimilated.

Today, unfortunately, there are a great many self-deprecating Jews, who mask their anxiety about being Jewish with self-righteousness, complacency, or inappropriate humor born of ignorance. In each generation, Jews have faced the immense challenges of anti-Semitism and assimilation. Being such a minority (approximately 0.3 percent of the world population and 2.2 percent of the United States),[14] we cannot afford to make matters more difficult for ourselves. Many leaders of the Jewish community focus daily on trying to win back this disillusioned segment of the Jewish population.

At the Passover seder, which is the most observed Jewish rite, the religiously secure and the not-so-secure all have an opportunity to remember and reexperience the dawn of the Jewish people. During the questions and comments of the Four Children, we can consider which of their attitudes most closely parallels our own. The questions help us to identify what it means to be a Jew, and they inspire us to determine the kind of Jew we would like to become.

THE THREE LEVELS
Peshat: simple, literal meaning
Derash: historical, rabbinical inquiry
Making It Personal: contemporary analysis and application

The Everlasting Ethical Imperative

B'khol dor va-dor .... In every generation each person is obligated to see himself as if he had come out from Egypt, as it says, *And you shall explain to your son on that day, "It is because of what the* LORD *did for me when I went free from Egypt"* (Exod. 13:8). Not only were our ancestors redeemed by the Holy One blessed be He, but even we were redeemed with them, as it says, . . . *and us He freed from there, that He might take us and give the land that He had promised on oath to our fathers* (Deut. 6:23).

—Haggadah, the *Maggid*[141]

Peshat

We encounter this paragraph toward the end of the *Maggid,* the narrative portion of the haggadah. It illuminates our understanding of the purpose of the seder by teaching us three important lessons about being Jews and about how we relate to our past and to our future. The first is that we did not personally live through the Exodus and the birth of the Jewish people, and thus our children will not immediately comprehend what it means to be a Jew. The second lesson is that we must teach this story in every generation. By explaining the foundational narrative of our people, our children will understand why continuing the traditions is a means of preserving our unique identity. The final lesson is that telling the story as if it were about our ancestors is not sufficient. We must personalize it, to see the story as continually unfolding and to see ourselves within it.

Derash

Because this paragraph demands that we tell the story in the first person, as if we had experienced the liberation from Egypt ourselves, it informs us of the pedagogical aim of the Jewish tradition in general. That is, when we transmit Judaism from one generation to the next, we teach the story as though we in fact had experienced it.

One important method of teaching, especially when teaching stories, is to help others empathize with the characters. Empathy develops insight into motivation and deepens our understanding. Personalizing the story, telling it as though we were there, goes a step beyond empathy to participation. This method, as the one used for formulating and conducting a seder, is also the method for teaching Jewish ethics and morality.

The great sage Hillel teaches: "Do not judge your fellow human being till you stand in his situation" (*Avot* 2:5). When we recite *b'khol dor va-dor*, we force ourselves to stand in the situation of our oppressed ancestors. Therefore, we know what it is to be a slave, to be needy, to be widowed, orphaned, and subjugated, not just because our ancestors were but because we, too, were. Medieval Torah and Talmud commentator Rashi adds to the verse "You shall not oppress a stranger, for you know the feelings of the stranger, having yourselves been strangers in the land of Egypt" (Exod. 23:9) by saying, "You know how painful it is when you oppress him." Personalization of the Exodus story is the basis for the perpetual, ethical imperative of Judaism.

Making It Personal
Joseph Campbell, 20th-century expert on comparative religion and comparative mythology, writes, "One of our problems today is that we are not well acquainted with the literature of the spirit. We're interested in the news of the day and the problems of the hour." Accordingly, he says, we do not listen to those "who speak of the eternal values that have to do with centering our lives."[142]

Teaching and learning Torah is the Jewish way of acquiring eternal values. It is not enough to merely know what is going on in the world. We must have a foundation of wisdom and forethought to guide our responses. If we envision ourselves within the annually repeated Exodus story of Passover, as though we ourselves had undergone the brutal treatment, we internalize the eternal value of *v'ahavta le-re'echa kamokha*, "Love your fellow as yourself" (Lev. 19:18). To remember that our ancestors were slaves is to remember that our God is compassionate and that the Jewish people, as God's representatives, must be, too.

✦ Passover ✦
Significance of the Holiday: Some Modern Perspectives

History and Memory
by Daniel Cotzin Burg

In his thought-provoking book *Zakhor: Jewish History and Jewish Memory*, written in 1982, Yosef Hayim Yerushalmi claims that memory, and not history or historiography, has been the primary lens through which the Jewish community has viewed its past. And yet, modern scholars endlessly debate the "historicity" of the Bible and the historical journey of the Jewish people. No holiday better reflects this tension, the continuing dialectic between history and memory, than Passover. It is one of the few holidays that retains its biblical ties to a particular historical event: the Exodus from Egypt. And it is this event, comprising the emergence from slavery, the theophany, and eventually the return to the Land of Israel, that has endured as the central story that defines the origin, purpose, and future of the Jewish people. As the Jewish theologian and philosopher Franz Rosenzweig (b. 1886–d. 1929, Germany) has said, "The welding of people into a people takes place in its deliverance."

There is ample evidence that throughout the ages Jews have continuously observed the festival of Passover, albeit in different and evolving forms. Biblical references include a Passover observance on the first anniversary of the Exodus[143] and again, 39 years later, as Joshua and his followers were encamped outside Jericho.[144] Hezekiah, king of Judah in the 8th and 7th centuries B.C.E., bolstered the holiday by insisting that the pilgrimage festival be observed,[145] as did King Josiah in the later 7th century.[146] When, in the 6th century B.C.E., Cyrus the Great of Persia allowed the Israelites to return to the Land of Israel, the priest and scribe Ezra led the people as they "joyfully celebrated the Feast of Unleavened Bread" (Ezra 6:22).

With the destruction of the Second Temple in 70 C.E., the focal point of the holiday shifted from the sacrificial order to the home-based seder and recitation of the haggadah. Much of the haggadah's content was fixed by the time the Mishnah (the first compilation of the Oral Law) had been completed in 200 C.E. While aspects of the seder were based on the framework of the Greco-Roman symposium, one can view the haggadah, in part, as a polemic against the frivolity and licentiousness of that feast. The Jews appropriate and adapt certain symposium customs and dedicate them to the recounting of God's essential role in the formation and endurance of the Jewish people. Among these adaptations are the ritual four cups of wine, the freedom to recline while eating, and the special portion of matzah known as the *afikoman*. The Talmud mentions additional or adapted compulsory rituals before and during the holiday celebration, including the searching for and burning of leaven (*bedikat* and *biur hametz*), the eating of *haroset* along with the bitter herbs, the chanting of *Hallel* (psalms of joy and gratitude), and the *Maggid* ("Telling") of the Exodus story. Perhaps the most significant line in the haggadah is the commandment that each participant see himself or herself as having personally gone forth from Egypt. The *Maggid* reflects this injunction—to experience empathy—with a commitment equal to the reenacted paschal offering of Temple times.

In the medieval period, Passover was met with mixed emotions. Beginning in Norwich, England, in 1144, Western European Jewry began to endure a sinister and fallacious charge known as "blood libel." This accusation of ritual murder, presumably to acquire Christian blood as an ingredient for matzah, has been used over the centuries to justify torturing, imprisoning, and slaughtering Jews. Jews became so fearful at Passover that, for a time, some rabbis ruled that only white wine should be used for the seder, so as not to arouse the suspicion of their Christian neighbors by imbibing a red liquid.

Today, Passover is the most commonly celebrated holiday in the Jewish calendar among North American Jews, surpassing even the awe-inspiring High Holy Days and the gift-flavored Hanukkah. Its rituals, melodies, and customs continue to evolve and grow. The rich symbolism of the seder and the dietary restrictions of the holiday lend themselves to new interpretations, ranging from our relationship with the modern State of Israel, to the role of women, to the Jewish response to modern slavery or human trafficking.

DID THE EXODUS REALLY HAPPEN?

For all the changes in the Jewish community's observance of the festival, the Exodus narrative, the story of Jewish deliverance, remains Passover's central and most compelling theme. This, of course, begs the questions: Does the biblical account hold up under scientific scrutiny? Given the lack of archaeological evidence along the route from Egypt to Canaan, the best hope in determining the historicity of the Exodus lies in a detailed analysis of the Israelite community that emerged in Canaan, after the Exodus. By studying its material culture (for example, unique pottery styles and living arrangements) as well as corroborating textual evidence from Egypt, we can learn much about the origins of the people.[147]

There are four prevailing theories regarding the Israelites' subsequent rise to power. The first of these suggests a planned, systematic conquest of the land that resulted in the destruction of Canaanite cities and the defeat of their inhabitants. This theory is best supported by the narrative in the Book of Joshua and by archaeological evidence, such as a burn layer uncovered at Tel Hazor dating to the end of the Late Bronze Period (approximately 1200 B.C.E.).[148] A second theory contends that the Israelites came to power through relatively peaceful infiltration—a slow settlement of Judea and Samaria with occasional skirmishes and power grabs. This account is more reflective of material in the Book of Judges and the absence of comprehensive archaeological evidence of destruction or conquest.[149] Two more theories suggest that the Exodus never happened, implying that the Passover narrative was developed and transmitted many years after the fact. The first of these is often referred to as the "Internal Revolution" or "Canaanite Revolt" theory. According to its proponents, the Israelite people emerged out of a peasant class of Canaanites who revolted against "the network of interlocking ... city states."[150] In recent years, another theory has emerged that questions the Israelites' Egyptian origins—the "Pastoral Canaanite" theory. Its primary proponent, the Israeli archaeologist Israel Finkelstein, claims that early Israelites were pastoral nomads, living in highland villages until the internal collapse of the Canaanite cities. In the ensuing years, these nomads began to settle, and they eventually reestablished the urban centers.[151]

Whatever the case, most scholars do claim that by the late 13th century B.C.E., the Egyptians had encounters with an autonomous people known as "Israel" who dwelt in Canaan.[152] This would suggest that the Exodus took place (depending on the rate of settlement) at some time between the 15th and early 13th centuries. It is especially intriguing, then, in regard to Passover, that we find reference to *Apiru* (or *Habiru*) in the Tel El-Amarna Tablets, a collection of 15th- to 13th-century B.C.E. clay documents. Scholars have speculated that these *Apiru*, who were perpetual thorns in the Egyptians' sides, may in fact have been the "Hebrews."

Speculation also exists about the identity of the "king who did not know Joseph" (Exod. 1:8) and then enslaved the Israelites, or, for that matter, his successor, the pharaoh of the Exodus itself. We can wonder whether the Israelites left en masse on a targeted journey for the land that God "swore to your fathers to give you" (Exod. 13:5) or whether a much smaller number, part of a "mixed multitude" (Exod. 12:38), left Egypt and later joined with native tribes of Canaan to form what became the Jewish people.

For the most skeptical among the scholarly community, potentially disproving the historicity of the Exodus does not necessarily undermine the meaning of the Jewish festival of deliverance. On the contrary, as Finkelstein has said: "To pin [the] biblical image down to a single date is to betray the story's deepest meaning. Passover proves to be not a single event but a continuing experience of national resistance against the powers that be."[153]

But even if the historical "truth" is someday revealed, the words of Yosef Yerushalmi in *Zakhor* are well worth keeping in mind:

> In effect, it is not modern Jewish historiography that has shaped modern Jewish conceptions of the past. Literature and ideology have been far more decisive. That this should be so seems to me sufficiently interesting to make one pause and reflect. . . . Those Jews who are still within the enchanted circle of tradition, or those who have returned to it, find the work of the historian irrelevant. They seek, not the historicity of the past, but its eternal contemporaneity."

The Freedom to Serve

by David Wolpe

The most famous verse in Exodus is incomplete: "Let My people go!" rings out the great truncated phrase. This verse fuels the popular notion of Passover—it is a holiday of freedom. From Passover we derive the Jewish people's rejection of slavery, bondage, cruelty, and domination that reaches down through the ages. "As I would not be a slave, so I would not be a master," declared Abraham Lincoln supported in flaming red letters by the spiritual force of "Let my people go."

Yet Passover is both deeper and subtler than this characterization. For what God instructs Moses to say reads in its entirety: "Let My people go that they may serve me"[156] (Exod. 7:26). In other words, let them go for a specific reason. Later, the Rabbis of the talmudic era reshape this idea to mean that one should be liberated for the higher servitude—that of God and God's purpose, rather than that of serving an empire or its ruler.[155] Somewhere in the background the raspy strains of Bob Dylan are heard, "You gotta serve somebody."

Passover enshrines this powerful truth. Its first message is not that human beings can be autonomous creatures. All of our experience tells us otherwise. We do not merely live; we live *for* something. The question is—will that purpose be compelling and noble?

In his masterpiece of psychology and history, *Man's Search for Meaning,* Viktor Frankl recounts what he learned during his experience as a concentration camp inmate. He looked to figure out who in the camps managed to survive. His conclusion was that meaning made the difference:

> Being human always points, or is directed, to something, or someone, other than oneself—be it a meaning to fulfill or another human being to encounter. The more one forgets himself—by giving to a cause to serve or another person to love—the more human he is. [156]

When the cause is unworthy, or limited, so is the sense of one's worth as a human being. Passover is about the turn from a limited human meaning to an unlimited, divine meaning. In other words, Passover is not only about being freed from slavery but also about gaining the spiritual freedom to access the deeper meaning of the human experience.

The symbolism of the matzah helps us to understand. Why of all the possible symbols of this holiday should a dried cracker be preeminent? What is it that the matzah represents?

The essence of freedom is control over time. Like the prisoner, the slave has no control over time: He rises at the bidding of his master, works when told, must sleep only when permitted. The free man is free in time. We often say "we must" in relation to our time—"I must go to this meeting" … "I must pick him up" … "I must get home"—but in reality these moments are choices, compelled by our system of values. We are free.

The mitzvot are crafted to shape time—not only Shabbat but also the holidays, the times for prayer, the cycles, and the seasons. All of them are in service to the Greater Master, the One who created time and gave it for our use. This is the deep underlying theme of Passover—how shall we each use our time? God entered history to permit the Israelites to set their clocks by Divine time.

If wise, we use our time covenantally. Life is measured by the quality of our relationships; and here too, the essence is freedom: we may attach ourselves to whomever we wish. Choosing wisely, Israel will create a sacred community. A covenantal relationship implicates both partners. Each freely chooses to bind himself or herself to the covenant. (Indeed, religion comes from the Latin, *ligare*, "to bind," which Jews enact each morning that they wrap their arms in tefillin.) The covenant is a statement of relationship, which is the most powerful drama of our lives. In the Ten Commandments, God is identified not as the One who created the world, but as the One who brought us forth from Egypt. For it is in relationship that love comes alive. The seder, with the family gathered together, beautifully illustrates this second message of Passover, when we became a nation, bound each to the other.

Relationship requires sacrifice. We think of the Passover sacrifice, which reminds us not only of the blood on the doorpost of each Israelite's house but also the inevitable truth of all love—that without sacrifice it cannot live. The measure of deep love, however, is that sacrifice does not feel like sacrifice. When we give something up for our children, it is easier than if we were to give up the same thing for a stranger, for love impels giving, and devotion demands sacrifice. So, at our best, when we make a sacrifice to God, it is not an act that depletes us, but rather one that fills us up.

Passover takes place in the spring. The season mirrors the truth about religious rites. For they happen in no time and at all times. The reality of the Exodus is not primarily a historical reality; it is fruitless to grow too preoccupied with the search for rusted chariots at the bottom of the sea. Rather the drama—that of slavery, liberation, the conquest over time, and the push to relationship—is a perennial feature of human life. It has no beginning and no end; but like spring, comes to us anew each year, deepening its resonance in our lives as we grow.

Renewal, time, and relationship all point to the seder's focus on children. A child is the human equivalent of spring—the promise of a new season. The thread of childhood is woven throughout the haggadah: the asking of the four questions, the metaphorical answers found in the Four Children, the songs at the end (such as "Who Knows One?" and "One Only Kid"), all designed to keep a child awake throughout the evening.

Passover is the keystone of Jewish history. The Exodus is celebrated not because it represents throwing off shackles, but because it represents the ability to choose obligations. The people were not destined for the desert, but for Sinai and Israel. No longer would other human beings determine their lives—individual and collective. Now the path to redemption begins.

So we end the seder with "Next year in Jerusalem!" For the events that began with the Exodus have not yet achieved their end. The goal remains elusive, somewhere in the mists of future history. Yet the chain that began with the simple declaration to Pharaoh has changed the world, and it continues to change the souls of those who understand this declaration in every generation.

You Were Strangers

by Bradley Shavit Artson

Like all Jewish festivals, Passover has its roots in Jewish history, in our connection to Creation, and in the rich spiritual and moral values of Judaism.

Agriculturally, Passover is a festival of the spring, a time of rebirth and of hope. In the spring, plants reemerge in the full bloom of their beauty. When we become aware of our connection to the earth and the importance of maintaining the balance of all living things, we learn key lessons of the season and of Passover itself.

Historically, Passover recalls that our ancestors were slaves in *Mitzrayim* (Hebrew for "Egypt"). It recalls our liberation from the abusive oppression of the pharaoh and his court. Under the leadership of Moses, Miriam, and Aaron, we learned that a free people must be willing to fight for its freedom, that no one is truly free until everybody is. Drawing on the memory of having been slaves, we Jews have a special obligation to empathize with any group who are outcasts, oppressed, or dehumanized. We, who experienced suffering, must always train ourselves to identify with those who suffer.

Finally, there is a religious message in Passover as well. Passover teaches us that

- God is a passionate and loving force on the side of the weak and the downtrodden;

- God is involved wherever and whenever people struggle to realize their fullest humanity;

• Jews were the first beneficiaries of God's liberating love, and we have carried that love with us throughout our wanderings.

In addition, Passover helps us to distinguish between two very different types of freedom. One notion of freedom—popular in many current venues—is "freedom *from* …." Such a view maintains that freedom means an absence of coercion; we are free not to do anything, or support anyone, unless we want to. That notion of freedom, however valuable as a beginning, is incomplete. It is not the full freedom of Passover.

Passover beckons us to a "freedom *to* …." Because we were liberated from *Mitzrayim*, from idolatry, and from slavery, we are now free to live as Jews and to build a sacred community. Our ancestors were willing to die for their faith; are we willing to live for ours? Passover beckons us to show that we accept the challenge and the privilege of living and growing as Jews. Part of our embodiment of such a commitment is through the mitzvot, the sacred commandments. And part of that commitment impels us to speak out for Jewish values, Jewish community, and human freedom and dignity around the world.

A mature freedom is not an escape from responsibilities. It is the acceptance of responsibilities that work *le-takken olam be-malkhut Shaddai*, "to repair the world under the sovereignty of God."

The promise of Passover leads us to its attainment at Mount Sinai. Liberation is the first step toward Torah—with its call to all of us to live as fully, as compassionately, and as meaningfully as we possibly can. Much of the wisdom and laws of our tradition can be understood only in the light of that passion for justice and that identification with the downtrodden, the lonely, and the oppressed.

In fact, one of the most frequently repeated explanations for a variety of laws in the Torah is the one found in Deuteronomy: "… for you were strangers in *Mitzrayim*, and the Holy One liberated you with an outstretched hand" (24:22). Because we were strangers in *Mitzrayim*, we recognize what it is like to feel unwanted or unnoticed. We are familiar with the pain of silent rejection and aware of the courage it takes to enter a room where we know no one.

Each of us, the haggadah reminds us, must feel as though we personally were liberated from *Mitzrayim*, a narrow, spiritually confining place. So, too, we must each reach deep down to painful moments of exclusion or invisibility to remember just how the stranger might feel in our midst.

This is no theoretical issue. Each Shabbat, and at every communal event, strangers summon up their courage to engage the Jewish community. Maybe they need to say *Kaddish* (the mourner's prayer) for a loved one, or perhaps they just want to learn Torah or to join in a social action initiative. Perhaps they don't feel they fit the mold (perhaps a vision of some perfect family). Whatever the reason, we always have strangers in our midst.

Who is supposed to greet those strangers? Whose job is it to make sure they have the right handouts, that they are not sitting alone, that someone is there to talk with them and to introduce them to people already established there?

Each one of us was a stranger in *Mitzrayim*, and each one of us must take the initiative to ensure that no stranger ever feels unwelcome at any Jewish gathering. The first step, then, is to realize that if you do not look for strangers, no one else will either. If you do not get up to say, "Hello, may I sit with you?" no one else will either. It all depends on you.

And in summoning the energy and the caring to approach a stranger and to make them feel welcome, know that you are doing more than just making a new friend. Know that you are an ambassador for the Jewish people and that the stranger's estimation of our community will be molded by your deed. Know, beyond that, that you serve as a *shaliach*, a "messenger" of the Holy Blessing One, the God who took a group of strangers into freedom—because someone had to do it.

From Slavery to Ecology

by Adam Naftalin-Kelman

The celebration of Passover usually focuses on history: the Egyptian enslavement of the children of Israel and their redemption by God. The festival also has a direct connection to the ecological cycle:

> You shall observe the Feast of Unleavened Bread—eating unleavened bread for seven days as I have commanded you—at the set time in the month of Aviv,[157] for in it you went forth from Egypt; …"
> —Exodus 23:15

In the Bible, this "month" of Aviv corresponds not to a month on the Hebrew calendar but to the ancient period in spring when the barley grain was just ripening. In Hebrew, this agricultural moment is called *aviv*, which is also the Hebrew name for the season of spring. The ecological aspect of Passover mingles with the background of the historical story.

> A new king arose over Egypt, who did not know Joseph. And he said to his people, "Look, the Israelite people are much too numerous for us. Let us deal shrewdly with them, so that they may not increase." ... So they set taskmasters over them to oppress them with forced labor.
> —Exodus 1:8–11

The origins of the Israelites' enslavement began long before their rapid population growth. It started at the end of the Book of Genesis when their ancestors, the sons of Jacob, first traveled to Egypt. What caused Jacob's sons to make this move? Throughout much of the world there had been an ecological disaster. Famine had struck the Fertile Crescent; and only because of the strategic planning of Joseph, who unbeknownst to his family had become viceroy to the pharaoh, did Egypt have food to provide for other nations in the region:

> When Jacob saw that there were food rations to be had in Egypt, he said to his sons, "Why do you keep looking at one another? ... Go down and procure rations for us there, that we may live and not die." So ten of Joseph's brothers went down to get grain rations in Egypt. ... Thus the sons of Israel were among those who came to procure rations, for the famine extended to the land of Canaan."
> —Genesis 42:1–5

Thus the biblical enslavement of the Israelites not only was caused by the change in Egyptian power but also was the result of an environmental disaster. In more recent eras, with Jewish life centered in urban communities, we have lost these environmental connections to Passover: its placement in the rhythmical harvest season of spring and its connection to a story of nature-induced famine. However, if we learn to pay attention to these associations, the holiday prompts us to reexamine our relationship with the land and the greater global environment.

Weeks before Passover begins, we start to thoroughly clean every place in which food may have been eaten—spring cleaning taken to the extreme. It is the time of the year when we search for *hametz*, both physical and spiritual leaven. But what about our environmental *hametz*? When searching for *hametz* to burn, why not also seek out the items in our homes that need to be removed or changed to strengthen our relationship with the environment? We can give the conventional Passover cleaning process an environmental tweak by establishing new practices and habits to make our homes more ecologically sound.

The connection between Passover and the earth can be extended to the items on the seder plate. It holds six items (or five, depending on custom). In this case, we look at *zeroa* (shank bone), *beitzah* (egg), *hazeret* (lettuce), *karpas* (spring vegetable), *haroset* (mixture of nuts, fruits, wine, and spices), and *maror* (bitter herbs). Each symbol represents some element of the Exodus story and connects Passover to its environmental roots.

Zeroa not only recalls the sacrifice of the pascal lamb but also prompts us to remember our responsibility for the humane treatment of animals. After God redeemed us from Egypt, we were given the Torah, which contains, among its other laws, instructions about our responsibility to animals. Because we were privileged to experience Revelation, we are responsible for following the Torah and its guidance about living things, such as the prohibitions against boiling a kid in its mother's milk and against yoking ox and ass together.[158]

Passover occurs during the vernal equinox, when daylight and darkness are of almost equal lengths; it is a moment in the cycle of the seasons when life begins anew, when we have a heightened sense of life because of the growth in crops and vegetation. The *beitzah, hazeret,* and *karpas* that are placed on the seder plate may be seen as representing a connection to spring and the renewal of life. These ritual items draw our attention to the global disaster that can occur when we neglect our ecosystem. If pollutants disrupt the regular course of the seasons, vegetation cannot grow during its appropriate time.

Haroset is placed on the seder plate as a reference to the mortar and bricks used by the Israelite slaves in building massive structures and cities for the Egyptians. It can symbolize the potential for disaster in a civilization that thinks only about building larger metropolises while it neglects the natural environment. When we consume the sticky yet crumbly mixture of fruits and nuts, it is a reminder that the outward expansion of cities and suburbs must never come at the expense of destroying the ecological balance.

The remaining item on the seder plate, the *maror,* may be a taste of the future. Traditionally the bitter herbs are used to draw our attention to the bitter lives the Israelite slaves lived, but they also resemble the bitterness a civilization ultimately tastes when neglecting its relationship with its ecological surroundings.

When the Children of Israel were redeemed from slavery, their relationship with God was renewed. They would forever be a people obligated by the laws given to them at Mount Sinai, including those about their relationship with the environment. As told in the Book of Genesis, the Israelites' journey had begun hundreds of years earlier in Canaan, when they fled from the near-global disaster of famine. Their redemption later, in the Book of Exodus, was not only that of leaving Egypt in freedom but was also a journey into a particular future, one where their relationship with the environment will either fall apart and contribute to enslaving them yet again or flourish and contribute to bringing about eternal freedom.

Experiencing the Haggadah's Message

by Marc Soloway

The Passover haggadah is perhaps the most fascinating and intricate of all Jewish texts—layered and nuanced, with the echoing cries of thousands of years of history. They permeate its pages. Many of us will open our haggadahs at the seder and find crumbs of matzah, wine stains, and various unidentifiable marks. Yet we also find the more subtle stains of memory seeping through the spaces between the words. Our stories and our recollections of previous Passovers mingle with the hidden and revealed messages of rabbis of many generations past.

The haggadah was never intended to be merely a book that is read and studied; rather, it is our guidebook to an extraordinary annual, ritualized journey from slavery to redemption. It is a book that is lived—through sensory and provocative experience— more than it is read. The obligation *l'haggid* (the basis of the word "haggadah"), "to tell the story," is one of the primary mitzvot (commandments) associated with this holiday; and yet we find the version of the story that appears in the haggadah to be elusive and obtuse. In its pages are the disputes of talmudic rabbis, spelling out for us that no one way exists for reading this book. There is a disagreement between two Babylonian talmudists of the 2nd to 3rd centuries— Rav (Abba Arika) and Shmuel (Samuel bar Abba)—about where the story begins and hence what the story really means.[159] Is it about personal, spiritual freedom or about a national struggle to escape a more literal, physical slavery? It seems that the story is neither and both at the same time. The *Maggid*, the storytelling section of the haggadah, includes some very strange and obscure elements—commentaries that are unfathomable for most modern readers and do not generally enhance the experience of the story. Anyone wanting to learn and understand the Passover story would be hard-pressed to find a straightforward style or a coherent configuration within the haggadah; although, at least in recent years, a movement has developed to bring much more flexibility and creativity into this night of storytelling.

Significant portions of the haggadah, as we have it today, appear in the very early Rabbinic text, the Mishnah.[160] One phrase in the Mishnah provides an important clue to the experience of the haggadah and is quoted in the text itself, *b'khol dor va-dor chayav adam lirot et atzmo k'ilu hu yatza mi'Mitzrayim.* "In every generation each person is obligated to see himself *k'ilu* (Hebrew for "as if") he had come out of Egypt." The experience of the haggadah is not complete until we have placed ourselves in its narrative and used our spiritual and emotional powers of imagination to mingle with the pages. In Maimonides' version of the haggadah, the wording of the sentence is changed from *lirot* ("to see") to *l'harot* ("to cause to see, to show"). Both of these words, derived from the same Hebrew verb root, are essential components of the night of Passover. Not only must we see ourselves in the story, we must also relive the story by acting it out with rituals and postures that awaken and enliven our senses. Our actions allow us to make the journey from slavery to redemption for ourselves. The Hebrew word *k'ilu* that appears in this Mishnah and other places in the rabbinical tradition is similar to the "magic if," a concept developed by the early-20th-century Russian actor and director Konstantin Stanislavsky. This technique, which became part of Method acting, demanded that the actor ask a series of questions, beginning with, "What if I were in this situation?" These questions open the actor's imagination, allowing an immersion into the reality of the setting that can be transforming. Each of us, then, is an actor in the drama of Jewish history presented in the haggadah; and we are invited to allow that "magic if" to expand our own experience as we embrace the reality of the narrative.

Another way to look at the haggadah is to study it with keen, scholarly eyes that can discern the layers of text, as would a geologist examining a rock formation or an archaeologist inspecting ruins. Each layer gives us sociological, theological, and spiritual hints to inform the journey. This trip through the haggadah spans some 4,000 years, beginning with the reference to God's covenant with Abraham (1742

B.C.E.). This covenant is followed by Jacob's dealings with his trickster father-in-law, Laban; Jacob's descent into Egypt; the enslavement of Jacob's descendants; the Exodus led by Moses; Revelation on God's holy mountain; entrance into the Promised Land; the physical and psychological suffering of the Rabbis of the Mishnah while under Roman occupation; and the piercing cries of medieval Jews facing continuing persecution. The trip continues all the way to right here and right now, as we add links in this eternal, narrative chain.

The medieval Hebrew poem[161] at the beginning of the haggadah contains the 15 steps of the seder, the order of our ritualized evening. Nachman Cohen, in his 2002 book *The Historical Haggadah,*[162] applies the personal growth model of a conventional 12-step addiction program to the seder. He calls the seder "a 15-step program for spiritual ascension." Cohen compares the stages in the seder—from the first prayer, *Kaddesh* (literally, "Sanctify") in which we sanctify the day, through the final prayer, *Nirtzah* (literally, "Accepted") in which we express our great hope for the future and for redemption—to the 15 steps leading us both physicially and spiritually to the upper courts of the Temple in Jerusalem. The experience of the seder, as guided by the haggadah, provides an opportunity for us to release ourselves from our personal addictions—our slavery in all its various forms—and to ascend the spiritual ladder toward redemption.

For each of us, this journey through the haggadah will be different from that of other people, even from those at the same table. And for each of us, this journey changes from year to year—sometimes personal and internal and sometimes deeply connected to our continuing collective suffering. Ultimately, how we experience this night of Passover and the message of the haggadah depends on how we experience ourselves in the layers of the story.

·✦· Passover ·✦·
Alternative Meditations

Thoughts on Cleaning for Pesach[163]

by Haviva Ner-David

When I was a child, my mother expended a lot of energy cleaning for Pesach [Hebrew name for Passover]. Our whole suburban New York home was turned upside down. Each room was cleaned in a search for *chametz* and for the dirt and junk that had piled up since that last big cleaning the year before. And all of this had to be done at least a few days before Pesach itself, in order to leave enough time for the cooking required to prepare for two seders.

As I came into my own as a young feminist I resented the fact that my mother (with the help of our house cleaner) was the one to do all of this cleaning and cooking, while my father was the one who led the seder. I told myself that I would never be subject to this inequity. I saw my mother as enslaved to an exaggerated notion of what was required by Jewish law in terms of ridding one's home of *chametz*, which I thought was totally antithetical to the notion of Pesach as a holiday of freedom. I decided that I would do the minimum amount of cleaning required by Jewish law and spend the rest of my precious pre-Pesach preparation time studying in order to be able to contribute to the content of the seder. I would stress the intellectual and spiritual side of Pesach preparation rather than the mundane, physical side.

However, as I grew as a religious feminist, married, had children, and set up a Jewish home in Jerusalem, I realized that this cleaning did have to get done by someone. Even if my husband and I (and our house cleaner) shared this work, I still had to focus much of my pre-Pesach energy on cleaning. The truth is, even if a search for *chametz* does not halakhically require turning one's entire home upside down, with small children it practically does—the chances of finding a half-eaten cracker almost anywhere in the house are pretty high with a toddler walking around. Therefore, once we were already cleaning to that degree, my husband and I figured we might as well do a real spring cleaning. I began to appreciate, then, my mother's motivations for turning Pesach preparations into a meticulous spring cleaning.

Moreover, when I began studying feminist theory seriously, I was exposed to the idea of gendered division of labor and introduced to the concept that societies often place a higher value on the work that those of a higher social status perform. As Judith Lorber explains in her book *Night to His Day: The Social Construction of Gender*:

> In a gender-stratified society, what men do is usually valued more highly than what women do because men do it, even when their activities are very similar or the same. In different regions of southern India, for example, harvesting rice is men's work, shared work, or women's work. A gathering and hunting society's survival usually depends on the nuts, grubs, and small animals brought in by the women's foraging trips, but when the men's hunt is successful, it is the occasion for a celebration. Conversely, because they are the superior group, white men do not have to do the "dirty work," such as housework; the most inferior group does it, usually poor women of color.[164]

Lorber's analysis suggested that the issue of Pesach cleaning was not as simple as I had assumed. I began to understand that I too had fallen into the trap of devaluing women's work simply because it was women who were doing it. I was underestimating the halakhic and spiritual significance of the work that my mother, her mother, and her mother's mother had been doing for generations of Pesachs. Ironically, my feminism had led me to disparage my own mother and the labor of her hands. The fact that I was not alone in having fallen into this trap did not convince me that I was vindicated in having done so. If it was the men who were cleaning the house for Pesach, perhaps I would have considered *that* the essence of the Pesach experience.

This realization did not lead me to accept all of the women's traditional roles in Judaism nor to defend woman's status or the way society has traditionally been divided along gender lines. Rather, it helped me to understand that all *mitzvot* are important: both lighting Shabbat candles and going to shul on Friday night, both cleaning for Pesach and participating in the seder. Of course, women should get more involved in the *mitzvot* and practices they have not traditionally considered their own, but that does not mean that they should abandon the customs of their mothers. And on the flip side of the same coin, men should become more involved in the spheres of Jewish life in which they have not traditionally been engaged, like cleaning for Pesach.

So there I was, doing a thorough spring cleaning before Pesach, much as my mother had done before me. And much to my surprise, I did not find it as burdensome as I had imagined it would be. In fact, I found it quite spiritually powerful—even transforming. As I sorted, wiped, and scoured I felt a spiritual cleansing taking place within me. Although I was engaged in an activity I had seen as an expression of women's servitude, I felt myself being psychologically and spiritually freed, much like the Jewish slaves were after they left Egypt.

I decided then to look in the Bible, where the prohibition against having *chametz* in your possession on Pesach originates, for some kind of reinforcement of what I was experiencing. But when I looked in Exodus 12 and Deuteronomy 16, where the explanation for this prohibition is found, all that I read about *chametz* and matzah was related to remembering the Exodus, when Jews had to leave in such a hurry that they didn't have time to let their dough rise. In order to reenact this experience each year, we eat no *chametz*, no dough that has risen. The Torah explains that we perform this *mitzvah* so that we can remember a national historical moment. I found nothing in the text to support the sense of personal, spiritual, and psychological freedom I felt in the actual act of ridding my home of *chametz*—the feeling that this cleaning was an important religious expression of one possible meaning behind Pesach.

Then I turned to the *Zohar*, a mystical commentary on the Bible that is the central text of Kabbalah. There I found much material to validate what I had experienced. In its commentary on *parshat Titzaveh*,[165] the *Zohar* associates *chametz* with the *yetzer harah*, that evil inclination, and *avodah zarah*, idol worship: "And such is the evil inclination like yeast in dough, because it enters into the insides of a person, slowly, slowly, and then it multiplies and grows more and more until all of the body becomes enmeshed in it. And that is idol worship, which is likened to the evil inclination." As we rid our homes of *chametz* we are ridding ourselves of the evil inclination, of all of the drives that are preventing us from being who we strive to be.

Then, when I did some reading to prepare for the seder, I came across a beautiful insight of the late Rabbi Shlomo Carlebach in the *Carlebach Haggadah*:

> What keeps us from becoming free sometimes is a very small thing. *Chametz* is *assur b'mashehu* [forbidden even in the smallest amount]. It is forbidden for us to have even the smallest amount of it in our possession, because sometimes one crumb can destroy your life. You know, friends, most married couples that get divorced do it not because of a major event, but because of small events, tiny crumbs. As Pesach comes we're getting rid of all those small tiny crumbs. Between redemption and slavery is *mashehu*

[literally, "something"], something so tiny. Real redemption comes when we walk around with a candle and find this tiny trait that's holding us back from being what we could be, this little thing that's in essence ruining us, when we find it and burn it.[166]

On that note, I would like to share a personal custom of a ritual that I perform each year before Pesach. As I clean I compile a list of all of my own personal spiritual and psychological *chametz*—the things that keep me enslaved to my evil inclination, the foibles that I hold on to that keep me from total, unencumbered, unfettered faith in the Almighty, the things that prevent me from being what I would like to or could be. Then, when I burn the *chametz* on the eve of Pesach, I toss that list into the fire and watch it burn.

However, I always keep in mind the difference between what is required by Jewish law and what is driving me to go overboard in my cleaning in order to reach the spiritual heights to which I aspire (as well as the level of spring cleaning I desire). I am not required to rid our home of particles that a dog would not eat. So, for instance, crumbs that are covered with dust are not *chametz*, and I do not need to buy toothpaste or dishwashing detergent stamped "Kosher for Passover." There is no need to cover shelves in the pantry with contact paper. A good cleaning to get rid of any visible pieces of *chametz* is enough—unless, of course, I were to cook directly on my pantry shelves! However, if you choose to cover your shelves because it reminds you of your own childhood Pesach experience, that is fine. You should just be aware that the halakhah does not require this of you. That way, you will be able to make educated decisions and prioritize appropriately in your Pesach cleaning if you begin to feel overwhelmed.

One helpful reminder rings in my head as I clean: Dirt is not *chametz*, and we are not the paschal sacrifice. If going overboard with the cleaning gets in the way of our ability to fully participate in the seder, then we are sacrificing our own souls spiritually, because we are preventing ourselves from the positive commandments associated with Pesach, such as remembering that we were slaves in Egypt, reenacting the Exodus, and eating matzah on the first night of Pesach. This is what the seder is about. But if we are too exhausted from weeks of cleaning to really participate fully in the seder, then we have missed out on an important aspect of Pesach. That is why it is crucial to remember what is actually required of us by Jewish law when doing our search for *chametz*. Perhaps the Rabbis realized that one can go overboard when cleaning and thus miss out on other important *mitzvot* related to Pesach; perhaps this was why they delineated exactly what is *chametz* and what is not, what one must be sure to find and expel from the house before Pesach and what one can leave alone. And so, while doing a thorough spring cleaning before Pesach can be spiritually fulfilling, we should keep the other positive commandments associated with Pesach in mind. If we don't, if we get so caught up in the cleaning that we lose perspective of the broader meaning of Pesach, have we really freed ourselves of the enslavement to idol worship that the *Zohar* talks about? Idol worship comes in many forms, and turning Pesach into nothing more than a spring cleaning may be one of them.

Welcoming Strangers to Your Seder[167]

by Mark I. Rosen

BEING THE STRANGER AT A STRANGE SEDER

Passover is a holiday of remembrance, a time to recall and retell the story of the deliverance of the Jewish people from generations of Egyptian bondage. But there is also a different kind of remembering that takes place each Passover, in which memory is personal, not scripted. We spontaneously recall, often vividly, the many different seders we have attended over the years, both as a child and as an adult.

My own memories begin in the early 1960s, when our family went to a seder or ritual Passover meal each year held at the Chicago home of my Aunt Fella and Uncle Morris. Almost every adult in attendance was from Eastern Europe; boredom among the children was rampant. My cousins and I would inevitably end up crawling under the table for a mischievous rendezvous, a distraction from the relentless Yiddish-accented recitation of the Maxwell House *Haggadah*. (Literally translated as the telling, the *Haggadah* recalls the Israelite Exodus from Egypt and indicates the rituals performed at the seder.) Eventually, our impatience was rewarded by my aunt's amazing Passover delicacies. I don't ever recall understanding what was going on, but I still looked forward to going. It was comforting and predictable—the same relatives came each year and the same food appeared on the table.

Because the seders I attended growing up always had the same cast of characters, it was an exciting break from routine when someone unfamiliar showed up. One year my older cousin brought a boyfriend, and it noticeably changed the seder dynamic. When I went away to college, it was my turn to become the unfamiliar face when I attended my first seder with a family other than my own. It was then that I really started to appreciate what a *mitzvah* or good deed it was to extend invitations to strangers, especially those unable to spend the holiday with family.

Since then, I've been a guest at many different seders. It is still a comforting ritual for me, even though the faces are new, the accents American and the dishes different. But it is never a predictable experience. While the *Haggadah* is always the roadmap, each new seder takes different side roads on which I never traveled.

It was a marvel the first time I attended a seder conducted by Jewish educators. While the seder was lengthy, everything was discussed, explained and analyzed. I acquired many new insights and went home fervently wishing that such an innovation had been introduced to my Chicago relatives.

Another seder, early in my career as a "Seder Stranger," caught me by surprise. Still fully in possession of childhood naivete, I was taken aback when I encountered non-Jews at the table, friends of the host family. Their questions reminded one of the simple child of the *Haggadah*, and it turned out to be a lovely experience to see the ritual through their eyes.

One year, my seder experience was a disappointment. I call this one seder-lite. It was a perfunctory *matzah* and wine tasting accompanied by a riffling of the *Haggadah* pages that figuratively stirred a cool breeze but didn't warm my heart. In a subsequent year, I was delighted and entertained at a seder orchestrated especially for children, with wind-up frogs and finger puppets.

Perhaps the most memorable seder I attended is the one I call, both wryly and fondly, the last supper. It was led in Manhattan by Rabbi Shlomo Carlebach at his Upper West Side *shul* or synagogue. Seventy of us from all over the country listened to stories and sang wordless chants until three in the morning. When I finally left, the seder still had a few hours to go. Reb Shlomo died the following fall. This seder turned out to be the last one he led.

PERFECT STRANGERS CAN MAKE PERFECT GUESTS

Drawing from my own enriching experiences, I am now an enthusiastic advocate of inviting strangers to one's seder. Many families do this routinely, reaching out to welcome various categories of Jews as well as non-Jews. Naomi Osher of Newton, Massachusetts, recalls her parents having twenty to thirty people each year at their

Cincinnati home, a number of them Christians. Her parents' born-again housekeeper always looks forward to the *tsimmes* or sweet carrot dish. Fred Kahn of Buffalo Grove, Illinois, remembers the time as a boy that his mother called the Hillel or Jewish Student Union at Northwestern University to see if any students wanted to come. On the night of the seder, seven students from the dental school showed up at the door, causing the family to scramble for seats and plates. Rabbi Sheldon Ever and his wife Reva, before making *aliyah* or immigrating to Jerusalem, made sure each year to invite local widows and widowers who had nowhere to go, drawing from the large elderly population of their Miami Beach neighborhood. On occasion, attendance at their seders was as high as forty.

Having strangers at the seder can generate some comical moments, especially when the guests aren't Jewish. Mary (not her real name), who grew up in Detroit, attended Catholic schools as a child and never learned anything about Judaism. As an adult, she befriended a man whose father was a cantor, and the family invited her to their Passover seder. She was very excited at attending her first Jewish event, and wanted to bring a very special gift. So she looked hard to find the one item that she knew symbolized Judaism. She still turns purple every time she describes the look on the faces of her host and hostess when she presented them with … a *challah* or loaf of bread.

Both guests and hosts benefit when strangers are invited. Individuals who are single, widowed, away from home, newly converted or unable to conduct their own seder are deeply grateful for an invitation. Unaffiliated Jews strengthen their connection to Judaism, and those experienced at seder participation pick up new insights and ideas for future seders. Guests who aren't Jewish often find the experience fascinating, although it is probably a good idea to prepare them in advance for the unfamiliar ritual aspects of the meal.

Hosts gain in a variety of ways. Jewish affiliations for young children are reinforced when they see strangers sing the same songs and perform the same rituals as their parents. Family tensions can be eased when strangers are present, as difficult relatives are more likely to be on their best behavior. Strangers contribute new songs, melodies, stories and interpretations, help out in the kitchen, and entertain the kids. Their questions can bring out new understandings and make the experience continually meaningful. New friendships and connections often emerge.

AN INVITATION

If you are inspired to invite one stranger or many, here are some people and places you might call to find guests:*

- A rabbi or synagogue office located in a neighborhood that is no longer predominantly Jewish. (where remaining members are likely to be elderly);
- An assisted living center or geriatric home;
- The Hillel or Chabad House at your local college or university to ask whether they know of students who would like to attend a home seder;
- Chaplains at local hospitals or military bases;
- Jewish Community Centers;
- Food pantries, social service organizations, and immigration organizations
- Organizations that conduct classes for people studying to convert to Judaism;
- Organizations that provide *tzedakah* (charity) or interest-free loans to the Jewish community.

Remember, by opening your home to others on Passover, you fulfill the appeal of the *hagaddah* liturgy: "Let all who are hungry, come and eat. Let all who are in need, come and share the Passover meal."

The Debate on Machine-Made Matzot[168]

by Philip Goodman

In about 1857, the first *matzah*-baking machine was invented in Austria, beginning a heated controversy that raged for half a century. Dr. Solomon B. Freehof has given us a full account of this dispute, which he calls "one of the most acrimonious discussions in the history of the responsa literature." However, this should not be surprising as this was, indeed, a radical innovation for the fulfillment of a duty whose execution had long ago been elaborately defined to the minutest detail.

The newly invented machine kneaded the dough and rolled it through two metal rollers from which it came out thin, perforated, and round. It was then placed in an oven. As the corners of the dough, cut to make the *matzot* round, were re-used, it was feared that the time elapsing until these pieces of dough were used again might

* List has been modified for this publication.

allow them to become leavened. A later machine was developed that produced square *matzot* so that there would be no leftovers. Other subsequent improvements in the machinery speeded up the entire process of production, leading to a general acceptance of the modern method. Meanwhile, many distinguished rabbis raised their voices in protest against the new machine, while others, equally respected, permitted its use.

Solomon Kluger of Brody, in a letter to Rabbi Hayyim Nathan and Rabbi Leibush Horowitz of Cracow, Galicia, where the machine was already in use, prohibited the eating of the machine-made *matzot*, especially for the *matzot* mitzvah [the commandment to eat matzah at the seder]. This letter and similar pronouncements by other rabbis were published under the title *Moda' ah le-Bet Yisrael* ("Announcement to the House of Israel," Breslau, 1859). In rebuttal, Rabbi Joseph Saul Nathanson published the pamphlet *Bittul Moda'ah* ("Annulment of the Announcement," Lemberg, 1859).

One of Kluger's most telling arguments was that the opportunity given to the poor to earn money for their Passover needs by working in matzah bakeries would be denied to them, as the use of machinery required fewer manual workers. He and his adherents also argued that *matzah shemurah* particularly, must be made with the intention of fulfilling the precept that requires the understanding of a mature adult. They also claimed that there was a suspicion that the pieces of dough left in the wheels of the machine, which were difficult to clean, would become leavened.

In the forefront of the rabbis who permitted the use of machinery was Joseph Saul Nathanson of Lemberg. … [Nathanson and his colleagues] refuted the arguments of the opposition seriatim. If concern need be expressed about the displacement of the hand-bakers, the same solicitude should be shown to scribes whose replacement by the printing press had been universally accepted. They also held that these *matzot* are baked with the intention to comply with the law, as it is necessary for an adult to start the machine. They had no fear that the dough would be left in the machines as they are cleaned well and often. Furthermore, they contended that the machine speeds the process and is more efficient than the men and women who worked in the bakery day and night. The views of Nathanson and those who sided with him have been accepted by most Jews.

PART 3

The Omer

*And from the day on which you bring the sheaf (omer) of elevation—
the day after the sabbath—you shall count off seven weeks. They must be
complete: you must count until the day after the seventh week—fifty days;
then you shall bring an offering of new grain to the LORD. You shall bring
from your settlements two loaves of bread as an elevation offering; each shall
be made of two-tenths of a measure of choice flour, baked after leavening,
as first fruits to the LORD. . . . On that same day you shall
hold a celebration; it shall be a sacred occasion for you; . . ."*

—Leviticus 23:15–17, 21

A Bridge of Time

THE JEWISH CALENDAR is made up of spiritual ebbs and flows, rises and falls. The gradual buildup to Passover climaxes with the seder, undoubtedly one of the high points of the Jewish year. However, Passover should not be experienced as a spiritual island. It is inexorably bound to the next major festival, Shavuot, by seven weeks; and within those weeks are the connecting days that possess their own inherent significance. For some people, this period is the most important span of time in the Jewish year.

These 49 days between Passover and Shavuot derive their original importance from a biblical directive. According to the Book of Leviticus, beginning on the second night of Passover, Jews are to count each day as it passes—for seven complete weeks—until Shavuot (The Feast of Weeks) is reached. This segment of the calendar is called *Sefirat Ha-Omer* ("The Counting of the Omer") or, more commonly, either of its two shortened names—"the Omer" and "the Sefirah." The Hebrew term for this period comes from the generic word *omer*, a reference to the sheaf, or bundle, of barley grain used to bake an unleavened offering for the second day of Passover. At Shavuot, the offering was two loaves of bread baked from new wheat. Coming at the end of the Omer period, this offering was the first time each year that wheat (the most desirable of grains) was part of the Temple service. At this turn in the season, the Israelites would begin again with fresh wheat, just as each year, we receive the Torah again at Shavuot.

Today, in addition to its biblical significance, this portion of the yearly calendar benefits from an historically rapid insertion of new commemorative days, interpretations, and innovations. It has evolved into a "Jewish season," adding holidays and meaningful observances, such as those related to the Holocaust and to the founding of the State of Israel, each of which gives unique expression to the historical and spiritual Jewish experience.

The Rabbinic Harvest

As the Bible makes only one simple directive about the Omer—that we mark the days between Passover and Shavuot—we must look at Rabbinic literature to learn what the connecting period means.

REINTERPRETING THE TRADITION

Shavuot was originally an agricultural festival. The Israelites marked the end of the spring barley harvest and the beginning of the summer wheat harvest by bringing crop offerings to the Temple in Jerusalem. These offerings were the first ripe fruit from any of the seven species praised in the Torah: wheat, barley, grapes, figs, pomegranates, olives, and dates. With the destruction of the Second Temple in 70 C.E., these pilgrimage festivals came to an end. In the Rabbinic era that followed, the nature of the holiday changed.

The Bible does not mention a specific date for when the Jews received the Torah at Mount Sinai. Later, in the Talmud (a work that was fully compiled by the 6th century), the Rabbis determine that the Torah was given to the Jews on the 6th day of the month of Sivan,[1] the date of the already existing celebration of Shavuot. Thus, rather than keeping Shavuot a mere agricultural festival, the Rabbis imbue it with the enormous spiritual value of *z'man matan Torateinu*, the time of the giving of the Torah. In turn, the Sefirah measures the days, not simply to a festival, but to the moment God revealed God's self to the Jewish people.

Furthermore, since Shavuot is the day the Torah was given, it becomes an integral part of the Passover story in the Book of Exodus. The Israelites' flight from Egypt occurred on the 15th of Nisan,[2] 49 days before Shavuot and the giving of the Torah. Thus the Sefirah is not merely seven weeks of mundane time to be ticked off between holidays; it is the temporal and spiritual connective tissue between the Exodus from Egypt and the giving of the Torah. The Sefirah represents both the physical and the spiritual passageways that the Israelites navigated as they moved from the painful depths of Egyptian bondage to the glory of God's voice at Mount Sinai.

LOSS AND SADNESS

One might think that the Sefirah—associated with two of the most inspirational moments in the Bible, the liberation from slavery and the giving of the Torah—would be a time of elation and celebration. On the contrary, the Counting of the Omer is actually a time of mourning and solemnity.

One reason for the serious mood may hearken back to our agrarian ancestors' experience of this season. The Sefirah, which occurs between spring and early summer, is the ripening time for many fruits; and we may assume that this was a period of great uncertainty for farmers. The Talmud reflects this doubt and yearning when it describes the culmination of the seasonal ripening, Shavuot, as the day on which the fruit trees are judged."[3] The verdict, of course, is not upon the trees themselves; it is upon us. After all, people are the ones who suffer if the trees do not bear edible fruit. Seeking a favorable judgment and a bountiful harvest, our ancestors most likely dedicated these weeks of the Sefirah to improving their behavior and raising their spiritual worthiness through prayer and self-reflection, in the belief that their personal state might influence the outcome.[4]

A more common and traditional explanation for the solemnity also comes from the Talmud. We learn it in this story about Rabbi Akiva, the renowned scholar who lived in 1st-to-2nd-century Israel (after the Temple had been destroyed), and his disciples.

> They said, "Rabbi Akiva had twelve thousand pairs of disciples from [the towns of] Gevat to Antipatris and they all died during one period of time because they did not treat each other with respect. The world was left desolate until Rabbi Akiva came to the south and taught them Torah. [Those who learned with him were] Rabbi Meir, Rabbi Yehoshuah, Rabbi Yossi, Rabbi Shimon, and Rabbi Elazar ben Shamu'a." A tanna [a rabbi of the time of the Mishnah] stated: "They all died between Passover and Shavuot." Rabbi Chana bar Abba, and some say Rabbi Chiya bar Avin, said: "They died a terrible death." What was it? Rabbi Nachman said: "Askerah" [a throat infection, commonly understood as diphtheria].[5]

Several aspects of this tragic tale are striking. First is the shear magnitude of the tragedy: 24,000 students died. Second is the unquestioned rationale for their deaths: the students treated each other disrespectfully, a difficult theological and moral concept that reflects on how we understand our relationship with God and the consequences of our behavior. Third is the timing: they died between Passover and Shavuot, which begs us to infer meaning from this period.

This story is so infused with symbolism that many scholars have difficulty accepting it as a factual historical event. Many historians believe it is really a metaphor for the persecutions of the Roman emperor Hadrian and the Bar Kokhba Revolt of the Jews in the 2nd century C.E., a time when the renowned Rabbi Akiva and many other rabbis were tortured and killed. Other talmudic and literary scholars suggest that this story is a blending of several earlier midrashic and talmudic elements, combined with the intention of heightening Rabbi Akiva's status. Ultimately, the only consensus among scholars is that the Sefirah has an aura of mournfulness; the origin of that mood remains very open for conjecture.

SPIRITUAL DIMENSIONS

The Sefirah has added significance for practitioners of Kabbalah—Jewish mysticism. Kabbalists understand Torah not as something that happened in the past, but, metaphorically, as something happening in the present—on a spiral, in which the spiritual vibrations from one time carry through to the next. When counting the Omer, Jews must prepare to receive the Torah this very year. Consequently, each day leading up to Shavuot, the day of Revelation, provides a mystical opportunity to improve oneself through meditation and proper intention.

The kabbalists align these 49 days with the chart of the mystical *sefirot* (dimensions of God; plural of *sefirah*), a central element of kabbalistic theology symbolized by the Tree of Life. The *sefirot* provide a way for us to understand God's anatomy and, therefore, God's will. Of course this is not a physical anatomy but a spiritual one, and one that we humans share with God. As such, this conception of God and spirit helps us to understand our purpose in the universe. All together the chart holds 10 *sefirot*. During the *Sefirat Ha-Omer*, however, the seven at the bottom—sometimes called the emotional *sefirot*—are emphasized. One is highlighted for each of the seven weeks that stretch from Passover to Shavuot. The *sefirot* are *hesed* (lovingkindness), *gevurah* (strength), *tiferet* (harmony), *netzach* (eternity), *hod* (Glory), *yesod* (foundation), and *malkhut* (God's presence or kingdom on earth).[6]

Besides being distinct parts of God's anatomy, these seven *sefirot* interconnect and combine with one another—for example, strength exists within lovingkindness. Consequently, during the Counting of the Omer, the kabbalists meditate and internalize certain combinations of these *sefirot* for each of the 49 days. The practice works every year as follows: on the first day of the first week, concentrate upon lovingkindness itself (*hesed she'behesed*); on the second day, the strength that is in lovingkindness (*gevurah she'behesed*); on the third day, the harmony that is in lovingkindness (*tiferet she'behesed*); and so on, until the second week begins. At that time, the pattern is repeated, but with strength as the principal *sefirah*. Through this meditative process, we try to unify within ourselves the divine elements of the *sefirot* and thus to prepare ourselves for accepting the Torah on Shavuot. For when we make this acceptance, we assume the moral responsibility and immense spiritual force that are manifest in the renewed covenant with God.

COUNTING AND MINDFULNESS

And from the day on which you bring the sheaf of elevation offering [*in effect, the second night of Passover*] *... you shall count off seven weeks. They must be complete: ... (Lev. 23:15). Then you shall observe the Feast of Weeks* [*Shavuot*] *for the LORD your God ... (Deut. 16:10).*

To observe the Sefirah, we simply and literally count each day from Passover until Shavuot. Every day, we say a blessing to sanctify the Torah-based commandment and then we make the count, for example, "Today is one day of the Omer" or "Today is eight days, which are one week and one day of the Omer" or "Today is 25 days, which are three weeks and four days of the Omer" or, finally, "Today is 49 days, which are seven weeks of the Omer." Because the counting must be done in terms of not only days but also of weeks and days,[7] the Talmud teaches that it is to be done at a set time—nighttime, when a "day" on the Hebrew calendar begins. Thus each day the full period is marked off and counted.[8] Medieval rabbis pondered the effect of the word "complete." If a person misses a day all together or forgets to count at night and catches up by counting during the following daylight hours, has the person thereby lost the opportunity to fulfill the commandment?

Opinions differ on this topic. The traditional and most stringent viewpoint suggests that the entire counting—all 49 days—constitute one commandment. According to this perspective, a person who forgets to count on any of the 49 days must halt the ritual because the counting could not ever be a "complete" one. Some medieval authorities disagree. They note that we say a blessing for each and every night, not one blessing for the entire seven weeks.[9] Thus each day's count embodies its own spiritual significance and is not merely part of one indivisible blessing.

▲   ▲   ▲   ▲   ▲   ▲   ▲   ▲   ▲   ▲   ▲   ▲

Weekly Chart of the Sefirot

WEEK	DAYS	SEFIROT	ALTERNATE TRANSLATIONS
One	1–7	*hesed* LOVINGKINDNESS	Love, Compassion, Grace
Two	8–14	*gevurah* STRENGTH (also known as *din*, JUSTICE)	Power, Judgment
Three	15–21	*tiferet* HARMONY	Beauty, Balance, Compassion
Four	22–28	*netzach* ETERNITY	Endurance, Victory, Fortitude
Five	29–35	*hod* GLORY	Majesty, Splendor, Humility
Six	36–42	*yesod* FOUNDATION	Construction
Seven	43–49	*malkhut* KINGDOM (also known as *Shekhinah*, PRESENCE)	Sovereignty

DESCRIPTION	IMAGERY AND SYMBOLS	MEANING
The generous and benevolent aspect of God	Right arm, white, Abraham, lion	Both God and humans create life through love. If we strive to see the divine image within each of us, we are enabled to find compassion and unity.
God's power, necessary to discipline evil and maintain control over the universe	Left arm, red, Isaac, serpent	Even though love and freedom are important, a need exists to set limits upon behavior and create structure.
The central component that unites and balances above and below, male and female	Spine and torso; purple and green; Adam, Jacob, and Moses; the sun and daytime	Truth and beauty are to be found in all things. Using compassion, we are able to discover and unite everything in truth.
God's continuous grace, creativity, and achievement in the world	Right leg, light pink, Moses, a pillar	Motivation and determination are significant forces for living our lives to their fullest and achieving our potential.
The channel through which God's judgment descends to earth. The complement to *netzach*	Left leg, dark pink, Aaron, a pillar	With determination and ambition must also come humility. We must recognize our own flaws and develop patience and a sense of gratitude.
The generative channel of the *sefirot* tree. A direct association with the masculine and the phallus	Phallus sanctified through circumcision, orange, Joseph, rainbow	We are brought together by the impulse to unify and bond. It is the impulse of covenant. This is seen explicitly in the act of sex and fertility.
The feminine aspect of God. The womb. The vehicle for all of the *sefirot* to be implanted and combined. The agent of fertility between male and female aspects of God. The immanent presence of God that each of us can experience	Mouth (sometimes feet), blue and black, Rachel, King David, the Land of Israel	To experience the presence of God, we must be conscious and accepting of these paradoxical ideas: we are in control, yet not in control; we are individuals, yet we are bound to others; we are self-assured, yet we are modestly doubtful; we are full of life, yet we die. This path leads to being openhearted and down to earth.

Since a Hebrew day begins at sundown, what would be the case if a person who has forgotten to count at night remembers and counts during the following daylight hours? Would the chain of counting remain intact? There are three schools of thought on this issue. The first opinion by Rabbeinu Tam (Jacob ben Meir Tam, 12th century, French Tosafist[10]) is no, one may not continue counting.[11] The second, supported by the revered medieval philosopher Maimonides, is yes, one may continue.[12] The third is cited by Joseph Karo in his 16th-century code of law, Shulchan Arukh (literally, "Set Table"). It says that one may count in the daytime so as to not break the chain, but without the accompanying blessing. Because there is doubt that this off-time counting is truly the performance of the mitzvah, a person does not want say a blessing in vain.[13] That evening, the recitation of the daily blessing begins again.

Because of the Jewish law that surrounds the Counting of the Omer, a certain amount of tension is generated. A person who observes this tradition does not want to be forgetful and fail to meet the stringent obligation of counting at nighttime. During biblical times and later in the Temple period, remembering may have been easier. Jews were directly connected to sunset because most of them led agricultural lives. They watched their crops grow to be ready for the sacrificial offering on Shavuot as an expression of spirituality. Their attentiveness and observance were links between their experiences on earth and their mindfulness of heaven. Nowadays, most of us do not live an agricultural life and do not have the inherent, natural reminders that were part of such a society. All we essentially have to pace our counting are the calendar and the clock, which are far more abstract reminders of our relationship with God than are the spiritual elements of nature. For many of us, remembering to count the Omer is more difficult today than in the ancient past and requires more deliberate focus. Yet such extra thoughtfulness may be just the sort of thing we need in the modern world, where we race against the clock and do our best to manage the stress of long, indoor workdays. During the Sefirah, it may be beneficial to deliberately create a level of tension to help us keep track of this ritual that is so much about time. We can then appreciate and foucs on what the ritual represents, something bigger and beyond time—the countdown to receiving the Torah.

Lag ba-Omer:
Mourning and Controversy

During the Sefirah, we observe several customs that capture the mournful spirit of this time. Each is a prohibitive custom—something we refrain from doing, for example, we do not hold weddings or other such joy-filled events,[14] and we refrain from getting haircuts.[15] While an ungroomed appearance is a traditional sign of mourning, allowing the hair to go uncut may also symbolize a pure status, similar to that of a newborn baby, or perhaps even a sanctified status, such as that of a Nazirite. This term, from the Hebrew word *nazir*, "consecrated" or "separated," refers to a Jew as described in the Book of Numbers, who took an ascetic vow "to set himself apart for the LORD,"[16] with certain abstentions. These include the prohibition "the hair of his head shall be left to grow untrimmed" (6:5), which applies only to men, some of whom extend the haircutting prohibition to shaving, as well.[17]

We pause only once during this period for a suspension from the prohibitions. The day is called Lag ba-Omer (literally, "33rd [day] of the Omer"), which falls on the 18th day of the Hebrew month of Iyar. Haircuts are allowed, and because joyous celebrations are permitted, many people choose this date as a wedding day. In Israel, Lag ba-Omer is a school holiday, replete with bonfires, picnics, and family outings.

The origin of Lag ba-Omer as an island of festivity, a kind of semiholiday, is obscure but generally connected to Rabbi Akiva and the time when his students were dying from a plague. One of the most significant references to Lag ba-Omer is in *Beit Ha-Bechirah* (literally, "The Chosen Building"), a commentary on the Talmud by 13th-century French scholar Menachem Meiri. He discusses an opinion of the Geonim, who were the heads of the Babylonian rabbinical institutes from the 6th to the 11th centuries. They had determined that Rabbi Akiva's students stopped dying on a specific day in the

A Numerical Translation

Lag ba-Omer is literally the "33rd [day] of the Omer." By modern standards, however, "lag" is not a conventional word. The ancient Hebrew language lacked numerals; instead, letters were used to represent numbers. The number 33 was written with the letter *lamed* (*l* sound, value 30) and the letter *gimel* (hard *g* sound, value 3) plus an *ah* sound in the middle for pronunciation. When we are counting, the prefix "ba" means "relating to." And, of course, Omer is Omer.

2nd century, and that date was Lag ba-Omer. Thus, the Geonim said, we have the custom to refrain from the practice of mourning on this day.[18]

Another description of Lag ba-Omer comes from the French rabbi Abraham ben Nathan of Lunel (France), who died in 1215. In his work *Sefer Ha-Manhig* (literally, "The Guide Book"), he states:

> It is the custom in France and Provence to marry from Lag ba-Omer on [i.e., to permit weddings which are prohibited from Passover until Shavuot because of mourning for the students of Rabbi Akiva]; I have heard in the name of Rav Zerachiah Rabbeinu Ha-Levi of Garonne that it has been found written ... "[F]rom Pesach until pros Ha-Atzeret [pros means half, and Atzeret is a term for Shavuot; that is, half of the time period referred to] ... in a mishnah, 'We ask concerning the laws of Pesach thirty days before Pesach'—and half of that is fifteen days; hence we forbid weddings until fifteen days before the Atzeret, and that is Lag ba-Omer."[19]

Notice that the passage from *Sefer Ha-Manhig* contains no description of Lag ba-Omer as a day with any special practices; it mentions Lag ba-Omer merely as the day the mourning ends and weddings are permitted. In the 16th century, Sephardic authority Joseph Karo (author of the Shulchan Arukh) and Ashkenazic authority Moses Isserles (author of the *Mapa*, literally, "Tablecloth") explore further the identity of Lag ba-Omer. Karo maintains that Lag ba-Omer is not a semiholiday; it marks the complete end of mourning during the Sefirah—that is, from the 34th day onward weddings and haircuts are permitted. Isserles, in contrast, takes the stance that Lag ba-Omer is merely a one-day suspension of mourning, and is thus not an end, but a semiholiday in the midst of this sad period. As a result of this divergence in opinion, Jews today follow two different ways of acknowledging and observing Lag ba-Omer, Sephardim recognize the teaching of Karo; Ashkenazim, the teaching of Isserles.

In yet another examination of the status of Lag ba-Omer, this one in more modern times, the Conservative stream of Judaism has made two official statements about the mourning customs during the Sefirah. The first is the 1949 decision to adopt the

Geonic tradition, as referenced by Meiri in the 12th century and upheld by Joseph Karo about two centuries later: Mourning practices need not continue from Lag ba-Omer onward, and marriages may be performed.[20] The second decision, which occurred in 1969, takes into account two historical events of the 20th century, the Holocaust and the subsequent establishment of the State of Israel. The decision notes that the textual basis for the mourning customs during the Sefirah lacks a firm origin and thus amendment is possible. Consequently, the conclusion was drawn that mourning customs must be upheld through the newfound Yom Ha-Shoah—Holocaust Memorial Day on the 27th of Nisan, the 12th day of the Omer. Beyond that date, according to the Rabbinical Assembly (the international association of Conservative rabbis), the prohibitions are lifted; however, a caveat expressed by Moses Isserles is emphasized as well, which states that we should make an effort to avoid conflicts within a community.[21] In other words, if an individual or a family is surrounded by people who follow a different custom, one that does not violate Jewish law, it may be advisable or even desirable to avoid isolation and to participate in the custom of the community.[22]

CELEBRATORY HAIRCUTS FOR BOYS

A ceremony known in Yiddish as *upfsherin* (literally, "cutting off") or in Hebrew as *chalake* (from the verb root *chet.lamed.kuf*, "to take parts") is especially prevalent in Hasidic communities. In this custom, parents refrain from cutting their son's hair until his third birthday. Around that time, they hold a celebration with guests invited to snip a lock of the boy's hair. The parents usually speak some thoughtful and hopeful words about their child and offer a *devar* Torah (literally, "a word of" Torah), meaning a Jewish teaching appropriate to the meaning of the day. Haircutting also has particular significance for kabbalists, as the great 16th-century mystic Isaac Luria was reported to have cut his son's hair at the grave of Shimon bar Yochai, who lived in 2nd-century Israel. One of the most eminent disciples of Rabbi Akiva, Bar Yochai is the reputed author of the Zohar. Although no date was originally associated with the Luria haircutting, it later was attached to Lag ba-Omer, the anniversary of Bar Yochai's death. People today continue to visit Bar Yochai's grave at Meron (northern Israel) on Lag ba-Omer, which is often the place and time when three-year-old boys are shorn for the first time.

The *upfsherin* practice is associated with the Torah's laws found in Leviticus concerning taking fruit from trees.[23] Just as we are prohibited from picking the fruits of a tree for its first three years of life, so we refrain from trimming the hair of a boy, to preserve a state of spiritual purity. Furthermore, a boy is traditionally initiated into his formal Jewish education at this time with the introduction of the Hebrew alphabet. In some circles, on a boy's third birthday, he begins wearing a *kippah* (Hebrew for skullcap, known as yarmulke in Yiddish) and tzitzit (ritual fringes attached to four-cornered garments). An *upfsherin* is a joyous occasion for many families; although, at the same time, there are rabbis across the different streams of Judaism who criticize the practice of this custom. Among their concerns is the limited knowledge that exists about its origins. Also, some feminists object to *upfsherin* because the custom excludes girls, for whom there is no parallel practice or ceremony.

From Shoah to Statehood

Shoah (literally, "calamity" or "destruction") is the Hebrew term for the Holocaust, the years just before and during World War II when Adolf Hitler and his Nazi Party systematically and diabolically carried out a plan to annihilate every Jew in Europe and—given Hitler's global ambitions—no doubt the world. During the period of the Sefirah, many Jews, and especially those in Israel, have begun to include days of remembrance for that horrid time as well as days of honor relating to the statehood that followed. These days are not technically part of the Counting the Omer, established at the time of the Bible; but, for many people, they flavor and bring additional meaning to the period.

LIVES SHATTERED

By 1938, Hitler had succeeded in legally excluding Germany's prosperous and assimilated Jewish community from the country's social and political life. Then on the night of November 9, the Nazis stepped up their campaign by unleashing a wave of pogroms. Groups of storm troopers and citizen thugs attacked Jewish homes and, in the space of a few hours, ransacked or burned nearly 2,000 synagogues (virtually all of them). They vandalized cemeteries and schools, looted and destroyed almost 7,500 Jewish businesses, brutally beat thousands of Jews, and killed about 100. About 30,000 Jewish men were sent to concentration camps.[24] This event, which became known as *Kristallnacht*[25] ("Night of Broken Glass"), was not only a tragedy unto itself[26] but also a visible turning point. It marked the most physical, widely observed beginning of the Holocaust, a moment when the shock and desperation of European Jewry sharply intensified.

▲ ▲ ▲ ▲ ▲ ▲ ▲ ▲ ▲ ▲ ▲ ▲ ▲

Yom Ha-Shoah

Seven long, excruciating years would go by until the Allies defeated the Nazis and then, surprisingly, just three more, albeit filled with tension and struggle, until 1948, when Israel declared its miraculous statehood. Thoughts about those who had died and about the suffering of those who had survived permeated the jubilation. In 1953, the Knessset (Israeli parliament) enacted into law an annual commemoration formally known as Yom Ha-Shoah v'Ha-Gevurah, The Day of the Holocaust and the Heroism, or simply "Yom Ha-Shoah." Choosing the date for Yom Ha-Shoah was no easy matter. Several proposals had been offered, each arguing for the appropriateness of a different date for a communal observance. The traditionalists and Orthodox rabbinate in Israel preferred to connect the anniversary of the Shoah with a preexisting day of mourning, to which would be added a recitation of the mourner's *Kaddish* (prayer said on the anniversary of someone's death) expressly for people whose date of death in the Holocaust was unknown or for people who died with no one left to say *Kaddish*. They chose the 10th of the Hebrew month of Tevet (which falls in early January), a minor fast day that commemorates the initial siege of Jerusalem that led to the destruction of the Second Temple in 70 C.E. As a result, some people today observe the 10th of Tevet as a general *Kaddish* day for victims of the Holocaust.

Far More Than One Too Many

No one knows for certain how many Jews were murdered in the Shoah. Adolf Eichmann, the Nazi known as "the architect of the Holocaust," proudly claimed the number to be 6 million. Recent studies put the Jewish death toll[27] somewhere between 5.3 and 7 million, of whom roughly 1.5 million were children. Estimates are based upon prewar and postwar population censuses as well as Nazi documentation on various deportations to concentration camps and subsequent killings. Yad Vashem, the Holocaust Martyrs' and Heroes' Remembrance Authority in Israel, has more than 4 million documented names from approximately 2 million pages of testimony. Whatever the exact death toll, we know that at least half of the world's Jews were murdered in the Holocaust and, along with them, the talents and contributions of their descendants who would never be born.

Young Zionists[28] in Israel, however, wanted to emphasize the heroism of the Shoah's victims. Now with their own country and army, Jews could be viewed as strong freedom fighters as opposed to frail victims from the cities and villages of Europe. For them, the day most worthy of memorialization would be the anniversary of the Warsaw Ghetto Uprising, which began in earnest on April 19, 1943. About three years earlier, the Nazis had begun herding Warsaw's 400,000 Jews into a small area of the city, from which they were deported to death camps. In the largest single revolt during the Holocaust, a group of Warsaw Ghetto Jews fought to the death to try to prevent the final deportations.

It so happened that April 19, 1943, was the 15th of Nisan on the Hebrew calendar—the first day of Passover as it would occur annually. As the debates about Yom Ha-Shoah wore on, the traditionalists insisted that the memorial day should not occur during Passover, a time of great joy with themes of hope and faith. They decided that a day of sadness and mourning for such a horrendous, pivotal event as the Holocaust should have a date all its own on the calendar. Ultimately, the Zionists and the traditionalists compromised, choosing the 27th of Nisan, with certain dissatisfactions remaining for each party. The traditionalists maintained the strict perspective of Jewish law, which contends that the entire month of Nisan is to be joyful.[29] They had lobbied for pushing Yom Ha-Shoah into the following Hebrew month, Iyar, which would be around the time the uprising was squashed. The Zionists, however, wanted the date as close to Passover as possible, to commemorate the beginning of the uprising, rather than its tragic ending, which occurred on May 16.

Thus today, the month of Nisan has a brake applied against its hitherto full-throttle enthusiasm, but perhaps that spiritual condition is appropriate for Jews in the reality of a post-Holocaust world. In fact to members of the Knesset, the most important factor in the choice of a date for Yom Ha-Shoah was not its relationship to the Warsaw Ghetto Uprising or to Passover. They wanted its place on the calendar to fall ahead of another day of commemoration, Yom Ha-Atzmaut, Israel's independence day. They understood the Shoah and the establishment of the State of Israel to be linked; after the sadness of Yom Ha-Shoah, Jews would do well to remind themselves of the founding of the state on May 14, 1948, the 5th day of the Hebrew month of Iyar. This sequence of days follows the pattern of history, in which the favorable vote in the United Nations (November 29, 1947) that established Israel was preceded by sympathy for the Jews after World War II, collective guilt felt by some remaining Jews for their own passivity, and international acknowledgment that Jews were always in danger living in the Diaspora. A majority of member nations (58 percent) saw a modern Jewish homeland as the best possible way of preventing another act of catclysmic anti-Semitism. In the end, Hitler's evil plan was upended by an amazing victory for Zionism.

CONTEMPORARY MEANING

Along with the traumatization and murder of millions of people, the Shoah distorted the advancements that had been made in the Western world, in fields such as science and technology. In Nazi hands, the fruits of those achievements became the efficient instruments of death and destruction used to inspire a methodical and thorough strategy to hasten the planned annihilation of Jews. Not wanting to waste money on bullets or time on individual murders, the Germans used their inventiveness for mass killing on an unprecedented scale. In the process, they betrayed their own culture and all of humanity.

World leaders who watched this horror remained silent and complacent for years (from before World War II to the very end) even though the Allies, including the Americans, had irrefutable evidence about what was happening to the Jews. We learned from the Shoah, in very modern terms, just how cruel people can be, whether through active or passive means; and we continue to struggle against the human inclination to be indifferent or nonreactive to the suffering of other people.

YOM HA-ATZMAUT

Although the United Nations General Assembly had voted in November 1947 to facilitate the establishment of a modern Jewish homeland, the months that followed were ones of escalating violence and diplomatic wrangling. Yom Ha-Atzmaut, Israel's independence day,[30] commemorates the events of May 14, 1948, when the Zionists' provisional council decided to wait no longer. On two days' notice and against a backdrop of imminent threat from hostile nations, council members gathered in Tel Aviv to hear their leader, David Ben-Gurion, read the Proclamation of the Establishment of the State of Israel:

The Land of Israel was the birthplace of the Jewish people. Here their spiritual, religious, and political identity was shaped. Here they first attained to statehood, created cultural values of national and universal significance and gave to the world the eternal Book of Books.

After being forcibly exiled from their land, the people kept faith with it throughout their Dispersion and never ceased to pray and hope for their return to it and for the restoration in it of their political freedom. . . .

[W]e . . . representatives of the Jewish community of Eretz-Israel [Land of Israel] and of the Zionist movement, are here assembled on the day of the termination of the British mandate over Eretz-Israel and, by virtue of our natural and historic right and on the strength of the resolution of the United Nations General Assembly, hereby declare the establishment of a Jewish state . . . .

The State of Israel will be open . . . for the ingathering of the exiles; it will foster the development of the country for the benefit of all its inhabitants; it will be based on freedom, justice and peace as envisaged by the Prophets of Israel; it will ensure complete equality of social and political rights . . . it will guarantee freedom of religion, conscience, language, education and culture; it will safeguard the holy places of all religions. . . .

We extend our hand to all neighboring states and their peoples in an offer of peace and good neighborliness. . . .

We appeal to the Jewish people throughout the Diaspora to rally round the Jews of Eretz-Israel in the tasks of immigration and upbuilding and to stand by them in the great struggle for the realization of the age-old dream——the redemption of Israel.

Rabbi Yehuda Leib Fishman[31] said a blessing, and each member of the council present[32] signed the document. As an orchestra played "Hatikvah" (the national anthem), crowds outside erupted in dancing and tears of jubilation.

Ben-Gurion soon addressed the breathless people of the United States in a live radio broadcast. While he was speaking, Egyptian planes swooped down and began bombing Tel Aviv. Within 24 hours, seven neighboring Arab countries had declared war on Israel in what was ultimately a failed attempt at destroying the tiny, infant nation.

Yom Ha-Atzmaut is a national holiday in Israel. In the evening, there are patriotic public shows and participation in folk dancing and singing. The following day, thousands of Israeli families go on hikes and picnics. Army camps are open for civilians to visit and see the latest military technology. Yom Ha-Atzmaut concludes with the Israel Prize in the fields of culture, science, art, and the humanities. Outside the country, Jews of different practices and ideologies join together to celebrate the day, as a way to show solidarity with the State of Israel. After 2,000 years of *galut* ("exile"), dispersion, and oppression, culminating in the severe trauma of the Holocaust, this day marks a time in history when Jews know there is a place they can live where they are free to speak their own language, create their own culture, and follow their own religion and dreams without fear of a ruling nation.

Heritage Site

Israel's declaration of independence was signed in a temporarily repurposed room of the Tel Aviv Museum. In 1971 this art museum moved to new quarters; and then in 1978, a re-created "Independence Hall" opened in the old building as the Eretz Israel Museum. Although the chairs around the long table are now a matched set (the originals were a hastily borrowed hodge-podge), the appearance is much the same, displaying many of the paintings and authentic artifacts from that day in May 1948. Above all, the spirit of Yom Ha-Atzmaut is fully present, especially when visitors hear a recording of the ceremony and spontaneously join the early statesmen in singing "Hatikvah."

REMEMBERING SOLDIERS AND HONORING A CITY

In Israel, two more national days of tribute have found places in the weeks between Passover and Shavuot.

Yom Ha-Zikaron

In Israel, Yom Ha-Atzmaut is preceded on the 4th of Iyar by Yom Ha-Zikaron, a memorial day to honor the men and women who have fought—often outnumbered and with minimal resources—to establish, protect, and preserve the land. Remembered are those who died under many circumstances, including the War for Independence (1948), the War of Attrition (1950s), the Six-Day War (1967), the Yom Kippur War (1973), the first and second *intifadas*, and two wars in Lebanon. As a country with a citizen army and with a history of fighting wars in every generation, just for the right to exist, Israel is a big family in which every member has been touched in some way by war and its terrible price. All places of public entertainment are shut down by law. Radio and television stations play programs about Israel's wars that convey the somber mood of the day. One televsion channel is devoted to airing only a procession of names—the tens of thousands who have fallen. The air raid sirens sound twice during Yom Ha-Zikaron. All activity, including traffic, immediately ceases. People get out of their cars, even in the middle of otherwise busy highways, and stand in respect. The first siren marks the start of this memorial day and the second is sounded immediately before to the public recitation of prayers in military cemeteries. Since the second *intifada*, many people have extended Yom Ha-Zikaron to include the security guards who have given their lives to save civilians during terrorist attacks.[33] Although Yom Ha-Zikaron is principally an Israeli day of commemoration, Jews worldwide may acknowledge their gratitude to the fallen heroes with prayers, songs of deliverance, and readings about Israel's struggles.

Yom Yerushalayim

We ran there, a group of panting soldiers, lost on the plaza of the Temple Mount, searching for a giant stone wall. . . . and suddenly we stopped, thunderstruck. There it was before our eyes! Gray and massive, silent and restrained. The Western Wall! Slowly, slowly I began to approach the Wall in fear and trembling . . . . I approached it as the messenger of my father and my grandfather, of my great-grandfather and of all the generations in all the exiles who had never merited seeing it . . . . I put my hand on the stones and the tears that started to flow were not my tears. They were the tears of all Israel, tears of hope and prayer, tears of Hasidic tunes, tears of Jewish dances, tears which scorched and burned the heavy gray stone.[34]

—Moshe Amirav, Israeli paratrooper

Yom Yerushalayim (Jerusalem Day) commemorates June 7, 1967, when the Israel Defense Forces reunited the eastern and western parts of the city, including the Old City, and reclaimed the *Kotel Ha-Ma'arivi*, "The Western Wall." Sometimes referred to as "The Wailing Wall,"[35] this sacred site is the extant retaining wall of the Second Temple, destroyed by the Romans in 70 C.E. Israelis celebrate Yom Yerushalayim on the 28th of Iyar (six weeks after the first Passover seder, one week before Shavuot). The chief rabbinate of Israel declared that *Hallel* (psalms of thanksgiving) should be recited on Yom Yerushalayim, just as on Yom Ha-Atzmaut; but observance, let alone acceptance, of this day has varied—largely for political reasons—since it was established by the Knesset in 1968. Many Israelis have gradually made Yom Yerushalayim into a pilgrimage day, when they travel, or even hike, to the city; and the Israeli education system devotes the week preceding this day to teaching the geography and history of Jerusalem, as do some Jewish schools and synagogues in other parts of the world.

◆— The Omer —◆
Pathways Through the Sources

Mishnah
The Original Reaping of the Omer

Judaism is able to send us back in time, back to the origins of civilization and the original response of humanity to changes of the season and arrival of a new crop to harvest. By emphasizing the study of ancient texts, we uncover vivid images of how our ancient ancestors conducted spiritual celebrations around the harvest; and these images ultimately provide insight into the character of our ritual or holiday practices today.

Interpreted by the Mishnah, the foundational text of Rabbinic literature and law, the following text describes the kickoff to the season of the Omer as it would have happened 2,000 years ago. It was clearly a tradition with much fanfare and public involvement, as well as a religious-political agenda.

> How did they prepare the omer? Messengers of the High Court used to go out on the eve of Passover and tie up bunches of the barley grain while it was still standing in order to make it easier to reap. Then all the townspeople assembled [at a particular field at the end of the first day of Passover] so that the sheaf of omer should be reaped with great ceremonial display. As soon as it became dark, the one assigned to reap the grain called out, "Has the sun set?" And they shouted, "Yes!" "Has the sun set?" [And they answered again,] "Yes!" [He then asked,] "[Should I reap it] with this sickle?" And they shouted, "Yes!" "[Should I reap it] with this sickle?" "Yes!" [He then asked,] "Into this basket?" And they shouted, "Yes!" "Into this basket?" "Yes!" If it was the Sabbath, he would further ask, "On this Sabbath?" And they shouted, "Yes!" "On this Sabbath?" "Yes!" [And finally he called out,] "Shall I reap?" And they shouted, "Reap!" "Shall I reap?" And they shouted "Reap!" Three times for each of these matters and they shouted back "Yes!" [and] "Yes!" [and] "Yes!"

> And why was it necessary for them to carry out the procedure like this? Because of the Boethusians [a group synonymous with the Sadducees in

Rabbinic literature], who maintained that the reaping of the omer should not take place upon the conclusion of the first day of Passover.
—Mishnah, *Menachot* 10:3

Maimonides
Restless Anticipation

The Counting of the Omer, the period between Passover and Shavuot, was undoubtedly filled with particular apprehension for our ancient, agriculture-centered ancestors, including the priests of the Temple, who were closely connected to concern about the forthcoming harvest. During the Rabbinic era, when the significance of Shavuot became associated with God's giving us the Torah at Mount Sinai, this period of anxiety evolved into one of eager anticipation. The general population was living a more urban way of life, and the Rabbis helped find new meaning in counting the days to Shavuot. As described here by Maimonides, the great thinker and interpreter of the Torah, they were days of restless joy.

> [Shavuot] is the day of the *giving of the Torah*. In order to glorify and exalt that day, the days are counted from the first of the festivals up to it, as is done by one who waits for the coming of the human being he loves best and counts the days and the hours. This is the reason for *the counting of the Omer* from the day when they left Egypt till the day of the *giving of the Torah*, which was the purpose and the end of their leaving.[36]
> —Maimonides, *Guide of the Perplexed* 3:43

Sefer Abudraham
Lest We Forget

We are all aware of the rigors of daily life. It is so easy to allow work responsibilities, packed schedules, household chores, and technological attractions to occupy all of our energy and thoughts. The Jewish tradition, however, especially in relationship to the Sabbath and to holy or commemorative days, insists that we carve out time from our secular lives to look beyond all that we appear to be. We are to remain mindful of the big picture—God's world—and be inspired by our partnership with our Maker. Counting the Omer is precisely such a responsibility and privilege.

Rabbi David ben Joseph Abudraham lived in Spain during the 1300s. In this text from his commentary on synagogue ritual and prayers, he provides rationales for and greater explanations about celebrating the period of the Omer. He is commonly known as Sefer Abudraham, which was also the title of his best-known work.

Since all Israel are occupied with the harvest and are all busy with the work of the fields and the people are widely scattered, He commanded us to count the days leading to the next pilgrimage Festival to ensure that none would forget.

The nation is anxious during the period between Passover and Shavuot that their crops and orchards be bountiful. The Talmud tells us in Tractate *Rosh Hashanah*: Why does the Torah command us to bring an omer offering on Passover? So that the grains in the fields might be blessed. And why does the Torah tell us to bring the two loaves offering on Shavuot? So that the fruits of the trees might be blessed. And why does the Torah tell us to perform the water libation [*simchat beit ha-sho'evah*] on Sukkot? So that they might be blessed with the rains of the year. God therefore commanded that we count these days so that we be reminded of the anxiety of mankind and so that we might return to Him with our whole hearts and plead to Him that He be merciful to us and all of Creation in providing sufficient harvests.[37]

—Sefer Abudraham

Sefat Emet

Fit to Receive

The Torah cannot be compared to any other book, nor can its Author be compared with any other author. The books that make up the Torah are the garments of the Divine, wherein every sentence, every utterance, is bursting with meaning and truth. The Torah includes all sorts of elements: history, anthropology, theology, ethics, lore, poetry, and law; and yet enveloped within its layers, infused with every letter and nuance, is truth. The truth of the Torah is eternal; and, therefore, it can be eternally discovered, interpreted, and reinterpreted; it can be continually given and received. In Judaism, the transmission of truth is conducted as a partnership with God, in which we must be responsible and take an active role. Each year, during the Omer, we ready our minds and hearts so that we will be fit to participate in the divine partnership of Shavuot.

Rabbi Yehuda Aryeh Leib Alter of Ger was born in Poland in 1847 and came to be called by the name of his five-volume work *Sefat Emet,* a commentary on the Torah and on the holidays.

> It is only in accord with one's personal purity that one can deserve to attain Torah. That is why the days of the Omer counting were given, as a period of purification to make us ready to receive the Torah. While it is true that anyone may study Torah, attachment to the innermost Torah, "utterances of the LORD" (Ps. 12:7), of which we say "Cause our hearts to cling to our Torah," indeed requires purity. This [inward attachment] in itself bears witness to the purity of the person's words for this Torah is attained only through purity.[38]
> —Sefat Emet

David Hartman

Remembrance and Hope

We often hear the expression, "Those who cannot remember the past are condemned to repeat it."[39] This statement, although extremely insightful, may perhaps be incomplete. We must not forget the past, but to avoid repeating it, we must affirm it while also having a hopeful vision for the future. If we know and accept who we were—for example, slaves in Egypt or victims of the Holocaust—that does not mean we are defined by those circumstances and events. We must continue to dream of the world we want for our future and must persistently work toward achieving it.

The events of the Holocaust and of independence closely followed each other historically, and Yom Ha-Shoah and Yom Ha-Atzmaut are now positioned next to each other on the calendar. Their proximity represents the act of looking back while looking forward. Yom Ha-Shoah is the culmination of thousands of years of Jewish subjugation—a past that the world in general and the Jews specifically must continue to accept; Yom Ha-Atzmaut is the hope and foundation from which we can develop the Jewish future.

Rabbi David Hartman, born in 1931 in New York, moved to Israel in 1971. Five years later he set up the Shalom Hartman Institute, dedicated in the name of his father, where a team of research scholars study and teach classical Jewish sources in relationship to contemporary Israeli society and the lives of Jews everywhere. As a leading Jewish philosopher and specialist in religious pluralism, his influence has been felt in the political arena: he has been an adviser to Israeli prime ministers and to the minister of education. The following text is from a 2002 article in which he discusses the theological and historical significance of Jews settling in the Land of Israel, in the face of continuous security challenges.

[T]he State of Israel is a collective affirmation of our determination to be defined not by the gas chambers of Auschwitz but by the hope of rebuilding a new Jerusalem. We will always mourn for Auschwitz. We will never become reconciled with our people's tragic suffering and losses. We will never forget how the homeland of Bach, Beethoven and Kant became the homeland of Himmler, Eichmann and Hitler, how the pride of Western music, poetry and philosophy became a synonym for barbarism and brutality.

Our return to Israel should be understood as a double affirmation: a "yes" to Egypt and a "yes" to Sinai. We will not forget Auschwitz but we will celebrate our new lives and hopes in Jerusalem. In returning to Israel we reaffirmed our determination not to withdraw from history but to continue believing in the possibilities of the future no matter how ambiguous, uncertain and precarious life is. We will not define our identity by our memories of suffering but by the moral spiritual quality of our daily lives.

The horror we feel when witnessing the brutality of terrorism must not lead to nihilism or negate the value of human efforts to build a just and peaceful world .... Despair and disillusionment are the refuge of the weak. Hope is a deep, characteristic Jewish impulse that was present throughout our history. Affirming life and potential for moral renewal despite the precariousness of the human condition express the ongoing power and significance of the foundational memories of Sinai and Exodus.[40]
—David Hartman

✦ The Omer ✦
Interpretations of Sacred Texts

The texts in these pages, each studied at multiple levels, are from two very different sources. The modern prayer for Israel, of mixed authorship, is found on many Web sites, in particular, that of the Israel Ministry of Foreign Affairs. The other, *Eleh Ezkerah* (These I Will Remember), is an aggadic midrash, from the nonlegal portions of Rabbinic literature, which includes moral lessons, prayers, legend, and folklore.

THE THREE LEVELS
Peshat: simple, literal meaning
Derash: historical, rabbinical inquiry
Making It Personal: contemporary analysis and application

Prayer for the State of Israel

Our Father in Heaven, Rock and Redeemer of Israel, bless the State of Israel, the first manifestation of the approach of our redemption. Shield it with Your lovingkindness, envelop it in Your peace, and bestow Your light and truth upon its leaders, ministers, and advisers, and grace them with Your good counsel. Strengthen the hands of those who defend our holy land, grant them deliverance, and adorn them in a mantle of victory. Ordain peace in the land and grant its inhabitants eternal happiness. Lead them, swiftly and upright, to Your city Zion and to Jerusalem, the abode of Your Name, as is written in the Torah of Your servant Moses: "Even if your outcasts are at the ends of the world, from there the Lord your God will gather you, from there He will fetch you. And the Lord your God will bring you to the land that your fathers possessed, and you shall possess it; and He will make you more prosperous and more numerous than your fathers."[41] Draw our hearts together to revere and venerate Your name and to observe all the precepts of Your Torah, and send us quickly the Messiah son of David, agent of Your vindication, to redeem those who await Your deliverance.

Manifest yourself in the splendor of Your boldness before the eyes of all inhabitants of Your world, and may everyone endowed with a soul affirm that the Lord, God of Israel, is King and His dominion is absolute. Amen forevermore.

—Israel Ministry of Foreign Affairs

Peshat

In 1948, the year the State of Israel was established, the first printing of this prayer appeared. It was composed by the two chief rabbis of Israel, Yitzhak Herzog (Ashkenazic) and Ben-Zion Uziel (Sephardic), with Israeli Nobel Laureate Shmuel Yosef Agnon perhaps playing a role.

This prayer includes three principles: (1) establishment of the State of Israel is part of God's plan for redeeming the Jewish people and the world, (2) securing the State of Israel is of divine significance, and (3) bringing all Jews from the Diaspora to live in Israel is an objective.

Derash

For thousands of years Jews have prayed for the welfare of their host governments. The Mishnah encourages this practice: "Pray for the welfare of the government, for if not for fear of the government, people would swallow one another alive."[42] Even though these same governments often swallowed the Jews themselves alive, actual wording for such prayers was published in Jewish legal codes by the 14th century. Our modern prayer, however, is for a sovereign Jewish government in the Land of Israel, which distinguishes it from any other prayer of this sort.

Making It Personal

In ancient times, primitive peoples and those unfamiliar with ethical concepts as passed on through literature hardly saw warfare as an absolute evil, but rather as an often inevitable part of the great chain of life and death. The view of the early Israelites, as described in accounts of war found in the Books of Deuteronomy and Joshua, differed in an important way from that of primitive peoples. This view painted war, whether for the elimination of professed enemies or for the acquisition of specific territories promised in the Torah, as a fulfillment of God's will and, therefore, as something waged for the greater good.[43] But after the trauma of the destruction of the First Temple (587 B.C.E.), and later, after the Israelites' return from Babylonian exile, Judaism pronounced something new—its hope for universal peace. This wish was informed by the apocalyptic messages of prophets Isaiah and Daniel, who said that ultimately the Messiah will come, and righteousness and justice will prevail.[44]

Thus latter prophets (in the Nevi'im part of the Bible, beginning with Isaiah) place the welfare of Israel at the epicenter of the struggle for peace. That peace is not simply geographical, but rather peace for all peoples. And although most Jews do not think their Torah-described status as the "chosen" people[45] means feeling superior or having a sense of moral arrogance, the well-being of the Jews and the Land or State of Israel is certainly at the core of Judaism's vision of the future. Israel is intended to serve as an example of God's goodwill and to uphold the moral principles of righteousness, justice, and love for all peoples. In praying for the security of Israel, we pray, too, for morality and peace everywhere.

THE THREE LEVELS
Peshat: simple, literal meaning
Derash: historical, rabbinical inquiry
Making It Personal: contemporary analysis and application

The Power of Silence

When the wicked Roman government decreed that the sages of Israel be put to death … Rabbi Shimon ben Gamliel and Rabbi Ishmael* the High Priest were seized to be executed …. When the executioner reached the place on Rabbi Ishmael's head where the tefillin are worn, he uttered a great and bitter cry, so that heaven and earth were shaken. When he cried a second time, even the throne of glory quivered.

Then the ministering angels spoke bluntly to the Holy One, "A man so righteous … that he should be put to death in such a horrible way? Such Torah, and such a reward?"

The Holy One said, "But what can I do for my son? … Then a divine voice came forth and said, "If I hear one more such cry, I will turn the world to void and desolation." When Rabbi Ishmael heard this, he fell silent.

Caesar said to him, "Do you still trust your God?" Rabbi Ishmael said, *"He may slay me; I may have no hope; yet I will argue my case before Him"* (Job 13:15). At that, the soul of Rabbi Ishmael left him.
—Midrash, *Eleh Ezkerah*

Peshat

This midrashic text, telling of the Hadrianic persecutions, is traditionally read on Yom Kippur during the martyrology, a section of the *Musaf* (extra prayers recited in the morning service). Nonetheless, the text resonates with the emotions of Yom Ha-Shoah, Holocaust Memorial Day. On Yom Ha-Shoah, we recount other martyrs: the 6 million Jews who were mercilessly slaughtered because of their Jewish heritage. This text, describing the execution of a revered sage, reverberates through the generations. It carries the cries emanating from all attempts to oppress or exterminate the Jewish people, from Egyptian slavery to the Spanish Inquisition; from the Chmielnicki massacres of the 1600s to the Shoah itself—one of Judaism's darkest hours.

Derash

The period of the Omer, during which Yom Ha-Shoah falls, is traditionally understood to be a time of mourning and loss. We maintain a somber disposition while we recall the deaths of Rabbi Akiva's students who, according to the Talmud, all perished during this period.

Considering the magnitude of his loss (the Talmud claims there were 24,000 students), one might have expected that Rabbi Akiva could not possibly rise from this devastation and reestablish the active presence of Torah in the world. Yet, by finding seven new students who became his disciples, he did. One might have expected that when the sages (including Rabbi Akiva) were martyred by the Romans, Judaism would die. In fact, it blossomed. One might have expected that after the Holocaust, the Jewish people would wither away. But within the decade that followed, the Jews had been given back their homeland, supported by the love and commitment of Jews worldwide, some of whom chose to move to Israel. And most significant, the 800,000 Jews exiled from Arab lands during that period and the European Jews who survived the Holocaust found an open door.

In this text, Rabbi Ishmael is murdered, yet in such a terrible moment, he hears God's voice and discovers that with silence he can save the world. That silence, like the silent aftermath of a bloody massacre, often marks not just an end to something terrible, but also the beginning of redemption. Yom Ha-Shoah ends and Yom Ha-Atzmaut begins; the Omer ends and Shavuot, the giving of the Torah, begins.

Making It Personal

In the wake of the Holocaust came many very difficult questions of faith, which cast doubt on the theological principle that God is merciful and good. Did God use Hitler and the Nazis as an instrument to inflict punishment on the Jews for past sins? Do the events of the Shoah prove that God is dead, as some have suggested? Or was God merely absent, seeming to have joined the rest of world in being deaf, blind, and mute when the Jews were most desperate for help. How do we find faith in light of such silence?

The answer is in the present: we are, in fact, here. Our very existence is the evidence needed for faith; and accepting that existence takes place silently. In the midst of the silent acceptance of the aftermath, we choose where and how to direct what we have and what we are. Such acceptance can be life-affirming or life-negating. We can choose, as did Rabbi Ishmael, to listen to and to partner with God to save the world. Or we can choose to negate life, silently pretending not to hear, see, or care.

---

* Shimon ben Gamliel was Nasi (literally, "prince"), the highest-ranking member of the Jewish community and head of the Sanhedrin (Jewish supreme court). Rabbi Ishmael was the *Kohen Gadol* (Jewish high priest) of the time. According to this story, they are the first two of the renowned 10 Martyrs whom Roman emperor Hadrian murdered for teaching Jewish law (Torah).

·✦· The Omer ·✦·

Significance of the Season:
Some Modern Perspectives

The Proximity of Despair and Hope

by Reuven Hammer

Yom Ha-Atzmaut (Israel's independence day) and Yom Ha-Shoah Ve'Ha-Gevurah (the date we commemorate the Holocaust) share a great deal, historically speaking. Both relate to momentous events that occurred within the same 10-year time period in the 20th century. And they also share the distinction of having their religious standing and level of observance as topics for debate. Otherwise, they could hardly be more different from one another in their moods and reasons for commemoration.

Yom Ha-Atzmaut is celebrated on the 5th of Iyar, the day when David Ben-Gurion proclaimed the establishment of a Jewish state in the Land of Israel. The holiday was enacted into Israeli law in 1949, with Zionists as the primary supporters of its election. But from the very beginning, they argued about whether it should have religious as well as secular status, and if so, how that religious status should be expressed. Members of the Religious Kibbutz Movement were out front, calling for religious observance and issuing a complete "Order of Prayer for Yom Ha-Atzmaut." One of the main features of their services was the recitation of the complete *Hallel*—a blessing followed by six psalms of praise—to be said in the evening as well as the more usual time in the morning. Many religious authorities, however, felt that the psalms of *Hallel* should be recited without first saying the blessing to avoid treating Yom Ha-Atzmaut as a God-ordained holiday with precedent in Jewish law; and that dispute continues to this day among Orthodox rabbis in both Israel and the Diaspora. Among some of those who conduct a religious service for Yom Ha-Atzmaut, two other features have been added: a Torah reading, Deuteronomy 7:12, about the promise of God that the Israelites will conquer the Land of Israel, followed by a haftarah (Bible portion from the Prophets) from Isaiah 10:32–12:6, promising a time of tranquillity and the restoration of justice in the Land of Israel.

The Conservative stream of Judaism, both in the Diaspora and in Israel (where it is called the Masorti movement) observe Yom Ha-Atzmaut as a religious holiday, for which they have added material to the siddur (prayer book). On this day, in addition to saying the complete *Hallel* and reading from the Torah, Conservative Jews insert into the *Amidah* (the central prayer of any daily or holiday service) a special paragraph—*al hanisim* ("for the miracles"), patterned after paragraphs that are traditionally recited for Purim and Hanukkah. This additional prayer acknowledges God's role in the miraculous deliverance of the new Jewish state from its enemies and for its establishment after 2,000 years of exile. For the Torah portion and the haftarah on this day, Conservative Jews read Deuteronomy 26:1–11, verses that speak of the laws the Israelites must follow when they enter the Land of Israel, and Ezekiel 37, a chapter that talks about reviving the people from a place of depravity and about reuniting the divided kingdoms of Israel. Included in the siddur is an excerpt from the proclamation establishing the State of Israel; a blessing, *Shehecheyanu* (an acknowledgment of gratitude to God for this holy season); and instructions to blow the shofar (a hollowed-out ram's horn used as a musical instrument) and to sing "Hatikvah" (the Israeli national anthem).

When Israel captured East Jerusalem in the 1967 Six-Day War, Shlomo Goren, an Orthodox Religious Zionist, was serving as the chief rabbi of the Military Rabbinate of the Israeli Defense Forces. He gave a prayer of Thanksgiving broadcast live to the entire country; and shortly after, he led the first prayer session at the Western Wall since 1948. For the 1978 30th anniversary of Israel's independence, Goren, by then the Ashkenazic chief rabbi of Israel, prepared text[46] for a Yom Ha-Atzmaut haggadah, modeled in some ways after the Passover haggadah (a book of historical storytelling, prayers, songs, and rituals). Later issued in English by the United Jewish Appeal,[47] that Yom Ha-Atzmaut haggadah has yet to find wide acceptance; but it has spawned more recent efforts at creating a Jewish family ritual for Yom Ha-Atzmaut. One is the haggadah published by the Frankel Center for Jewish Family Education in Jerusalem to be used for a Yom Ha-Atzmaut seder that includes prayers, songs, stories, and rituals laden with symbolism. The seder table holds a Zionist seder plate in the form of the Star of David, which bears a number of things: foods representing different aspects of the state; four cups of wine, each accompanying a different chapter in the history of Zionism; and a fifth cup, not for Elijah, but for Theodor Herzl (b. 1860–d. 1904), founder of the political Zionist movement.

BEFORE THE JUBILATION

In contrast to Yom Ha-Atzmaut, instituted as a day of festive celebration and thankfulness, Yom Ha-Shoah was established by the State of Israel as a national day of mourning to commemorate a tragedy. The date, the 27th of Nissan, was chosen because of its connection with the Jews' uprising in the Warsaw Ghetto during World War II. Religious authorities, however, chose not to add Yom Ha-Shoah to the ritual calendar and chose another day for remembrance. The 10th of Tevet was already long established on the ritual calendar as the date for a public fast commemorating the day the king of Babylonia laid siege to the ancient city of Jerusalem. And so the Israeli rabbinate designated the 10th of Tevet[48] as Yom Ha-Kaddish Ha-Klali (literally, "the Communal Day for *Kaddish*"). On any yahrzeit (anniversary of death), Jews recite a prayer called the Mourner's *Kaddish*; in this case we mourn all those whose date or place of death is unknown and all those who were killed in the Holocaust.

For many synagogues and Jewish organizations outside of Israel, Yom Ha-Shoah—or a convenient Sunday near it—became a day to hold primarily nonreligious programs commemorating the Holocaust that usually involved presentations by survivors of the horror.[49] As time has gone by, other approaches have been added. Many groups and individuals have published pamphlets and other materials suitable for communal readings. The Rabbinical Assembly, in cooperation with the Schechter Institute of Jewish Studies in Jerusalem (the academic center of the Masorti movement), has undertaken changing the nature of the day from secular to religious and thus having it permanently entered into the ritual calendar of Judaism. To this end, in 2003, the two groups commissioned the writing of *Megillat Ha-Shoah*, "The Holocaust Scroll," a text suitable for reading on Yom Ha-Shoah year after year. It is intended to convey the essence of the Shoah in the same way that reading Lamentations does, with its feelings of mourning about the destruction of the Temple, when read on Tisha b'Av, the solemn day of fasting and mourning that commemorates many sad events in Jewish history.

Taken together, these two seasonally proximate days—Yom Ha-Atzmaut and Yom Ha-Shoah—present a paradox of Jewish existence, one in which we continuously pray for a time of complete peace in Israel and in the Diaspora, while, nearly simultaneously, we stay in touch with the harsh realities of the world in which we live. Yom Ha-Atzmaut is a day that makes evident the undying hope of the Jewish people. It is a day when we commemorate the world's having acknowledged the importance of all Jews, when nations put aside millennia of anti-Semitism and agreed to support the existence of a Jewish homeland. Thus it is a day that many believe is a testament to God's sacred relationship with the Jewish people. In contrast, Yom Ha-Shoah is a day for remembering an unspeakable tragedy. It is a day of despair, a day that recounts a time when the world stood silent, ignoring the march toward annihilation of the Jewish people. And it is a day that many believe represents God's "hiding" and lack of presence in the world.

Fear and Response: Inside Yom Ha-Shoah and Yom Ha-Atzmaut

by Bradley Shavit Artson

Theology is not science; it does not transcribe into words some neutral, objective assemblage of facts (if, indeed, that is what science does). Theology is, above all, engaged, reasoning from within, highlighting relationships as perceived by participants, scrutinized and challenged and clarified. In that sense, when people intertwine the theology of Yom Ha-Shoah, which memorializes the tragedy of the Holocaust, and Yom Ha-Atzmaut, which celebrates the independence of the State of Israel, this connection approaches the level of obscenity.

It would be an obscenity to see the establishment of Israel as reparation for the Shoah. Standing on the outside—presenting an ordering of facts, offering the creation of the State of Israel as compensation (or worse, justification), for the murder of 6 million Jews and the persecution and deaths of countless other victims of Nazi barbarism—is atrocious. As a matter of historical record, such a link is also false: Zionism, the national liberation movement of the Jewish people, preceded the Holocaust by a good 50 years (and is rooted in Jewish tradition from the Torah and antiquity). Jews had been organizing settlements in the Land of Israel on a Zionist basis from the late 1800s, and Nazi ideology was neither more nor less opposed to Zionism than it was to any other facet of Jewish civilization. If the context is "just the facts, ma'am," then linking the two events is both historically false and theologically repugnant.

But intuited from the inside, from the heart of Jewish vitality and the association of Jewish sentiment, the two are inextricably linked, not as cause and effect, but as starkest fear and vital response. Yom Ha-Atzmaut, the day the State of Israel was founded, is our existential and theological response to the events of the Shoah: the assertion of social and communal order in contrast to state-sponsored chaos, of the power of goodness in the face of sheer evil, of the possibility of hope despite the reality of unimaginable tragedy. Yom Ha-Atzmaut celebrates the survival of the Jewish people, indeed of the promise of humanity, in a world that descended into sanctioned lawlessness, organized mass murder, and glorified crime.

And, psychologically again, the two are linked. The horror of the Holocaust did persuade a shocked world of the necessity for a political state the Jews could call home, and did arouse the Jews to the need to reclaim power in their own national interest. Existentially, then, Jews do experience the season as one of *me-afela le-orah, me-avdut le-herut,* "from darkness to light, from bondage to freedom."

And the theological significance of these two momentous pivots of 20th-century Jewish life?

- The Jewish People still plays a cosmic role: What befalls us is not an obscure back alley of human life, but engulfs and implicates all of humanity in its wake. We remain a bellwether of human liberation and dignity, and the canary in the coal mine announcing the eclipse of a broader humanity. In the medieval period, Rabbi Yehudah Ha-Levi labeled the Jewish people the heart of humanity, first to show signs of affliction when the body politic becomes ill.

- The ancient aspiration of Torah—establishing the Jewish people in a commonwealth of righteousness on our own soil—continues to inspire and to infuse Jewish life everywhere with purpose, vision, and service.

- Godliness can be found even in the whirlwind. Humanity can be lost even in the midst of the highest civilization and the most rigorous education.

- The enemies of human dignity and equality are not wrong to view themselves as enemies of the Jewish people. Freedom and liberation continue to speak with Hebrew accents.

- God works through human effort and through united humanity. Together, we can turn back Nazi domination and the Nazi denigration of human worth. Together we can advance the sovereignty of God through the establishment of societies devoted to justice, peace, and inclusion. Therefore, both Yom Ha-Shoah and Yom Ha-Atzmaut summon us to take responsibility for each other and for every other.

The Mystical Path to Lag ba-Omer

by Pinchas Giller

The conclusion of the last volume of the Zohar, the great literary classic of Jewish mysticism, recounts the death of its hero, the 2nd-century rabbi

Shimon bar Yochai. On the day he is dying, Bar Yochai spends hours describing the secrets of Kabbalah—the deepest mysteries of the emanations of divine energy into the universe. At his death, Bar Yochai's astonished students look up to see angels bearing his soul aloft to heaven as flames of unknown origin surround his body and its earthly attendants. There is a brief dispute regarding Bar Yochai's burial, but eventually the residents of a place called "Merona" claim his body. More than 1,000 years after the time frame of that story,[50] in 1272, the Jewish traveler Petachiah of Regensburg, Germany, passes through the Galilee in northern Israel. He notes in his memoirs that the local Jewish population is praying for rain at the caves on "Mount Meron," where Hillel and Shammai (two renowned Jewish scholars from the 1st century B.C.E.) are buried; and he notes that the "[former] study house of R. Shimon bar Yochai" has been identified on the mountain's slope.

By the 16th century, these kabbalistic traditions regarding the death of Bar Yochai had become the focus of Jewish religious practice. It was a time when kabbalists, newly arrived to the Galilee after their expulsion from Spain, explored the spiritual possibilities to be found in the hilly areas in and around Tzfat and Tiberius. The famed kabbalist of that era, Rabbi Isaac Luria, is said to have traveled to Mount Meron on the 33rd day after Passover, during the Counting of the Omer. By that time, a site had been identified as the place where Bar Yochai was buried, and Luria came there to celebrate his kabbalistic master. This event was reported by Rabbi Chaim ben Yosef, Luria's principal disciple, who then established the kabbalistic practice of visiting Meron on Lag ba-Omer. According to variant manuscripts of *Gate of Intentions,* a book by the great kabbalist Chaim Vital (b. 1543–d. 1620),[51] the 33rd day of the Omer is the day that Shimon bar Yochai died, or alternatively, the "day of his rejoicing." These two descriptions are of essentially the same thing, because classical Kabbalah takes a positive, transformative view of the death of the righteous. It sees death as the release of their divine souls to their real home in heaven. Because the 33rd (Lag, from the Hebrew letters *lamed-gimel,* which equal 33[52]) is a day of sweet release and rejoicing for all concerned, it is a day to suspend the regular observances of mourning that are otherwise part of the Omer and celebrate Lag ba-Omer.

The rainbow is a sign of God's protective covenant that the world will never be wiped out by a flood. One talmudic tradition notes that as long as Bar Yochai was alive, there were no rainbows in Israel.[53] Accordingly, the tradition concludes, Bar Yochai's very presence must have been enough to guarantee the covenant during that period. The Hebrew term for rainbow is *keshet,* which is the same word for the bow used in archery. Thus it became a custom on Lag ba-Omer for children to go out into nature to shoot toy bows and arrows.

Another association with the life of Bar Yochai is an honored site in northern Israel about which many stories are told. According to the Talmud, Bar Yochai criticized the Roman government that was ruling the Land of Israel and had to flee Jerusalem with his son, Eliezer. Legend says they hid in a cave for 12 years, where they were nourished by a carob tree and water from a nearby spring. The Zohar variously cites the cave as being in "Lod" or in a place called "Beki'in." It so happens that in northern Israel an isolated Druze village exists with the similar-sounding name of "Peki'in." It possesses a spring, and a cave and, perhaps, it once had a carob grove. So Peki'in, which coincidentally has had continuous Jewish settlement since the Second Temple period and retains an ancient, still-in-use synagogue, has become the traditional site identified as Bar Yochai's hiding place. Jewish mystics today venerate this site as the place where Bar Yochai, according to talmudic midrash, wrote the Zohar and where his mystical ascension took place.

Lag ba-Omer, we see, began as a rugged holiday linked to the land, evoking the activities of the Rabbis of the Mishnah whose transcendent concerns were acted out through ramblings across the soil of Israel. Between the 13th and the 17th centuries, the Tzfat kabbalists studied the Zohar's depiction of these Rabbis as peripatetic wanderers who had their mystical visions while traveling. They sought similar experiences for themselves by scouring the mysterious hills of the Galilee for spiritual clues. In one example, Solomon Alkabetz, the composer of the hymn Lekha Dodi and his brother-in-law, the kabbalistic master Moses Cordovero, made a practice of gerushim (self-imposed "exiles") into the hills to ponder mystical subjects. In another example, Isaac Luria, renowned teacher of Kabbalah and halakhah, combed the Meron and Dalton districts and the upper Galilee for gravesites of ancient spiritual masters. He envisioned each location as a portal to the upper worlds of Kabbalah.

This attachment to the land evolved as Judaism approached modernity. The naturalism of the Zohar and Tzfat Kabbalah was appropriated by Hasidism, which took advantage of a newly mobile, financially independent population in order to further its own growth. Hasidism spread through Eastern Europe via new channels and connected formerly isolated communities. It likewise made use of the romance of the road. The experiences that the Hasidim had on journeys going to and from their masters inspired many Hasidic tales and parables in which the founder of the movement, the Baal Shem Tov, is yet another wandering holy man.

Zionism, clearly a concept attached to the land, began in the salons of Vienna but was not realized as a mass movement until it expanded into Eastern Europe, running on the paths already cut by Hasidism. Beyond mere mobility, Zionists explored the physical and erotic possibilities of the Jewish body. In both of its major forms—socialist and revisionist—Zionism was repelled by the conventionally envisioned physical weakness and pallor of the Talmud scholar. The utopian socialists sought to transform the Jewish physical self through physical, agricultural labor, while the revisionists saw war and physical struggle as the way to redeem the Jewish soul.

Each of these approaches was exemplified on Lag ba-Omer in the encampments of the young Zionists. The toy bows and arrows evolved into the weapons of the Jewish revolt, as Zionism sought a literal link with the heroic, doomed warriors of late antiquity: They anointed the rebels of the Jewish revolt as their immediate historical forebears. The bonfires traditionally held on Lag ba-Omer no longer evoked only the flames that surrounded Shimon bar Yochai's funeral bier, but became, as well, representatives of the campfires of the Bar Kokhba Revolt against the Roman Empire. The Zionists drew upon their Lag ba-Omer bonfires as inspiration for the establishment of the State of Israel.

Hence Lag ba-Omer represents the dovetailing of mystical and natural elements in Judaism. It links ancient and modern Judaism through the medium of the actual soil of the Land of Israel. This soil is viewed as the portal to Judaism's most transcendent realities, a vision shared by a wide variety of Jews, including Zionist youth groups, families with backgrounds that are Sephardic or Mizrachic (literally, "from the East," meaning the Arab lands east of Israel), and Hasidim of the more romantic sects. In the countryside of the Galilee, as Jews light bonfires to commemorate the adventures of rabbis and sages of the past, they become part of a tradition that has inspired generations of spiritual pioneers and seekers.

·✦— The Omer —✦·
Alternative Meditation

Facing History[54]

by Arnold M. Eisen

I don't think I could have fully appreciated the stark opening chapters of Exodus, their moral choices so clearly delineated, without the encounter with Holocaust and Israel. I certainly would not have felt the full force of Pharaoh's behavior. His initial warning to his nation concerning my ancestors is frightening: "Behold, this people, the Children of Israel, are too numerous and powerful for us. Let us deal wisely with him lest he multiply and, when war breaks out, he too will be counted among our enemies, and fight against us, and rise up from the land." It soon gets worse. "Dealing wisely" leads to an order that midwives kill male Israelite infants at birth, and when that policy fails, Pharaoh orders his entire people to cast male Israelite babies into the Nile. We are talking, in modern terms, about genocide. One nation sets about murdering another.

Readers who are so inclined can of course dismiss the decrees presented in the text as Israelite or Jewish ideology, constructed after the fact to rationalize God's drowning of Egypt's army in the sea and/or (if that too is a mere fiction) the Israelite conquest of Canaanite territory, which Egypt at that time claimed. Pharaoh's order to kill the Israelites could also be seen as a plot device which sets in motion the chain of events resulting in the birth of a "holy nation." The king can be viewed as a mere puppet who helps to set the stage on which God—the producer, director, and lead actor in this show—will enter history as Redeemer. I myself used to read Exodus this way—suspiciously, keeping my distance—before encountering the Holocaust, in Israel.

That encounter did not persuade me that the narrative is factually accurate. The Exodus story might well be fiction. The sea might never have split, the miracle or tidal wave. The Israelites might or might not have been slaves for Pharaoh and freed. But genocide, as we all know by this point in the human story, *is* a fact. That cannot be doubted. Its origins perhaps go back even further than the Egypt of the Pharaohs. Nor did the barbarity of the Nazis suffice to bring genocide to an end. Its most recent objectives have included Bosnian Muslims who were the victims of "ethnic cleansing" by Bosnian Serbs while the world at large (myself included) stood by and did nothing.

In the shadow of such events one has to pause at Pharaoh's political rhetoric in the first chapters of Exodus. A Jew in particular must take stock of the facts of the twentieth-century Jewish situation to which the king's words point. A sentence very similar to Exodus 1:22, ordaining the murder of my people, was uttered a little more than a half a century ago by a leader who carried it out with brutal efficiency. Whatever one makes of the plagues and the sea turning into dry land, *that* part of the Exodus story had proved too real and recurrent. And if the wonder at the sea did not happen this time around, as wondrous salvation failed to arrive on most of the occasions when it was most needed, that too has to figure in our reckoning. Experience of the world must always be brought to the reading of Torah. This century's history makes it far more difficult to read the opening chapters of Exodus with composure, and harder still to get through and reach Sinai, which might well have proved a mountain difficult for moderns to scale in any event.

Israel has for me as for other Jews of this generation played a crucial role in this effort. The Jewish State has stood, during my entire adult life, at the very center of my identity, whereas the Holocaust, perhaps for reasons of biography, has never been at the forefront and is not today. Growing up in the fifties and sixties, I like most American Jews at the time hardly ever heard the Holocaust mentioned. It was in my consciousness anyway, of course: not a topic of study or conversation, but a constant shadow in the near-distance of my mind. As a child it hit me with some force that I had been born a mere three years after Israel, and a mere six after the shutdown of the death camps. I took for granted reading *The Diary of Anne Frank*, that nothing of my food fortune could ever be taken for granted. I could not assume that people were "basically good at heart," never underestimate the horrors we are capable of visiting upon one another. For I too might have been among the Holocaust's victims, and wondered whether, had I been a German, I would have had the courage to resist the Nazis' decree.

It was in Israel that I first felt the full impact of the chronological coincidence linking me to the Jewish state as well as to Auschwitz, and linking them to one another; there too that I had my first nightmare featuring Nazis. One could not avoid the connection in the mid-seventies, when I first spent extended time in Israel. Survivors and their children made up a significant share of the population. Their stories were on TV, in the arts, in living rooms. Even now, when the Holocaust has reached the forefront of Jewish consciousness everywhere, its place in Israeli Jewish culture seems unique. A few years back, on sabbatical, I sat in the Jerusalem Cinemateque and watched a film called *Because of That War*. It concerns (and stars) two leading Israeli rock musicians, both the children of Holocaust survivors. The background permeates their music, and the music, like the film, is searing. My immediate response when light came on was thanksgiving that I was able to encounter it in the original Hebrew, in Jerusalem. I knew its subject concerned me. This was my fate. These were my people. All the more important to have direct access to it and to them, without subtitles.

My second response, almost as immediate, was to affirm the centrality of Israel in contemporary Jewish history—still an issue of live debate between American Jews and Israelis these days, but which for me at that moment was resolved. The previous chapter of Jewish history ended at Auschwitz. Although America is not peripheral to what has followed, the main event, the gathering of what remains of the Jewish people after Hitler, the Jews' most defiant building of a collective future, is underway in Israel. One feels the continuity all the more powerfully because the threat to collective Jewish existence has not ended in the world's only state with a Jewish majority. Hence the nightmare, I suspect. It is a new and disturbing sensation for an American to be surrounded by so many people who would like one's own people, removed, or dead....

American Jews must *choose* to direct their attention to history, Jewish or American, whereas Israelis know that the covenant of fate has already chosen them. Though bombs always claim their victims indiscriminately and have recently begun to explode on American streets as well, Israeli Jews cannot escape the realization that they are, because they are Jews, almost always the intended targets. War and bloodshed intended to eliminate their presence are virtually unceasing. The covenant of fate is as a result self-evident. And the covenant of destiny is more apparent in Israel as well. When one rides a public bus and looks at the varied faces of the Jews on board, one realizes: so this is Jewish peoplehood, this is the place in the world where all Jews come together, to live and quarrel and manage their affairs in close proximity.

The perception—often forceful—perhaps accounts for the sense of homecoming reported by many American Jewish visitors, who cannot speak Hebrew, find the landscape and the food unfamiliar, and are disturbed by the lack of civility in ordinary human interactions, yet somehow feel at home. It is not just that sides have obviously been drawn up before they arrived, and like it or not they belong to one of them: the covenant of fate. Nor is it just the pride at collective achievement: the sight of blooming deserts roads clogged with traffic, and immigrants who have been absorbed by the hundreds of thousands—the marks of collective Jewish action, the covenant of destiny. The point is that Jews are here, before one's eyes, not only individually but as a people.

Hitler did not end the Jewish story. Life has in this instance at least defeated death. "Am Yisrael Chai"—the people of Israel lives.

That above all is the meaning of Israel for me, as it is perhaps for other American Jews. I know the reality of Israeli society, politics, and culture fairly well, but I treasure the place because its significance is mythic, larger than life, transparent to the depth of meaning. The two, myth and reality, are inextricably intertwined. I need Israel to exist— and it does, thank God. Its vitality so deeply satisfies me because vitality is, as it were, existence squared and magnified. Auschwitz, by coming so close, threatens my very being, as it literally threatened the existence of the people whom I most love in this world. Had my wife's maternal grandmother not been sent out of Poland in place of her brother, who was originally supposed to leave, my partner in life, the mother of my children, would never have been born.

But they were born, their voices fill my days with happiness, we are here to tell this tale. Judaism too lives. Torah still speaks—and, as Israel demonstrates, can actually matter in the world. That is true in America too, of course, but in Israel it is far more obvious. People argue over Torah endlessly, on television and in living rooms. They criticize each other mercilessly for failures to live up to its teachings. Stone cars on the Sabbath in its name, perform surpassing acts of justice because God commanded them—and sometimes parade injustice as divine imperative, or reduce profundity to schmaltz and kitsch, and then with the very next breath prove capable of everyday kindnesses in the name of God that are far more valuable to me than profundity. The Holocaust too is not merely remembered but used as motivation for great effort, even heroism, even as it is all too often flung against anyone not of the speaker's political or religious persuasion. This is the price one pays for vitality. We find ourselves cursing the abuses to which Torah is subject, now that Jews have the power to commit them, and blessing the fact that this power is now ours, that life is ours, to use for good, to make Torah live.

Israel, then—even while it does not in any way "solve the problem of the Holocaust," does not compensate for it, does not close the wounds in Jewish psyches which half a century after Auschwitz have barely begun to harden into scar—can nonetheless help one to get around the awful history that threatens to block the path to Sinai. It does so by providing a graphic experience of the life opened up by covenant, a sense of what Jews can accomplish when fate and destiny are joined. And if that gift is effective, as it was in my case, it brings us face to face once more with the difficulties which Jews would likely have had with faith and covenant in any case, even had the Holocaust never occurred.

PART 4

Shavuot

שבועות

You shall count off seven weeks; start to count the seven weeks when the sickle is first put to the standing grain. Then you shall observe the Feast of Weeks for the LORD your God, offering your freewill contribution according as the LORD your God has blessed you.

—Deuteronomy 16:9–10

Mutually Dependent Partners

SHAVUOT (LITERALLY, "WEEKS") was traditionally a harvest festival. In the days of the Temple, Jewish farmers made pilgrimages to the Temple to offer the first grains and fruits of spring. Although such a festival may seem foreign to our modern sensibilities, Shavuot is one of the most profound holidays mentioned in the Torah, and it was certainly experienced as crucial to the welfare of our ancient ancestors. Imagine the farmer who, with feast-or-famine anticipation, had anxiously counted the seven weeks of the Omer until the time when he could harvest the first produce of the season—the result of his own intense labor, but, as he realized, more truly a gift from God. When that farmer offered his *bikkurim* (literally, "first fruits"), it was not merely as a token of thanksgiving or a tribute. As anthropologist Theodor Gaster explains in his book on Jewish festivals, this offering "is the payment to God of the dividend on His investment. To withhold that payment is an act not of impiety but embezzlement."[1]

A Grain of Intelligence

At Passover, the grain brought as a sacrifice was the just-harvested barley, which in ancient times was used as fodder for animals. The grain offering at Shavuot was wheat, which often serves allegorically as a symbol of human intelligence. While an animal satisfies its hunger simply with "ready-made" fruit or leaves, God gives people a particular intelligence and creativity that can be used to make bread for human sustenance. At Passover, we fulfill our yearning to be free, to have the same kind of freedom that an animal desires. By Shavuot, we become spiritually free as well.[2]

This presentation of first fruits is a deep expression of the relationship between humankind and God—a relationship defined as one of partnership, rather than one of master and servant. The seeds that the farmer sows depend upon the fertility of the soil and upon the cooperation of the right balance of wind, rain, and sunshine. Indeed, the process of agriculture is a mutually dependent partnership, with God and people as co-owners of the field and its crop. God gives us life and is invested in our existence and our progress. To succeed—to reach our potential—we must accept all that God grants us and participate fully in the bountiful possibilities of nature.

The first part of the Rabbinic era, after the destruction of the Second Temple, was the time of the sages. They expanded the inherent spiritual value of Shavuot—its celebration of the agricultural partnership between God and God's children—into *z'man matan Torateinu*, "the time of the giving of the Torah." As with agriculture, the Rabbinic emphasis was not solely on God's giving of the Torah, but included the other half of the partnership—the Jews' receiving it. After all, the Torah is a covenantal contract that requires acceptance before its terms can be fulfilled.

The Rabbis wisely did not restrict our perception of the giving of the Torah to one static moment. As with the never-ending flow of planting and harvesting, the experience of receiving of the Torah is constantly renewed in God's partnership with us. Although the giving of the Torah may have happened on one day and at one place, each Jew—in each generation, in his or her own way—receives it, for the wisdom of the Torah is limitless and eternally applicable. With this understanding, the Rabbis remarked, "Turn it and turn it, for everything is in it."[3]

Shavuot in the Bible

The Torah describes Shavuot solely as an agricultural festival; it never connects the holiday to the historical narrative as it does with the other two pilgrimage festivals, Passover and Sukkot. In other words, the Torah never specifically identifies Shavuot as the day God gave the Torah. The festival's association with the giving of the Torah—its most poignant source of significance and spiritual weight for us today—is not made until the Rabbinic era, which begins after 70 C.E., the year the Second Temple was destroyed.

The Torah uses three different names for Shavuot, each one imbuing the festival with another distinctive characteristic. The first is found in the Book of Exodus, where the laws for the three pilgrimage festivals are given. Shavuot is referred to as *Hag Ha-Katzir*, the Feast of the Harvest (Exod. 23:16). Falling in the Hebrew month of Sivan (May–June), when wheat, the most important crop of the season, begins to ripen, Shavuot is the time to reap the harvest and bring to the Temple an offering to God of *lechem tenufah sh'tayim*[4]—two special loaves of bread made from the newly cut wheat.[5]

The second name, *Yom Ha-Bikkurim*, commonly spoken of as *Hag Ha-Bikkurim* or Feast of the First Fruits, is found in the Book of Numbers, which directs the Israelites to bring an offering of new grain to the Temple, on the Feast of Weeks (Num. 28:26). Thus first fruits were brought as offerings to the Temple in Jerusalem starting on Shavuot and continuing in the same fashion until Sukkot in the fall. According to Rabbinic interpretation, the *bikkurim* were any of the "seven species" (*shivat minim*)—the staple foods of the biblical Land of Israel: olives, grapes, wheat, barley, figs, dates, and pomegranates. Every Israelite who possessed the means of agricultural productivity was under the obligation to make these offerings. The first fruits were given to the priests after the donor had recited a confession taken from Deuteronomy (26:1–11) acknowledging God as the One who redeemed the Israelites from Egyptian bondage and expressing gratitude to God for bringing the Israelites to the Promised Land. A farmer could bring *bikkurim* as late as Hanukkah, but after Sukkot, no declaration was made.[8]

We are most familiar with the third name, *Hag Ha-Shavuot*, The Feast of Weeks, used in the Book of Deuteronomy (16:10). Because the name references a period of time, the choice suggests that the most essential characteristic of the festival is its place on the calendar: the culmination of counting the seven weeks after bringing the Omer (an offering of sheaves of grain), which began on the second day of Passover. The 49th day is Erev Shavuot, the last day we make the blessing and count the Omer. The 50th day of the Omer is a day that is celebrated in its own right, rather than by "counting." It is Shavuot, which falls on the 6th of Sivan. Some scholars have pointed out that during biblical times, when the beginning of each month was based upon witnessing the new moon, Shavuot occurred on the 5th, 6th, or 7th of Sivan. The date depended on whether, in any particular year, the months of Nisan and Iyyar were *malei* ("full," 30 days) or *chaser* ("deficient," 29 days). Because the name of the festival is simply "Weeks," without a particular date attached, we see that the Torah is hinting at some calendrical flexibility, while nonetheless retaining Shavuot's "date"—the date that caps off the preceding 49 days, the seven weeks that we have been counting. This date is not based on counting from the new moon, as are the dates of many other holidays, but on counting from harvest to harvest (the barley of Passover to the wheat of Shavuot). The day of Shavuot, although not "counted," is the culmination of the Omer.

Three Trips by Foot

After Israel broke into two kingdoms in the 10th century B.C.E., many Israelites stopped bringing their offerings to the Temple in Jerusalem; they used unregulated, local altars, where pagans also worshiped. In the late 7th century B.C.E., Josiah, the king of Judea, instituted a reform,[6] to help unite the Jewish nation in its spirituality. He obligated his citizens to again bring all their sacrifices to the Temple as directed in the Torah, and that requirement would include making pilgrimages on Passover, Shavuot, and Sukkot.[7] These festivals are called the *Shalosh Regalim* (*shalosh* means "three," and *regalim*, "pilgrimage," is derived from *regel*, "foot"), thus istinguishing them from the nonpilgrimage festivals, such as Hanukkah and Purim.

From Fruit of the Earth to the Fruit of Heaven

After the Roman conquest, Jerusalem, the city that is the geographical heart of the Jewish people, lay in ruins, and the Temple, the physical center of Jewish ritual expression, was gone. Judaism emerged from this violent storm into a new period. The Jews who were not killed or enslaved, escaped to northern Israel or to Babylon, the two places where the Rabbinic sages compiled the Mishnah and the Talmud. They taught Torah, restored tranquillity, regenerated ideas, and infused meaning back into Jewish life. In the process, observance of temple-centric holidays such as Shavuot did not get destroyed along with the Temple; rather these holidays were reborn during what became known as the Rabbinic era, which spanned, approximately, the 1st through 6th centuries C.E.

Teacher–Student Relationship

During the time of the Temple in Jerusalem, the religious leaders were priests, the Kohanim and the Levites. In 70 C.E., when the Romans destroyed the Second Temple, the functions of the priesthood vanished along with the building in which these rites were performed. A religious sect called the Pharisees had already developed a system of learning in which a student moved from apprentice to master or teacher. From the Pharisees grew the concept of "rabbi" (Hebrew for "my master" or "my teacher"), which evolved over centuries into Rabbinic Judaism as we know it today.

Two of the three annual pilgrimage festivals, Passover and Sukkot,[9] were perhaps fairly easy to reinvigorate. They were inherently connected to the historical narrative of the Exodus, the central story of the Jewish people, and thus the Rabbis could find details and layers of meaning from which spirituality and new traditions could be drawn. A fresh approach to Shavuot, however, was difficult, because this pilgrimage festival had hardly any ties to Judaism beyond the harvest-based offerings once brought to the Temple in Jerusalem.

The Rabbis delved into much intellectual argument and spiritual examination while working to settle on a date and develop meaning for a new Torah-connected Shavuot. Part of this process can be traced back to the Second Temple era, when Shavuot was still solely an agricultural festival, to one of many debates between the Sadducees and the Pharisees, the two leading Jewish sects of that time. The Sadducees (Hebrew, *Tzadukim*), made up of aristocrats of priestly lineage, believed that the sacrificial practices and a literal reading of the Torah were the hallmarks of Judaism. In contrast, the Pharisees (Hebrew, *Perushim*), a party of scribes and sages, believed that prayer and study were just as valuable as the practices of the Temple priesthood. They held that the Torah must be interpreted on varying levels, so that Jews could embrace the full extent of their ongoing partnership with God.

This particular disagreement is the background against which the Rabbis, centuries later, would settle on a date for Shavuot as we now celebrate it. The argument concerns the date on which to begin counting the Omer. Because the Sadducees and the Pharisees did not interpret the Torah the same way, the two groups celebrated the agricultural-based Shavuot at substantially different times. Passover is a weeklong occasion—on that they could agree; but the beginning of the Omer was a challenge. The Torah says from "the day after the sabbath—you shall count off seven weeks. . . . [Y]ou must count until the day after the seventh week—fifty days" (Lev. 23:15–16). What and when is "the day after the sabbath"? The Sadducees argued that the "sabbath" to which the Torah was referring was the first Shabbat after the first night of the Passover celebration. They concluded that the counting should begin the day after that Shabbat, meaning that Sunday. The Pharisees, from whom our Rabbinic sages descended, interpreted the "sabbath" not as our weekly day of rest, but as the first day of the Passover festival itself, on which no work was permitted (following very similar restrictions as those for Shabbat). According to the Pharisees' logic, the counting of days toward Shavuot should begin on the second day of Passover. This arguing did not end with the two sects, but lasted into the Rabbinic era and beyond.[10] The most passionate defense of the Pharisees' position was that of the mishnaic sage Rabbi Yochanan ben Zakkai (1st–2nd century, Israel), the youngest and most distinguished disciple of the acclaimed Rabbi Hillel.

During this period the Rabbis were looking at the other issue that would affect when and why we celebrate the Torah-based Shavuot. On what date was the Torah given by God? Only one verse in the Torah even hints at a date for the giving of the Torah: "On the third new moon after the Israelites had gone forth from Egypt, on that very day, they entered the wilderness of Sinai" (Exod. 19:1). Since we know that the Israelites left Egypt in Nisan, the Rabbis of the Talmud agree that the Israelites arrived at Sinai on Rosh Hodesh (literally, "the Head of the Month") of the month of Sivan. They agree, as well, that the Torah was given on Shabbat.[11] One could assume that such an understanding means the Torah was given on the 7th of Sivan.

Rabbinic Name for Shavuot

The Rabbis of the Talmud most often refer to Shavuot as *Atzeret* (generally translated as "Solemn Gathering"), a word primarily associated with Shemini ("Eighth") Atzeret, the concluding day of the fall festival of Sukkot. They drew a parallel between the relationship of Shemini Atzeret to Sukkot and the relationship of Shavuot to Passover. That is, they understand Shavuot to be a part of Passover—its finale—and the seven intermediary weeks as a prolonged *hol ha-mo'ed*. Some commentators suggest that Atzeret is appropriate for Shavuot beause Moses gave the Torah to the Israelites in a gathering or assembly. Other commentators give weight to the Hebrew root of *Atzeret, ayin.tzadee.resh— la'atzor,* meaning "to stop." They claim the Rabbis were emphasizing that without the Temple, Shavuot retained no commandments other than the cessation of work.

Yet another dilemma looms that provokes another question—was that date in fact the 7th of Sivan, or was it the 6th? This dilemma is based on a directive from Moses. The Torah says he warned the Israelite people that before the events at Mount Sinai, they should "stay pure [husbands and wives temporarily separated] today and tomorrow."[12] Because of the way a "day" is calculated on the Hebrew calendar, it is difficult to tell whether "today and tomorrow" means one day or two. The number affects how we count the days from the first of Sivan to the giving of the Torah, and the Rabbis of the Talmud began to debate this issue. Discussions and studies about the date continued for many centuries, certainly as late as the 17th century,[13] even though the argument had become essentially academic: In the 4th century, Hillel II and the Sandhedrin had fixed the Hebrew calendar and chosen the 6th of Sivan as the official date for Shavuot. Perhaps this choice tells us that the Rabbis of the 4th century had consciously chosen to downplay the exact date of Revelation and were subtly emphasizing the connection of Torah to our everyday lives; because each time we learn Torah or fulfill a commandment, God is giving us the Torah and we are receiving it. Today, when we consider the Rabbis' discussion about the date for Shavuot, we see that its relationship to the giving of the Torah is indeed important to us, but the day's primary significance, if we peel back the layers of Jewish history, is as the capstone of the Omer.

Customs and Observances

FLORAL DECOR

Decorating the home and synagogue with flowers and greenery is likely the oldest custom still associated with Shavuot. The custom once included bringing trees into the synagogue, but Lithuanian rabbi Elijah ben Shlomo Zalman, known as the

Ga'on (literally, "Genius") of Vilna, basically banned that practice as an adoption of Christian rites based on pagan rituals.[14] There are three traditional explanations for the custom. The first goes back to the *bikkurim* brought to the Temple as offerings. *Bikkurim* were the evidence of a successful growing season, made possible through a partnership with God. This concept relates to an assertion in the Mishnah: Shavuot is the day on which God judges the trees and their fruits and determines scarcity or abundance.[15] By decorating with flowers and plants, we enhance the intention of our prayers and remember that we rely upon God for the sustenance of life.

A second explanation for the floral motif relates to the association of flowers and plants with Moses, the leader of the Jews when God gave them the Torah. That story begins much earlier, on the day Moses was born. The Rabbis of the Talmud identify this day as the 7th of Adar. The Torah says that Moses' mother hid him for three months and then placed his wicker basket among the reeds on the Nile riverbank where Pharoah's daughter finds him. The Rabbis point out that counting three months from the 7th of Adar brings us to the month of Sivan—and the date of Shavuot.[16] The plant decorations we use today symbolize that connection and remind us of Nile reeds and the events that unfold, from Moses' adoption all the way to the giving of the Torah.

Finally, the Shavuot decorations remind us of Mount Sinai itself, where the Torah was given.[17] Although traditionally we maintain that Mount Sinai is located somewhere in the heart of a desert peninsula, some interpretations indicate that it was miraculously covered with grass and flowers. This understanding is based on the interpretation of a verse in Exodus (34:3), wherein God commands Moses to prohibit flocks and herds from grazing at the base of the mountain.[18] That is to say, if God was prohibiting grazing, the place must have been grassy and fertile rather than barren. By placing flowers in the synagogue, we are reminded of the lushness that some commentators say surrounded Mount Sinai.

TIKUN LEIL SHAVUOT

As with Passover and many other holidays, the number of days for celebrating Shavuot varies according to the geographic location of the celebrants and/or their stream of Judaism. Generally speaking, Shavuot is one day for Reform Jews in the Diaspora and for all Jews in Israel. For Orthodox and Conservative Jews in the Diaspora, an extra day is added. Whatever the practice, once Shavuot arrives, the first, or in many cases only, night of Shavuot includes the holiday's most noteworthy custom, *Tikun Leil Shavuot*, "Set Order of Study for the Night of Shavuot." It begins with the evening prayer service, which starts a bit later than usual on the first night. To meet the Torah's requirement of counting seven complete weeks before Shavuot,[19] we wait until the stars are out, similar to the way we end Shabbat, to ensure that the 49th day is undeniably completed.[20]

Developed by kabbalists, the *Tikun* is an all-night study marathon. The Zohar, the core text of Jewish mysticism, claims that the custom is of ancient origin and describes the premise for the practice: "The early Hasidim did not sleep on this night and occupied themselves with the Torah."[21] As Kabbalah spread, the custom gained popularity throughout Europe, and eventually a special study text was created for it. Rabbi Isaiah Horowitz (b. 1565–d. 1630, Prague and Tzfat) was known as the Shelah, an acronym for his best-known work, *Shnei Luchot Ha-Brit* (literally, "The Two Tablets of the Covenant"). He suggested specific selections from the Torah that would be appropriate for people to read during the *Tikun*. In the mid-1700s, a printer gathered this material together and published it as *Tikun Leil Shavuot*. This compilation contains passages from each of the 54 *parshiyot* (portions) in the Torah, each tractate of the Mishnah, the entire Book of Ruth (which is customarily read on Shavuot), and excerpts from the Zohar.

Three of the earliest sources to mention the *Tikun* hold that the custom is meant to inspire a sense of restless anticipation and awe on the night preceding the giving of the Torah. One source is a midrashic legend that tells of the Israelites sleeping soundly— with a casual lack of anticipation—the night before the Torah was given. Indeed, they had to be awakened for the momentous event.[22] To show how much we love the Torah and feel that receiving it is awe-inspiring, we stay up all night, wide awake and on alert.

Another midrashic account expands upon the Rabbinic tradition that not only the Written Torah (The Five Books of Moses) but also the Oral Torah[23] (the teachings of the sages in the Mishnah, Talmud, and Midrash) were given to Moses at Mount Sinai.[24] The legend describes the Israelites accepting the Written Torah but, at first, refusing to accept the Oral Torah. God threatens them with destruction.[25] The Israelites have a change of heart, and upon their acceptance of the Oral Torah, they are saved. Accordingly, the *Tikun* shows our own willingness to keep and study the laws of the Oral Torah; and, in light of the midrashic legend, many groups emphasize the study of Rabbinic literature on this night.

▲　　▲　　▲　　▲　　▲　　▲　　　　▲　　▲　　▲　　▲　　▲　　▲

The Zohar provides a third midrashic reason for the custom.[26] It portrays Shavuot as the wedding day between the Israelites (the bride) and God (the groom). In getting ready for this holy union, the Israelites had to prepare spiritually; we, in turn, spend the night studying Torah to be better equipped to appreciate the virtue of what the daylight will bring. This interpretive image of Shavuot as a wedding day has led some Sephardic communities to hold public readings of a "Shavuot *ketubah*" (marriage contract).[27] The most commonly used *ketubah* was composed by the mystic and poet Israel ben Moses Najara, who lived in Tzfat, Israel, from about 1550 to 1625.[28]

DAIRY DELIGHTS

At a *Tikun Leil Shavuot* or at a traditional Shavuot meal, chances are the food will be rich in dairy, with everything from blintzes to cheesecake. Eating exclusively meatless meals with lots of dairy dishes is a prevalent custom on Shavuot, and a wide variety of reasons are given for this practice. Here are four.

The first is one of the most commonly reported reasons, although some scholars have criticized it for being "facetious."[29] It concerns kashrut (Jewish dietary laws). According to this explanation, in receiving the Torah on Shavuot, the Israelites learned the laws of kashrut, including the proper slaughter of animals and the prohibition against consuming blood. After leaving Mount Sinai with this new knowledge and returning to the camp, they realized that their meat and their cooking vessels were not proper. They had no choice, for the immediate moment, but to eat a dairy meal.[30] We pattern our menu choice today in commemoration of this event.

Confirming Responsibility

One of the newest life-cycle events, confirmation, originated in early 19th-century Germany with Israel Jacobson, nominal father of Reform Judaism. He introduced then-radical reforms such as the use of an organ and mixed male-female seating. Each boy in the congregation had a confirmation ceremony, which took place on the Shabbat of his 13th birth-day, as a replacement for the traditional Bar Mitzvah (brought back by popular demand in the 20th century). By 1822, boys and girls were being confirmed together as a graduation ceremony held either at a home or in school during Passover or Hannukah. Shavuot became the designated holiday when the German rabbi Samuel Egers saw a spiritual link between the acceptance of Torah at Mount Sinai and the modern affirmation of the same responsibility. The first American confirmation ceremony was held in New York City in 1846. Confirmation is practiced today by some Conservative, most Reconstructionist, and nearly all Reform synagogues.

Food Makes
the Holiday

"What's my favorite
Jewish holiday?
Definitely Shavuot."
"Why?"
"It's simple: on Pesach you
can't eat what you want;
on Sukkot you can't eat
where you want;
on Rosh Hashanah you
can't eat when you want;
and on Yom Kippur you
aren't allowed to eat at all."
—attributed to Chaim
    Bermant[31]

A second possible reason is found in a medieval collection of Jewish ritual and civil law, *Kol Bo* (literally, "All Is in It"). This book suggests that part of a verse in The Song of Songs—"Honey and milk are under your tongue" (4:11)[32]—alludes to the Torah. Thus on this day that celebrates the giving of the Torah, its words should be as pleasing to our minds and hearts as milk and honey are to our tongues.

A third explanation is one offered by the 16th-century Ashkenazic authority Moses Isserles, who links the giving of the Torah on Shavuot with the Exodus from Egypt on Passover.[33] On Passover we have two ritual food items on the seder plate that symbolize distinctly different sacrificial offerings at the Temple: the shank bone representing the paschal sacrifice (*korban pesach*) and the egg representing the festival sacrifice (*korban hagigah*). As a reflection on the ritual items of Passover, the festival of Shavuot needs to have two contrasting categories of food (in this case, food that we actually consume, as Shavuot does not have a tradition of ritual food items). The most extreme expression of this idea would be meat and dairy.[34] However, because Jewish law forbids Jews to eat meat and dairy foods in the same meal, Shavuot would require two separate meals. Jewish holiday meals are usually centered around meat; but at Shavuot, we highlight the duality between the two different sacrifices by making the most central and celebratory meal one that focuses on the eating of dairy-based foods. Therefore, Isserles asserts that emphasizing dairy helps us to remain mindful of the association between the Passover Exodus and the giving of the Torah at Shavuot. At the same time, it highlights the unique status of Shavuot in our tradition.

The fourth explanation offered here may be the most logical. It associates the practice of limiting Shavuot meals to dairy foods with self-control and discipline. The manner in which Judaism distinguishes between the mundane and the holy is often through ritual acts of separation. By sorting aspects of the physical world into categories, we can also separate and differentiate aspects of the spiritual world: sin and virtue, pleasure and suffering, blessing and desecration. Recognizing such distinctions is part of the human process that enables us to exercise self-control, particularly regarding the visceral aspects of life (for example, eating or sex). We have the power to set limits on our behavior based upon our understanding of what category a certain action fits into. Is the action healthful and reasonable or harmful and excessive? Self-control is a demonstration of integrity and strength of spirit. By limiting ourselves to having a solely and noticeably dairy meal on Shavuot, we stress the spiritual value of a life guided by moderation and temperance rather than by the seeming freedom of limitlessness and gluttony.[35]

READING RUTH

For each of the three pilgrimage festivals, we read a megillah ("scroll") from Kethuvim (The Writings), the third section of the Hebrew Bible: on Passover, The Song of Songs; on Sukkot, Ecclesiastes; and on Shavuot, Ruth. The first mention of reading the Scroll (or Book) of Ruth on Shavuot comes from a medieval work called Tractate *Soferim* (Scribes):

> *The first half of Ruth is read on the night after the first day of Shavuot and it is completed on the night following the second day of Shavuot. Some say that all of the [festival] readings should begin on the Saturday night preceding the appropriate festival. And this is the custom that the people have adopted, for no* halakhah *(legal precedent) becomes law until it has been established as custom.*[36]

Because this source mentions two days of Shavuot, it is referring to the two-day observance as practiced in the Diaspora after the destruction of the Second Temple. Jewish legal authorities today agree that, although *Soferim* is a relatively late source, the custom of reading Ruth on Shavuot is of ancient origin and should be continued.[37] Most also agree that Ruth should be read on the second day of Shavuot in the Diaspora.[38] They have struggled, however, to establish a uniformly accepted practice for conducting the reading.[39] To this day, practices in reading Ruth vary from community to community. Some congregations read Ruth only during *Tikun Leil Shavuot* and not during the prayer services. In some communities, people read Ruth to themselves before the formal Torah reading of the morning service. In others, Ruth is read aloud by a designated person just before the Torah reading, but customs differ on the medium— whether the reading is done from a Torah scroll or simply from a book version.

The story of Ruth is set at the time of the biblical judges (c. 1200–1000 B.C.E.). It focuses on the relationship between two women: Naomi, an Israelite from Bethlehem, and Ruth, her Moabite daughter-in-law. After 10 years spent living in the land of Moab, during which time her husband and her two sons—both married—die, Naomi decides to return to Bethlehem. One widowed daughter-in-law, Orpah, returns to her Moabite family, while Ruth insists upon staying with Naomi. Despite Naomi's attempt to dissuade her, Ruth dramatically pledges her allegiance to Naomi:

> *Do not urge me to leave you, to turn back and not follow you. For wherever you go, I will go; wherever you lodge, I will lodge; your people shall be my people, and your God my God. Where you die, I will die, and there I will be buried.*
>
> — Ruth 1:16–17

As the story unfolds, the impoverished women are living together in Bethlehem when Boaz, Naomi's kinsman by marriage and a wealthy landowner, allows Ruth to glean in his fields. She acquires enough grain to sustain herself and Naomi for a long time. Boaz is impressed with Ruth, who has shown so much devotion to her mother-in-law, and he treats her very respectfully. Naomi decides that Ruth should pay a surprise visit to Boaz while he is winnowing barley on the threshing floor and remind him of his responsibility to his uncle's family. Boaz redeems Naomi's land and marries Ruth. They have a son, Obed, who is identified as the grandfather of King David.

On the most basic level, the Book of Ruth is appropriate reading for Shavuot because the story has a strong connection to harvesttime.[40] At a more complex level, it is appropriate because of the spiritual connection demonstrated in this midrashic teaching:

> *What is the relationship between Ruth and Atzeret [i.e., Shavuot], such that it is read on Atzeret, the time of the giving of the Torah? It is to teach you that the Torah is only acquired by means of suffering and poverty."*[41]

Affirming one's faith is often initiated by trials and challenging situations. Ruth, after she faces widowhood, loss of her sons, and poverty, affirms her faith in Naomi, in Judaism, and in the Jewish people. So, too, on Shavuot, we remember and reaffirm the events at Mount Sinai and the foundation of Jewish beliefs, as we experience our connection as a people bound together through Torah.

Because Ruth is the great-grandmother of King David, some people say we read the Book of Ruth on Shavuot to honor his lineage.[45] One of the most important and impressive individuals in the Hebrew Bible (although not without personal faults), David had successes as a warrior and as king of Israel that were unprecedented. He was responsible for uniting the two kingdoms (Judah and Israel), for establishing Jerusalem as the capital of the United Monarchy, and for laying the plans for the First Temple. Rabbinic scholars credit him with authoring the Book of Psalms, perhaps the most popular book of the Bible after those in the Five Books of Moses. As a further connection to King David, the Talmud deduces that the dates upon which he was born and died fell on Shavuot.[46]

Revelation Revealed

AWE AND AMBIGUITY IN THE TORAH

During Shavuot, we celebrate the events at Mount Sinai, as described in the Book of Exodus. Amid thunder and lightning and loud blasts of the horn, Moses descends from the cloud-covered mountaintop and brings with him everything God told him and the Tablets of the Pact (Ten Commandments). He addresses a sea of millions of Israelites. This climactic event in the biblical drama of the Exodus story describes "Revelation": the communication to the Jewish people of the will of God, through laws, moral

Wherever You Go

Ruth is considered the first true[42] convert to Judaism; and from her famous biblical interchange with Naomi,[43] the Talmud derives the laws of conversion: "Our Rabbis taught: One who comes to convert at this time, they say to him: 'Why did you come to convert? Do you know that Israel at this time is afflicted, oppressed, downtrodden, and rejected, and that tribulations are visited upon them?' If he says, 'I know, but I am unworthy,' they accept him immediately."[44] Some people interpret this statement to mean that converts are not welcome, but most understand it as a hard-hitting interview to test the convert's sincerity. Choosing to become part of the Jewish people requires intense education and commitment. The attendees at the culminating ceremony hope the convert will be as successful as Ruth in experiencing the deepest elements of both the religious and social aspects of Jewish life.

instruction, and a plan for their future. The Torah is traditionally considered to be the product and content of the Revelation at Sinai.

The telling of this story has a share of ambiguity, leaving us with a hazy image of what exactly happened on the mountain and what Judaism ultimately means by the term "Revelation." Is Revelation solely theophany: God's appearance to the Jewish people visibly and audibly? Is Revelation just the Ten Commandments, which are communicated in that specific biblical narrative, or is Revelation the entire Torah? Is Revelation an ongoing event—still happening—or did it happen only at Sinai long ago?

Furthermore, Moses ascends the mountain two more times in Exodus (chapters 24 and 34) without any clear distinction between each experience of Revelation. The timing of Revelation is not necessarily clear. In the Book of Numbers (two books beyond Exodus), for example, there are occasions where the law is unknown to Moses, and he must seek God's guidance, such as the discussion about the man who violates Shabbat (chapter 15) and the inheritance case of the daughters of Zelophehad (chapter 27). In the final book of the Torah, Deuteronomy, Revelation appears to be something that will continue to happen after Moses is gone; God informs him that future prophets will also reveal God's will. God explains that the falseness or trueness of a prophet will be discernable only when that prophet's oracle does or does not come true.[47] Thus God acknowledges that Torah alone does not account for all future situations, and it will sometimes be difficult to know God's will.

RABBINIC INNOVATIONS

By the time the Second Temple was destroyed in 70 C.E., the Bible had been canonized. But now the priesthood was gone, the age of prophecy had ended, and the Rabbinic era had begun. If we look at certain Jewish texts from that time, the already ambiguous concept of Revelation becomes even more so. The sages of the Rabbinic tradition alter the biblical concept of Revelation by boldly proclaiming that "from the day the [First] Temple was destroyed [586 B.C.E.] prophecy was taken away from the prophets and given to the sages [of the Second Temple era]."[50] In the opinion of the Rabbis, the chain of Revelation passed from the prophets to the Temple-era sages to the Rabbis themselves. In other words, the voice of God now comes through the Rabbis' text-based teachings and interpretations. The Rabbis begin to speak of a dual Revelation: the word and will of God given to Moses at Mount Sinai, called the

Written Torah (the Five Books of Moses), and the collected teachings and rulings of the sages, called the Oral Torah (Midrash, Mishnah, Talmud, and so forth). As expressed in the Talmud, these sages position themselves unequivocally as the final and most authoritative link in the chain through which Revelation is transmitted:

> *What is the meaning of the verse,* and I will give you the stone tablets with the teachings and commandments which I have inscribed to instruct them *(Exod. 24:12). "Stone tablets" refers to the Ten Commandments; "teachings" refers to the Five Books of Moses; "commandments" refers to the Mishnah; "which I have inscribed" refers to the Prophets and Writings; "to instruct them" refers to the Gemara [Talmud]. Therefore, the verse teaches that all of those sources were given to Moses at Sinai.*[51]

Thus the sages maintain that their teachings and rulings are part of the original Revelation and have always been an integral part of Judaism. A talmudic teaching directly supports this assertion when it states, "even what a distinguished student is destined to teach in the presence of his master was already revealed to Moses on Sinai."[52]

Perhaps the most important Rabbinic claim to authority, one that might be described as radical, is expressed in a talmudic dispute that happens to be about whether or not a particular oven is kosher, but it could be about anything. Rabbi Eliezer is on one side of the argument; the rest of the sages, led by Rabbi Joshua, are on the other.[53] The Talmud recounts that when neither side is able to convince the other of its opinion, Rabbi Eliezer resorts to the performance of nature-defying miracles in hope of persuading his

Where in the World Is Mount Sinai?

The location of Mount Sinai, also referred to as Mount Horeb,[48] is shrouded in debate and mystery. Sinai is where Moses meets God at the burning bush; where God gives the Israelites the Torah (and where they continue to live for nearly a year); and where Elijah, fleeing from King Ahab and Queen Jezebel, encounters God in "a still, small voice."[49] Yet for all these connections, Jews did not retain specificity about this physical location, although they have identified and venerated other biblical sites. In the 4th century, Christian monks claimed a site in the Egyptian Sinai peninsula as the mountain, and later the Byzantine emperor Justinian built a monastery at its foot. Muslims call the site Gebel Musa (the mountain of Moses). Other candidates in the quest for the "real" Mount Sinai include Gebel el Shaiira in Egypt and others in Israel, Jordan, and Saudi Arabia.

colleagues, but to no avail. Finally God's voice calls down from heaven and declares that Rabbi Eliezer is correct! Unmoved, Rabbi Joshua rises up and shouts the following verse from the Torah: "It [the law] is not in heaven."[54]

God laughs and concedes, "My children have defeated me." The Talmud clarifies this statement by explaining that when we try to determine God's will, we do not heed a "heavenly voice," but instead adhere to a majority decision.

This talmudic legend illustrates the Rabbinic stance that the Torah, standing alone—or any "heavenly voice" for that matter—is not the only source of authority from which we understand God's will, God's truth, and what God demands of us. The sages contend that once the era of prophecy, with its top-down transmission, ended, revelation became something more horizontal, conveyed through a scholarly, rigorous, democratic process of textual study and interpretation. This ideological advance—the intertwining of theology and the philosophy of law—is one of Judaism's greatest strengths. With the study and interpretation of texts as the keys to understanding God's will, each generation can determine for itself how to discern truth and Jewish law.[55] In other words, we continually grow in our understanding of God's will. And according to the legend, in the joyous concession to "My children," God approves of the Rabbinic innovation.

STEPS TOWARD MODERNITY

The medieval period witnessed another shift in the Jewish conception of revelation. With the advent of Christianity and Islam, Judaism found itself part of a triumvirate of monotheistic traditions, each claiming its own divine authority. Jews (as well as Christians and Muslims) were pressed to prove why their faith was the most reliable and their claim to God's will through revelation was relevant and true. Moreover, when the Arabs conquered a huge part of the world stretching from Spain to India, a process completed by the middle of the 8th century, the work of philosophers such as Plato and Aristotle became available to Jews, Christians, and Muslims through translations into the commonly shared language of Arabic. This interchange allowed each religion to communicate and assert its own tenets, using philosophy and reason as arenas for the debate.

At this time, many Jewish luminaries, including Sa'adia Ga'on, Yehuda Ha-Levi, and Maimonides,[56] composed philosophical masterpieces. Each, in his own way, argued that although Revelation is certainly important to understanding God, it is not the only way. Judaism is a reasonable system of belief, and through the faculties of our minds, we have the ability to understand the overall reason for following the Torah and observing the mitzvot. At the same time, Revelation is especially essential under two circumstances. One is when people do not have the intellectual or philosophical capacity, or the means or opportunity, to know God without Revelation. The other is when someone wants to address issues that go beyond reason, such as those regarding the eternal existence of God.

Another occurrence during the medieval period was the growing, popular acceptance of Kabbalah and the teachings found in the Zohar. In contrast to the inclinations toward reason and philosophical inquiry undertaken by many of the Jewish masters of the era, Kabbalah insists that only the Torah can be trusted. Kabbalists believe that reason is easily misleading and will prevent us from discovering the deepest truths hidden in the Revelation of the Torah at Mount Sinai. Furthermore, in addition to the Written and Oral Torahs given at Sinai, to which the sages refer, medieval kabbalists submit that a third, "hidden" Torah was revealed there and can be discovered only through study of kabbalistic texts and mystical practices, such as meditative prayer.

With the dawn of the Enlightenment, the Western world embraced an ideology that supported individual rights for all and celebrated the value of scientific reasoning and technology. Judaism once more examined its conception of revelation by using reason as the guiding principle. Jewish theology was certainly influenced by reactions to Immanuel Kant, the German philosopher, born to a Pietist family, whose ideas spread across Europe throughout the second half of the 18th century. On the one hand, Kant did not believe in the classical concept of Revelation, and he thought Judaism was morally abhorrent and contradictory of reason. On the other, Kant asserted a position similar to that of certain Jewish philosophers, especially Sa'adia Ga'on and Maimonides: Reason and intellectual faculties can provide a sufficient basis for faith and morality, but Revelation is a necessary basis for people who lack philosophical aptitude.[57]

Jewish existentialists Martin Buber (b. 1878–d. 1965, Austria) and Franz Rosenzweig (b. 1886–d. 1929, Germany) contributed the most radical transformations to the classical image of the Revelation at Mount Sinai. They do not interpret Sinai as a historical occurrence but rather as a poetic expression of how the individual experiences and responds to a divine encounter. Accordingly, the most important factor they see in Jewish life is the relationship an individual has with God. That relationship is deepened and expressed through the understanding and performance of mitzvot, which are, in this interpretation, defined and determined primarily by each person's unique connection with the Divine. Nonetheless, Buber and Rosenzweig also say that certain social responsibilities are drawn from the Jewish tradition and are communally defined, and it is encumbent upon each individual to honor them.

AUTHORSHIP: CHALLENGE AND RECONCILIATION

Generally speaking, the traditional perspective on Revelation holds that God dictated the Torah to Moses who transcribed it word for word.[58] The Torah was then meticulously copied by scribes and passed down from one generation to the next. The earliest noteworthy challenge to the divine nature of Revelation comes from Baruch Spinoza, the renowned 17th-century Dutch philosopher of Portugese-Jewish origin. He suggests that the Torah was not divinely dictated. In his opinion, the 5th-century B.C.E. biblical figure "Ezra the scribe,"[59] for whom the Book of Ezra is named, is the primary author of the Torah, Moses having written only certain important parts. Of course, Martin Buber and Franz Rosenzweig, in their time, would also challenge the idea that there was a divine handing-down of a document to Moses at Sinai, but they discuss the Torah as a metaphor rather than as a document to be examined from a literary or literal perspective.

The most serious challenge leveled against Torah as Revelation came much later, in the early 20th century, when new approaches were taken to studying the Bible, such as archaeological, literary, linguistic, and cross-cultural examinations. Although these disciplines brought about major shifts in thought for some biblical scholars, they were not necessarily used by Jews as a means to supersede or replace the traditional methods of study. Rather, they were thought to serve as complements that could offer additional insights and meaning to the text.

One theory, known variously as the Documentary Hypothesis, the Critical Approach, or Form Criticism, suggests that the Torah as we know it was written over time and comprises at least four documents, written by four different unnamed authors.[60] These were linked together, edited, and compiled by a single redactor in the 5th century B.C.E.[61] This theory has gained majority acceptance among 20th-century scholars of biblical literature and has caused many Jews to question the authority of the Torah and its directives to follow Jewish law. Our conception of Revelation determines how we perceive the authority of the Torah, and this theory of nondivinity has, on the one hand, become a central issue dividing the different streams of Judaism from one another. On the other hand, for certain people, the literary approach has deepened their insight into Torah and has actally been the inspiration to begin practicing Judaism and observing Jewish law.

In the 20th century, rabbis and theologians responded in different ways to the conflicting views of Revelation. Most traditionalists and Orthodox Jews reject the critical approach. As Rabbi Norman Lamm, chancellor of Yeshiva University, writes:

I believe the Torah is ... God given. ... [God's] will was communicated in discrete words and letters ... in as direct, unequivocal, and unambiguous a manner as possible. Literary criticism of the Bible is a problem, but not a critical one. Judaism has successfully met greater challenges in the past. ... [It] is chiefly a nuisance but not a threat to the enlightened believer.[62]

Other thinkers, particularly those in the Conservative stream, take approaches that attempt to reconcile the disparate views of revelation—both the classical and critical views. Such approaches span a wide array of perspectives, which, to varying degrees, hold that the Torah is both divine and human. At one end of the Conservative spectrum, scholars such as Joel Roth, professor of Talmud and Jewish Law at the Jewish Theological Seminary,[63] acknowledge evidence that the Torah comprises several documents, but that it is nonetheless the word of God. The other end includes scholars such as Abraham Joshua Heschel, the great 20th-century theologian and professor of ethics and mysticism. He describes the Torah as an expression of the sacred partnership between humankind and God,[64] a response to the overwhelming, personal experience of the Divine.[65] Rather than defining the Torah as the direct word of God, he calls the Torah a human "midrash," a human-made description of the contents of Revelation. Although there are theological nuances that distinguish these thinkers' positions, they all assert that, even though revelation involves human influence, Jewish law is binding.

Most theorists in the Reform stream embrace the critical approach. For these thinkers, the emphasis that Buber and Rosenzweig place on individual experience of God is a fundamental theological principle. Thus Reform Judaism largely maintains that each person's conscience dictates whether and to what extent one follows the mitzvot. At the same time the Reform stream strongly endorses the position that individual decisions be based on the study of Judaism, guided by the classical tradition.

No matter what theory of Revelation we may accept, the centrality of the Torah to Judaism—in any and all of its beloved shades—is undeniable. The story told in the Torah is forever our own and the lessons within it are eternal, providing the core elements of Jewish identity. A lifelong commitment to the study of Torah, with its ever-evolving variety of interpretations, remains fundamental to Judaism. And even when there is intellectual conflict and tension, there is also certainty that in each generation, our encounter with Torah is the source of inspiration and growth for the Jewish people. Shavuot celebrates that gift.

·✦— Shavuot —✦·
Pathways Through the Sources

Mishnah
Bringing Fruits to Zion

It is hard to picture what life was like for our ancestors and to imagine taking the awesome journey to Jerusalem during the pilgrimage festivals. Yet these expressions of spiritual commitment, embarked on millennia ago, laid the foundations for our modern experience celebrating holidays such as Shavuot. This text from the Mishnah presents snapshots of the past and insight into why we perform some of our rituals. Ultimately, it is a source of inspiration, giving us a taste of the soulful encounters that throughout time have characterized the path of the Jewish people.

How do they take up [to Jerusalem] the *bikkurim* [first fruits]? All of the townsmen within the same region assembled and lodged for the night in the street without entering the houses. Early the next morning the official would say, "Come, let us go up to Zion, to the Lord our God!"

Those who lived nearby brought figs and grapes and those who lived far away brought dried figs and raisins. And an ox led them with its gold crowns on its horns and olive wreath around its head. The flute played as they came up to Jerusalem and when they arrived they sent messengers ahead and they adorned their *bikkurim*. The Levite wardens, the chiefs, and the treasurers went out to greet them. The pilgrims entered according to their rank and all the craftsmen of Jerusalem aligned before them with the greeting, "Our brothers of such and such a place, welcome!"

The flute played before them until they arrived at the Temple Mount. When they reached the Temple Mount even King Agrippa would set his basket over his shoulder and go in until he reached the Temple Court. Upon arriving at the Temple Court, the Levites would sing, *I extol You, O LORD, for You have lifted me up, and not let my enemies rejoice over me* (Ps. 30:2).
—Mishnah, *Bikkurim* 3:2-4

Midrash

Transmitting Torah

When Jews speak of learning Torah, they do not necessarily mean it literally—that is, studying from the Five Books of Moses. Rather "Torah" is a general term and can refer to all sorts of traditional Jewish literature. In fact, classic Judaism does not have the word "religion." The closest equivalent is simply Torah. But Torah does not only exist in texts; it exists in people. That is, we all have the ability to transmit Torah and, in doing so, to link us together all the way back to Mount Sinai. The Rabbinic sages who compiled the Talmud and Midrash were the first proponents of this idea, and when we accept it, our connection to God through Torah remains alive and dynamic.

Sifrei (literally "Books" in Aramaic) is a two-volume set, completed by the sages of the 3rd century, that comprises midrashim from the School of Rabbi Ishmael. (a 1st- to 2nd- century sage who developed a system of religious interpretation more logical and less mystical than that of his contemporaries). Mostly halakhic in nature, the midrashim provide verse-by-verse Hebrew exegesis of the biblical books Numbers and Deuteronomy.

> *My commandments which I command you this day* (Deut. 11:13). Where do you learn that even if one learns an interpretation from the least learned of the Israelites, he should consider it as if he had learned it from a sage? From the verse *which I command you* (11:13). And, more than that, it is not as if he had learned it from only one sage, but as if he had learned it from many sages, as it said, *the words of the sages are as goads* [pointed rods] (Eccles. 12:11): just as a goad guides a cow along its furrows, thus producing livelihood for its owners, so do the words of Torah guide a person's thoughts toward knowledge of God.
>
> And more than that, it is as if he had learned it not from many sages, but from the Sanhedrin [the highest court of the land] itself, as it is said, *masters of assemblies* (Eccles. 12:11), "*assemblies*" meaning the Sanhedrin. ... And more than that, it is as if he had learned it not from the Sanhedrin, but from Moses, as it is said, *they are given from one shepherd* (12:11). ... And even more than that it is as if he had learned it not from Moses but from the Almighty One, as it is said, *they are given from one shepherd* and *Give ear, O Shepherd of Israel, You lead Joseph like a flock* (Ps. 80:2) and *Hear O Israel, the LORD our God, the LORD is one* (Deut. 6:4).[66]
> —*Sifrei*, Deuteronomy 41

Midrash
The Voice of God

What does it mean "to hear the voice of God"? What does God's voice sound like? What power does it carry and how might one be affected by it? Since first learning the story of the Revelation at Mount Sinai, mystics and believers have asked such questions, which truly touch upon what we believe about the nature of God and our relationship with God. Judaism maintains that we each hear God in our own unique way, appropriate for each of us.

Midrash Rabbah (Great Midrash) is a series of books that expounds upon and further illustrates each book of the Torah as well as five books from the third part of the Bible, Kethuvim (The Writings). The works were edited and redacted between the 5th and 10th centuries.

> *I the LORD am your God* (Exod. 20:2). And it is written, *Has any people heard the voice of a god . . . ?* (Deut. 4:33).
>
> A heretic asked Rabbi Simlai,[67] "Are there many gods in the world?"
>
> He asked, "Why?"
>
> They answered, "Because it is written, *Has any people heard the voice of elohim*, in the plural [i.e., *elohim*, the word for God, is grammatically in the plural form]!"
>
> He told them, "But it does not say 'God speaking—*medabrim'*—in the plural, but '*medaber*'— in the singular!"
>
> His students then said to Rabbi Simlai, "You have put them off with a broken reed of an answer [i.e., easily]. But what answer do you give us?"
>
> So Rabbi Levi[68] explained again, "*Has any people heard the voice of a god . . . ?* If it had said, 'the voice of the Lord is in *His* power,' the world would not have been able to stand. But the text says, *The voice of the LORD is power* (Ps. 29:4)—that is, according to the strength of each individual—young men, according to their strength, and the old, according to their strength, and children, according to their strength. Thus, God said to Israel, 'Just because you heard many voices, do not think that there are many gods in heaven, but be aware that I the Lord am your God,' as it said, *I the LORD am your God . . . .*"
>
> —*Midrash Rabbah, Exodus Rabbah* 29:1

Babylonian Talmud
The Anxiety of Innovation

We in the present often feel burdened with living up to the authority of those who preceded us. Are we doing the rituals in the proper manner? Are we teaching Torah the way Moses taught Torah? Are we as knowledgeable as even our recent ancestors? One of the most common rationales for following a particular custom or observance is for a Jew to say, "This is the way my grandfather did it," as the conclusive evidence of authenticity. The truth is, our sages seemed to be burdened with the same kinds of questions. As this text teaches, the sages understood that to be genuinely traditional, we must go beyond what came before us. With the courage of a sage, we must interpret and go deep into the text, even if it leads to certain innovative conclusions. In this way, we each play a role in the design of the tradition.

The Babylonian Talmud is divided into 63 tractates. This text is from *Menachot* (Grain Offerings), which encompasses both obligatory and freewill offerings at the Temple in Jerusalem. Even though a talmudic tractate may be primarily dedicated to one area of Jewish life, it will likely digress into tangential and even seemingly irrelevant topics, because it is the recording of Rabbinic conversations, which are not necessarily linear. This fascinating and important text about interpreting the Torah is but one example of such a digression.

Rav Yehuda[69] said in the name of Rav [Abba Arikha]:[70] When Moses ascended on high, he found the Holy One, Blessed be He occupied in affixing crowns to the letters [of the Torah].

Moses said, "Master of the Universe, who stays your hand?" [i.e., why are you attaching crowns to the letters; are they really necessary?]

God answered, "There will arise a man at the end of many generations named Akiva ben Yosef, who will be able to make heaps and heaps of interpretations and laws based on each of those crowns."

"Master of the Universe," Moses said, "allow me to see him."

"Turn around," God said.

Moses [found himself in the academy of Rabbi Akiva] and he went and sat at the back, eighteen rows [from the front of] an ongoing class. However, as he was unable to follow the discussion and arguments, he felt very uncomfortable. Finally they came to a certain subject and one of the students asked the teacher [Akiva], "From where do you know this?' and he replied, "It is a law given to Moses at Sinai," and Moses's discomfort was eased.

Moses then returned to the Holy One, Blessed be He, and said, "Master of the Universe, You have such a man and yet You give the Torah through Me?!"
—B. Talmud, *Menachot* 29b

Maimonides
United in Faith

The Jewish people claim that because of Revelation, we have a relationship with the Holy One, the Source of All Life. This perspective is the basis for everything in our sacred tradition. Every observance, every custom, and every philosophical discourse, in some way or another, hearkens back to the origin of our covenant with God. The covenant as expressed in Revelation must be studied and taught, because it is an indispensable part of what makes us one people. At the same time, our covenant with God raises grave questions. We wonder about the purpose of our dispersion or about the reason for our massive suffering. Nonetheless, faith in the Torah—given to us on Shavuot as a product of our sacred relationship with God—remains a cornerstone of Judaism.

In his renowned and inspiring letter to the Jewish community in Yemen, Maimonides uses the concept of Revelation as encouragement to people, during their time of despair, to have faith in God and remain steadfast in their commitment to the Torah.

It is imperative, my fellow Jews, that you make this great spectacle of Revelation appeal to the imagination of your children. Proclaim at public gatherings its momentousness. For this event is the pivot of our religion, and the proof which demonstrates its veracity. Evaluate this phenomenon at its true importance, for Scripture has pointed out its significance in the verse, "For ask now of the days past, which were before you since the day that God created man upon the earth and from the one end of heaven to the other, whether there has been any such thing as this great thing is, or has been heard like it?" (Deut. 4:32).[71]

Remember, my coreligionists, that this great, incomparable, and unique historical event is attested by the best of evidence. For never before or since, has a whole nation witnessed a revelation from God or beheld His splendor. The purpose of all this was to confirm us in the faith so that nothing can change it, and to reach a degree of certainty which will sustain us in these trying times of fierce persecution and absolute tyranny, as it is written, "For God is come to test you" (Exod. 20:17)[72] in order to give you strength to withstand all future trials. Now do not slip nor err, be steadfast in your religion and persevere in your faith and its duties.[73]

—Maimonides, Epistle to Yemen

Zohar
The Significance of One

The specific identity of Shavuot within the three pilgrimage festivals is experienced in many ways, including custom and liturgy. The most obvious difference is that Sukkot and Passover are each a week long (plus one extra day for many Jews in the Diaspora), whereas Shavuot is merely a single day (two in the Diaspora). It might appear that Shavuot is therefore less important than the other two festivals. On the contrary, the Zohar, the core text of Jewish mysticism, sees the single day of Shavuot as being filled with supreme significance.

> Rabbi Yehudah [bar I'llai][74] said to him, "Why is it that Passover and Sukkot have seven days [in the Torah], but not Shavuot, which really ought to have more than the others [since the Torah was given on that day]."

> He replied, "It is written, *And who is like Your people Israel, a unique* [literally, "one"] *nation on earth …?* (2 Sam. 7:23). Now why is Israel called 'one' here as opposed to in any other place? It is because the text here is praising Israel, because it is the pride of Israel to be 'one.' Furthermore, the junction of the upper and the lower takes place at the place called 'Israel,' which is linked with what is above and what is below, and with the community of Israel. It is there that the whole is called 'one,' and in this place faith becomes manifest complete union and supernal holy unity. The Tree of Life [the Torah] is also called 'one,' and its day therefore is one. Therefore, we have Passover and Sukkot and [Shavuot] between them [uniting them]. This is the manner in which the Torah is honored, that it should have this *one* day and no more."

—Zohar, Leviticus 96a

Tanchuma Buber

Overwhelming Goodness

When we think of Revelation—the unveiling of the majesty of the Almighty—as it is described in the Book of Exodus, we wonder how people experience such an awesome occasion. Perhaps witnessing Revelation is pure, ecstatic elation. Or, perhaps the event is too overwhelming for a mere mortal. The Jewish tradition discusses the latter as a state of anxiety filled with dread that in the presence of God, we would be overcome. Yet it concludes that a merciful God reveals only what we can handle.

Tanchuma Buber is a collection of midrashic material collected, edited, and published in 1875 by Solomon Buber (b. 1827–d. 1906, Ukraine), scholar, philanthropist, and grandfather of the famed philosopher Martin Buber. This collection includes ethical teachings and rabbinical stories and interpretations based upon the weekly Torah portions.

> When God revealed His presence to the Israelites, He did not display all His goodness at once, because they could not have borne so much good; for had He revealed His goodness to them at one time they would have died .... When Joseph made himself known to his brothers, they were unable to answer him because they were astounded by him (Gen. 45:3). If God were to reveal Himself all at once, how much more powerful would be the effect. So He shows Himself little by little.[75]
> —*Tanchuma Buber*, Deuteronomy Ia

Abraham Joshua Heschel

Torah as Midrash

The Torah accounting of the Revelation at Mount Sinai is among the most poetic and eloquent in all literature. Its language and imagery capture and convey an experience that would otherwise seem impossible to grasp. And yet with all of the Torah's force and descriptive splendor, does it tell us what Revelation truly is? Perhaps the Torah begs us to interpret and celebrate Revelation rather than know it in literal terms.

Abraham Joshua Heschel was born in 1907 in Poland, where he received a traditional yeshiva education and became learned in Talmud. In 1933, he obtained a doctorate in philosophy from the University of Berlin. After being deported by the Nazis four years later and then fleeing their invasion of Poland, he founded the Institute for Jewish Learning in London and eventually became a professor and social activist in the United States. This text is taken from his 1955 book *God in Search of Man: A Philosophy of Judaism,*[76] which examines biblical thought and how that thought becomes faith. Heschel died in 1972.

> The nature of revelation, being an event in the realm of the ineffable, is something which words cannot spell, which human language will never be able to portray. Our categories are not applicable to that which is both within and beyond the realm of matter and mind. In speaking about revelation, the more descriptive the terms, the less adequate is the description. The words in which the prophets attempted to relate their experiences were not photographs but illustrations, not descriptions but songs. A psychological reconstruction of the prophetic act is, therefore, no more possible than the attempt to paint a photographic likeness of a face on the basis of a song. The word "revelation" is like an exclamation; it is an indicative rather than a descriptive term. Like all terms that express the ultimate, it points to its meaning rather than fully rendering it ....

> We must not try to read chapters in the Bible dealing with the event at Sinai as if they were texts in systematic theology. Its intention is to celebrate the mystery, to introduce us to it rather than to penetrate or explain it. As a report about revelation the Bible itself is *a midrash.*

> To convey what the prophets experienced, the Bible could use either terms of description or terms of indication. Any description of the act of revelation in empirical categories would have produced a caricature. This is why all the Bible does is to state *that* revelation happened; *how* it happened is something they could only convey in words that are evocative and suggestive.[77]
> —Abraham Joshua Heschel

Emmanuel Levinas
A Divine Symphony

The act of revelation is often understood to be a process that works in one direction only—from God to people. However, revelation is truly realized when that communication happens through each of our individual communications and our relation to God is put into place by each of us. In other words, each of us is a guarantor of revelation and each of us has his or her own unique way of conducting it into the world. With this understanding, we could say that God continues to speak to us all through the diverse symphony of our lives.

Born in Lithuania in 1906, philosopher and religious thinker Emmanuel Levinas began studying in France at age 17, As a naturalized citizen, he was drafted during World War II and ended up in a German prisoner-of-war camp. His wife and daughter survived by hiding in a French monastery; his family in Lithuania were murdered. Levinas, who died in 1995, focused on personal ethical responsibility as his starting point for philosophy, rather than pursuing the more traditional exploration of the nature of existence and the validity of knowledge.

> The Revelation as calling to the unique within me is the significance particular to the signifying of the Revelation. It is the multiplicity of persons—is not this the very meaning of the personal?—were the condition for the plenitude of "absolute truth"; as if every person, through his uniqueness, were the guarantee of the Revelation of a unique aspect of truth, and some of its points would never have been revealed if some people had been absent from mankind. This is not to say that truth is acquired anonymously in History, and that it finds 'supporters' in it! On the contrary, it is to suggest that the totality of the true is constituted from the contribution of multiple people: the uniqueness of each act of listening carrying the secret of the text; the voice of Revelation, as inflected, precisely, by each person's ear, would be necessary to the "Whole" of truth. That the Word of the living God may be heard in diverse ways does not mean only that the Revelation measure up to those listening to it, but that this measuring up measure up the Revelation: the multiplicity of irreducible people is necessary to the dimensions of meaning; the multiple meanings are multiple people. We can thus see the whole impact of the reference made by the Revelation to exegesis, to the freedom of this exegesis, the participation of the person listening to the Word making itself heard, but also the possibility for the Word to travel down the ages to announce the same truth in different times.[78]
>
> —Emmanuel Levinas

·✦— Shavuot —✦·
Interpretations of Sacred Texts

The texts in these pages, each studied at multiple levels, are from three sources: the Book of Exodus and two tractates of the Babylonian Talmud.[79] Exodus, the second of the Five Books of Moses, recounts the Israelites' enslavement by the Egyptians and subsequent escape to freedom, and God's giving the Israelites the Torah and instructing them on how to build the Tabernacle. The Babylonian Talmud is a collection of Torah-related writings that explains all aspects of Jewish life. Of its many tractates, one is called *Shabbat,* which deals with all the laws of the Sabbath; another is called *Berakhot,* which deals with prayers and blessings.

THE THREE LEVELS
Peshat: simple, literal meaning
Derash: historical, rabbinical inquiry
Making It Personal: contemporary analysis and application

Upturning the Barrel

. . . and they took their places at the foot of the mountain (Exod. 19:17). Rabbi Abdimi bar Hama bar Hasa* said, "This teaches that the Holy One, blessed be He, turned the mountain on its head like an upturned barrel and held it over them, and said to them, 'If you accept the Torah, all will be well; if not, this will be your grave.'"
—B. Talmud, *Shabbat* 88a

Peshat

This talmudic text describes God threatening Israel with destruction if it rejects the Torah, thus implying the nation was resistant. The passage contrasts sharply with Rabbinic teachings that depict an enthusiastic Israel, identified as the only nation that would accept the Torah.[80] A Rabbinic paradox unfolds. In the interpretation we have here, God coerces Israel to take the Torah— that is, God chooses Israel. Yet in other interpretations, Israel freely accepts the Torah—that is, Israel chooses God. This dichotomy recalls the old homily: "How odd of God to choose the Jews. It's not so odd, the Jews chose God."

Derash

Later rabbinical interpretations of this text state that Israel had to be coerced to accept the Torah for the agreement to be binding. The Maharal of Prague (born in 1525) suggests that if Israel had been able to accept the Torah on its own, it would also have had the authority to annul the agreement.[81] In other words, if acceptance were a real option for Israel, then rejection would also have been a real option, which was untenable to God. Therefore God had to have a coercive, permission-giving role. The Israelites could then never say the acceptance was by their choice alone.

The Talmud, as well as the illustrious commentator Rashi (born in France in 1140), make another point. Although Israel may not have willingly accepted the Torah in the wilderness, it finally and permanently did so centuries later during the events that take place in the story of Purim.[82] This concept is based on a verse in the Scroll of Esther, the biblical book that tells the Purim tale. It says, "the Jews undertook and irrevocably obligated themselves …" (9:27).

Making It Personal

Revelation in much of Rabbinic literature is likened to a stage in the process of Creation, whereby the Jewish people and the world itself are born anew. For birth, indeed Creation, to occur, it must be preceded by the removal of something preexisting. Kabbalah uses the term "contraction" or "emptying"—emptying an existing vessel to make room for something new to occupy the space. In the case of Revelation, however, we are speaking of nonphysical space: the spiritual, emotional, and intellectual space that it takes to fit the teachings of the Torah into the world. The Midrash alludes to this idea, saying: "When God gave the Torah … the whole world stood hushed into breathless silence, and the voice of God went forth …."[83] Here, we learn that the voice and presence of God filled the vacant space left open by the silence.

But what does it take for silence to occur so that we may accept a revelation—something that will spiritually change our lives?

In our personal lives, many of us are set in familiar ways; and it is simply easier to not change, even if we know a change might be helpful in the long run. These changes can be as elemental as getting more exercise every day or as complex as conquering a chronic, immoral behavior. Therefore, to force the change, the situation must often be stated in drastic terms. To get an addict's attention, a doctor may need to say, "This will kill you in a year if you don't stop now." If the addict chooses to heed the doctor's warning, he or she must empty the place where the addiction lives, to make room for something new. This is the spiritual process of assuming responsibility.

The Talmud uses a dramatic visual description of God hanging a mountain above the head of Israel. The purpose of this drastic scenario is to force the Israelites to empty out their spiritual past and make room for Revelation and their spiritual future. The Talmud expresses a crucial turning point in the spirit of Israel, the precise point when the Israelites were ready to be born anew, emptying out the past life of the nation and filling it with Torah.

---

* Rabbi Abdimi (also known as Abdima) was a 4th-century sage who lived in Israel and later in Babylonia.

THE THREE LEVELS
Peshat: simple, literal meaning
Derash: historical, rabbinical inquiry
Making It Personal: contemporary analysis and application

Deep into the Words of Torah

What blessing is said [before the study of Torah]? Rav Yehudah[*] said in the name of Samuel,[**] "[Blessed are You …] who has sanctified us by His commandments and has commanded us to engross ourselves in the words of Torah." Rabbi Yochanan[***] would conclude the blessing, saying, "Please make sweet, God our God, the words of Torah in our mouths and the mouths of all Your people Israel. May we, our children, and all the children of the House of Israel come to know You and study Your Torah. Blessed are You, God, who teaches Torah to His people Israel." Rav Hamnuna[****] would [instead say the blessing], "[Blessed are You …] who chose us from all the nations and gave us His Torah. Blessed are You, God, who gives the Torah." Rav Hamnuna said, "This is the finest of blessings, therefore, let us say all of them."

—B. Talmud, *Berakhot* 11b

Peshat

Before studying Torah, we recite a blessing that ends with *la'asok b'divrei Torah*, "to engross ourselves in the words of Torah." The ruling to use that blessing is based on this talmudic discussion and the opinion of Rav Yehudah. Two other talmudists, Rabbi Yochanan and Rav Hamnuna, differ about which blessing to say. Rav Hamnuna finally asserts that the endings of all three proposed blessings should be merged into one extended ending, because the blessing over Torah study is the "finest of blessings." As a result, in the preliminaries of the daily morning service, we say all three endings as now written in the prayer book.[84] We begin with the ending "to engross ourselves in the words of Torah." We then add the words of Rabbi Yochanan, from "Please make sweet" to "who teaches Torah to His people Israel." We conclude with the final words of Rav Hamnuna's prayer "who gives the Torah," which is also the blessing a person says when given an *aliyah* (literally, "ascension"), the honor of being called upon to recite the blessings before and after a Torah reading.

Derash

For centuries, the intellectual world has recognized that to become a so-called educated person, a student must become familiar with a core curriculum of thinkers, including Plato, Shakespeare, Kant, and Freud. These and other important thinkers have responded to the perennial questions about the conditions of life. Their contributions have infiltrated society and become a part of our collective identities and our collective education and vision.

Judaism has its own core curriculum with a vision that originates in our study of Torah. To be an educated Jew, one must have a certain breadth and depth of knowledge based in these texts. Rabbi and contemporary scholar Daniel Gordis calls Jewish texts the "collective diaries" of the Jewish people and, he says, by studying them, "we learn that the human condition is not a modern condition but a timeless, existential one. And we learn that being Jewish is most profoundly about thinking through the questions that the human condition begs us to ask."[85]

Making It Personal

How should the study of Jewish texts be a part of our lives today? The great German philosopher Franz Rosenzweig said that we have discovered a new way of learning:

It is a learning in reverse order. A learning that no longer starts from the Torah and leads into life, but the other way round: from life, from a world that knows nothing of the Law … back to the Torah. That is the sign of the time."[86]

Rosenzweig suggested that this approach is necessary because in contemporary society, so many Jews find their spiritual home outside of Judaism. Although his suggestion may work for some, it is not the optimal relationship for Jews to have with their texts. The study of Torah and life should be intertwined; we should understand each in light of the other, each reflected in the other. Phrases from the text should resound in our experience and guide our Jewish identities. This method shows us the way to truly live the blessing "engross ourselves in the words of Torah" and tells us how to engage God, who gives and teaches Torah.

---

* Rabbi Yehudah II was a 3rd-century sage who lived in Israel. He was the grandson of Yehudah Ha-Nasi, renowned redactor of the Mishnah.

** Samuel (Shmuel) bar Abba was a 2nd- to 3rd-century talmudic sage in Israel.

*** Most likely, this is Yochanan bar Nafcha, a late-3rd-century talmudic sage who lived in Israel and traveled often to Babylonia. He laid the foundations of the Jerusalem Talmud.

**** Of the several talmudic sages called Hamnuna, his one most likely lived in early 4th century Babylon.

THE THREE LEVELS
Peshat: simple, literal meaning
Derash: historical, rabbinical inquiry
Making It Personal: contemporary analysis and application

More Than Commandments*

verse 1 God spoke all these words, saying: verse 2 I the LORD am your God who brought you out of the land of Egypt, the house of bondage [1st commandment]: verse 3 You shall have no other gods besides Me. verse 4 You shall not make for yourself a sculptured image, or any likeness of what is in the heavens above, or on earth below, or in the waters under the earth. verse 5 You shall not bow down to them or serve them. . . . [2nd] verse 7 You shall not swear falsely by the name of the LORD your God; for the LORD will not clear one who falsely swears by His name [3rd]. verse 8 Remember the sabbath day and keep it holy. . . . [4th] verse 12 Honor your father and your mother, that you may long endure on the land that the LORD your God is assigning to you [5th]. verse 13 You shall not murder [6th]. You shall not commit adultery [7th]. You shall not steal [8th]. You shall not bear false witness against your neighbor [9th]. verse 14 You shall not covet your neighbor's house: you shall not covet your neighbor's wife, or his male or female slave, or his ox or his ass, or anything that is your neighbor's [10th].
—Exodus 20:1–14

Peshat

This passage, the Torah reading on Shavuot, is commonly referred to as the "Ten Commandments." The term was derived from the Hebrew *Aseret Ha-Devarim*[87] (literally, "The Ten Statements") and from the Greek rendering *Deka Logoi* (literally, "Ten Words"). In truth, "commandments" is an inaccurate English translation, because the Hebrew word for commandments is mitzvot, which never appears in the passage.

The Torah states that these pronouncements were inscribed on two stone tablets and placed in the Ark of the Covenant.[88] The Talmud also claims that the inscription miraculously went completely through the tablets, wherein the letters hung, unattached to the surrounding stone.[89] Moreover, it says that they were legible from both sides as an exact image, not reversed.

Originally, the Ten Commandments were recited as part of the daily public liturgy.[90] And yet the Torah contains hundreds of commandments—the Talmud claims 613.[91] The Rabbis decided to eliminate the practice because of concern that overemphasizing these 10 would diminish the significance of the other 603.[92]

Derash

Judeo-Christian faiths have different traditions for dividing the 13 biblical verses (2–14) into the Ten Commandments, particularly regarding the first three commandments. The prevailing Jewish division begins with verse 2 ("I the LORD am your God") as the first commandment; verses 3–6 ("You shall have no other gods besides Me") as the second; and verse 7 ("You shall not swear falsely by the name of the LORD your God") as the third.

In addition, in the Jewish tradition the Ten Commandments have two inherent groupings based on style and content. The first five commandments—a mixture of statements, positive directives, and prohibitions—are about the relationship between humankind and God. The second five commandments—all prohibitions—are about the relationship between a person and his or her fellow.

Making It Personal

To fully grasp the significance of the Ten Commandments, it is helpful to understand how this code compares with other approaches from long ago. Ancient codes of law typically expressed laws in terms of retributive justice, describing the crime and its proportionate punishment: "If one does this, then that will happen." The only reason to follow the law is the threat of sanction. In contrast, the Ten Commandments simply present civil, moral, and religious laws, without sanction. We follow the laws because God wants us to do certain things and not do other things.[93]

The verbal composition of the Ten Commandments tells us that they are not laws or commandments at all; they are *devarim*, which means both "words" and "things of substance." They are elements of universal certainty that require neither explanation to understand nor punishment to cultivate obedience. They are presented as conditions of the universe, just like the laws of gravity or the suspension of stars in the sky. Inscribed in the structure of absolutely everything, they require only our acceptance and cooperation.

---

* The verses in this passage are numbered to aid the reader in studying and understanding their relationship to the Ten Commandments.

·◆— Shavuot —◆·

Significance of the Holiday: Some Modern Perspectives

From Ordinary to the Most Holy

by Alan Abrams

At first glance, Shavuot might seem to be the poor stepsister of Judaism's three pilgrimage festivals, the *Shalosh Regalim*. The Torah assigns seven days of celebration to Passover and Sukkot; Shavuot only gets one.[94] Shavuot does not even get a fixed date in the Torah. And Shavuot is also lacking the very thing that helped lift the other festivals out of the ordinariness of their agricultural roots into the spiritual heights that we now know. That is, it has no biblical association with the Exodus, the great historical event in the story of the Israelite people and their encounter with God.

After the Second Temple was destroyed in 70 C.E., these seeming limitations put the future of Shavuot in jeopardy; the festival appeared to be solely without hope for an ongoing existence. The destination for the pilgrimage—the place for making the offering of first fruits—was gone. Shavuot had no additional aspects to its celebration, as did Passover with its grand seder meal or Sukkot with its ritually built huts—connections that could survive beyond the destruction of the Temple and take root in the Jewish home, wherever it might be. Shavuot was truly in danger of withering away. Yet this holiday did anything but whither. Instead, in every generation, Jews sought to find their own particular way of crowning Shavuot with new rituals and spiritual associations. Those new elements developed out of diverse associations with the holiday, some modern, some ancient.

Reconnecting to the Land

The kibbutz movement (Zionism fascilitated through land-based labor collectives), flourished in the first half of the 20th century when pioneering Jewish farmers began intensely revitalizing and working the land. As they revived the practice of agriculture in Israel, they also sought to revive the agricultural element of the Jewish holidays. They wanted to express the deep meaning they found in the tie between the people "Israel" and the Land of Israel. Shavuot, associated with the first fruits of the harvest, was a natural opportunity. On the kibbutzim, people created *bikkurim* festivals, albeit usually secular in nature, featuring children dressed in blue and white, and carrying flowers and produce. Ironically, the very thing that might make Shavuot seem impoverished—its relative failure to develop beyond an association with the agriculture of Israel—reinvigorated Shavuot on that very land.

Shavuot had remained available and could be reassociated with old traditions in striking new ways. Besides the agricultural experience, something else would also become possible again: a large-scale pilgrimage of worshipers to the site of the Temple in Jerusalem. One of the most dramatic of these reassociations occurred in the wake of the Six-Day War in 1967. Jews had been denied any access whatsover to the Western Wall, or Kotel, since late 1947 when the Jordanians had taken control of the Old City section of Jerusalem. But on June 7, 1967, Israeli paratroopers arrived at the Kotel, and Shavuot arrived just a week later. Nearly messianic euphoria accompanied Israel's seemingly miraculous deliverance from the destruction that had been feared at the hands of the surrounding Arab armies. On that Shavuot, amid this atmosphere, some 200,000 Jews streamed through the city on a pilgrimage to the Kotel. The *Jerusalem Post*[95] reported:

> Every section of the population was represented. Kibbutz members and soldiers rubbing shoulders with Neturei Karta [Aramaic for Guardians of the City, an Orthodox Jewish group that opposes Zionism and the existence of the State of Israel]. Mothers came with children in prams, and old men trudged steeply up Mount Zion, supported by youngsters on either side, to see the wall of the Temple before the end of their days.

From then on, it became the practice among a great many people to walk to the Kotel for prayer during the early morning hours of Shavuot.

RECONNECTING TO THE TORAH

Other apsects of the holiday hearken back to the ancient Rabbis' choice to associate Shavuot with the giving of the Torah. For this reason, on Shavuot, the Torah reading highlights two things in particular: the verses in the Book of Exodus that describe the appearance of God to the people Israel at Mount Sinai and the verses that include the Ten Commandments. Over many centuries, other rituals and spiritual associations have arisen. In the Middle Ages, amid the terror of crusades and expulsions, Jewish mysticism was blooming. It gave us, among other things, a striking Aramaic poem composed to introduce the Torah reading. This poem—the 11th-century *Akdamut Millin* (literally, "An Introduction to the Words," referring to the Ten Commandments)—is still recited in many Ashkenazic synagogues. Its

90 acrostic lines conclude with a description of a great cosmic battle featuring the primeval beasts Leviathan (of the sea) and Behemoth (of the land). God approaches them with sword in hand and then creates a great feast for the righteous, including wine that had been preserved from the day of Creation. The final words of *Akdamut Millin* urge the worshipers to listen to—and to heed— the great commands that will be read following the poem.

Another medieval addition to Shavuot was the kabbalist's creation of the all-night Torah study session called *Tikun Leil Shavuot,* This practice has found new life in recent years as today's Jews embrace many of the mystical practices of Shavuot, although sometimes in blended ways that might be surprising to their creators. One Shavuot in Jerusalem, I participated in such an eclectic observance. In the style of the kabbalists, all night, we went from home to home, studying. And then, in those early morning hours before the sun made itself known, we walked the paths our biblical ancestors, laden with their first fruits, may have taken to the Temple. We joined a huge stream of people heading toward the Kotel. When light came, in our own style, we were praying with men and women side by side. We were, like the generations before us, increasing the spiritual meaning of this once purely agricultural holiday by making it our own.

Speaking in Thunder

by Arthur Green

Among Jews in North America, Shavuot is surely one of the least-known and least-observed Jewish holidays. Here we have another irony of Jewish history: the holiday of the book, forgotten by the People of the Book (*Am Ha-Sefer*).

Shavuot, which commemorates the giving of the Torah at Mount Sinai, should, by rights, be the apex of the Jewish festival cycle. Passover, the time of liberation, leads up to it. We count the days from Exodus to Sinai, as though liberation itself were just a prelude. In order to be wedded to our God at the mountain, we have to be free from bondage to all our inner and outer pharaohs. Sukkot, the third partner in the pilgrimage cycle, basks in the afterglow of Sinai. In it we celebrate our wandering through the wilderness and our eternal preparation to enter the Promised Land. Neither of these makes any sense without the main event, the Revelation of God at the holy mountain.

Sinai takes us to the heart of Jewish faith. It claims three things:

- God communicates with humans;
- Such communication took place during the wilderness encounter between Moses and the Israelites and *yud heh vav heh*—the unutterable Hebrew name for God, understood here as an impossible form of the verb "to be," best translated "is-was-will be";
- Revelation makes known the divine will.

In one form or another, this set of claims pervades all of classical Judaism.

If the Revelation and covenant of obligation at Sinai are the heart of Jewish faith, they are also the most difficult and "scandalous" claims made by the religious traditions of Israel. Taken at face value, they form the very essence of Jewish supernaturalism and seeming theological arbitrariness. The Creator of the universe, *yud heh vav heh,* chooses at a particular moment to reveal God's self uniquely to the Jewish people, addressing them in words and pledging eternal loyalty in a covenant with them, if they will accept God's specific will as manifest in the practice of Judaism. Both mind and conscience reel at such a thought! What does it mean to say that God speaks? Does God speak to Israel in a language that Israel understands, commanding through a Torah made up of laws, ethics, rites, and traditions that seem remarkably related to those of the pagan nations in whose midst Israel lives? Can we imagine a God so arbitrary as to choose one nation, one place, and one moment in human history as a set of cirumstances in which the eternal divine will is to be manifest for all time? How can we attribute to *yud heh vav heh,* who becomes personified only through our encounter, this sort of arbitrary willfulness? For these reasons and others, thinking Jews in our time, including many who seek a serious approach to questions of the spirit, balk at accepting the so-called yoke of Sinai.

But hear another voice from within the classical tradition. "Moses spoke and God responded in a voice"[96] (Exod. 19:19). The Rabbinic commentators explain: God responded "in the voice of Moses." This seems to say that the one and only voice heard at Sinai was that of Moses, sometimes speaking on his own and sometimes possessed by the divine spirit—God responding from within Moses's own voice. Rather than a "voice from heaven," the voice was that of a prophet transformed by an inner encounter that can only be characterized as "heaven." Jews over the centuries have debated how to refine the naive biblical depiction of Sinai and the experience of Revelation. For example, the phrase "*Shekhinah* [Divine Presence] speaks from within his throat" was often applied to prophets. As for the content of Revelation, modern Judaism has buried the truth the Jewish mystics knew centuries ago. All God "reveals" at Sinai is God's own self, the self of the universe. The entire Torah is naught but this, God's own name. All the rest is commentary.

The fact is that any sophisticated theory of Revelation recognizes a moment in which the divine and human minds flow together. Indeed, we speak of the "mind" of the Divine only by analogy with the human mind. If *yud heh vav heh* is the incorporeal essence of the universe and mind or soul is the incorporeal essence of the person, we "call" God the mind or soul of the universe. God as *yud heh vav heh* knows no distinction between matter and spirit. In seeking to comprehend Revelation, we may, however, speak of *yud heh vav heh* as a cosmic mind, present in the depths of each human mind and impressing itself in a unique way upon consciousness. The universal One seeks to be known by the human—this manifestation of its own self that is also, paradoxically, its "other." The "seeking" or "calling out" to its other (the human) is not in the form of language. It is only humans who can make the Divine articulate in words, because words are the human tool for communication. In fact, the most recent translations of Exodus 19:19 render it, "As Moses spoke, God answered him in thunder."[97] *Yud heh vav heh* speaks in thunderclaps; it takes a Moses to translate God's thunder into words.

If the Jewish imagination regards the Divine and human as separate, God living in heaven and humans on earth, Revelation is the act that comes closest to bridging this separation. Moses goes up to the top of Sinai, according to the Torah, and God comes down upon the mountain (Exod. 19:3,20). But at that moment, the entire top of Sinai is covered by thick cloud—as though to say that the border between the "upper" and "lower" realms had been lost. (Some later accounts of Revelation are more fanciful; they actually depict Moses as riding on the clouds, entering the heavenly realms, and holding on to God's throne of glory.) Moses returns from Revelation still human, but his face glows with the light of that encounter, in which the upper limits on human spiritual attainment had been momentarily cast aside. He returns from an experience of transcendent unity to the "world of separation." The Torah is now "translated" within Moses: His words and God's thunder are now one.

Throughout its history, the Jewish people has accepted the task of forming a communal religious existence and creating a civilization that stands in response to the events of Sinai. This undertaking is what we mean by "accepting the Torah." What we accept is the reality that divinity is present in humans—manifest in human language and human institutions. We accept the challenge to create a society, with all its institutional trappings, which embodies this presence. We are no less charged with that task today than we were thousands of years ago.

The single commandment to which Jews are most committed is that which comes directly from the teaching of Shavuot: *ve-shinnantam le-vanekha,* "teach them diligently to your children." In general, Jews today care more about giving their children at least some smattering of Jewish education than they do about any aspect of religious observance or about maintaining specifically Jewish values in their own lives. We have an overpowering sense that we come from a long line of tradition, one that has been forged and deepened by much suffering. To break the connection, to let the next generation have nothing of this legacy, is almost unthinkable. That is why mixed marriage remains such a source of heartbreak among many Jews, even those who have little sense of what it is that the tradition actually teaches. This pull to preserve the legacy is a positive aspect of our collective culture, and one that we celebrate on Shavuot. In traditional communities and, recently, far beyond them as well (even in secular Tel Aviv), there is a custom called *Tikun Leil Shavuot*—staying awake all night on Shavuot to study Torah. The kabbalists originated this practice in the Middle Ages. Like *Kabbalat Shabbat* (special prayers and songs to welcome the Sabbath), it is a mystical practice that is now widespread among many Jews who know little of its original meaning.

Tikun Leil Shavuot helps to keep alive another aspect of Shavuot. The receiving of Torah is an experience, not just a body of teachings. A *tikun* for Shavuot night is not a superlong graduate seminar! Sinai is understood by the tradition to be an eternal moment. Precisely because God as *yud heh vav heh* ("is-was-will be") exists beyond time, the moment when Torah is transmitted from the heart of the One to the Jewish people can be re-created in each and every moment of our existence. The "awakeness" of Shavuot night is not just a lack of sleep. It should be a deeper wakefulness as well, a willingness to hear God as the Beloved knocking on the door of each person's heart, waiting to be welcomed in, so that the holy teaching—Torah—is truly "upon your very heart."[98] The great sage Rabbi Akiva insisted that The Song of Songs, the poetic declaration of God's love, was given to Israel at Sinai, at the very heart of Revelation. It takes an open heart as well as an open mind to receive the Torah, which we do again each year on Shavuot.

Out of that openness we are also ready to "hear" a Torah that calls upon us to not only faithfully preserve old traditions, but also to devise ever newer and more creative ways to celebrate God's presence in our midst. Some people interpret this idea as the need for new expressions of faith, created in music or other artistic forms appropriate to our age. Others offer new interpretations to our ancient texts and help remold them to confront new challenges as they arise. Yet others, being no less innovative than the mystics were hundreds of years ago, will create new ritual forms. Every generation has to do this in order to keep the fires of Sinai alive, to keep them from becoming merely ash, merely the memory of a once-vital faith. Maintaining the sense of balance between these two, preserving old traditions while creating new ones, and doing both in awareness of God's eternal voice—that is the challenge of Shavuot, the time when we re-receive our Torah.

Chosen Together

by Bradley Shavit Artson

Why is the festival of Shavuot called "the time of the giving of our Torah" and not "the time of the receiving of our Torah"? Because the giving of the Torah happened at one specified time, but the receiving of the Torah happens at every time and in every generation.[99]
—Rabbi Meir Alter of Ger

Each generation must make its own way back to Sinai, must stand under the mountain and re-appropriate and reinterpret the Revelation, in terms that are both classical and new. We recognize change as part of the continuing process of tradition itself.[100]
—Rabbi Gerson D. Cohen

The least-known of the *Shalosh Regalim* is Shavuot. A victim of schedule, Shavuot comes at the shift from spring into the recreation time of summer. People are busy with graduations, weddings, and vacation plans. Furthermore, it currently lacks any special rituals to excite widespread observance.

In the biblical period, Shavuot celebrated the conclusion of the barley harvest and the beginning of the wheat harvest. By the time of the Mishnah and the Talmud, some thousand years later, the Rabbis expanded Shavuot beyond its agricultural origin to incorporate a foundational event as well, the giving of our Torah—the token, record, and pathway of the special love between God and the Jewish people.

It comes exactly seven weeks after the second day of Passover, the festival that marks the liberation of the Jews from Egyptian slavery. Passover and Shavuot are linked not only by the cycles of the calendar (based on the Torah's insistence that Shavuot occur precisely 50 days after Passover) but also by the nature of the stages of human liberation.

Passover, however popular, is just a beginning: the initiation of Jewish freedom. As our ancestors were liberated from Egyptian slavery, they took their first halting steps toward freedom and independence. No longer saddled with the burdens and oppression of Egyptian taskmasters, the Jews entered the wilderness of Sinai, where they experienced their independence as little less than anarchy. Theirs was a freedom from control, a freedom from limits. Such liberty, by itself, is the freedom of adolescence, one that bridles at any restraint. It is fine as a first step, but it ultimately cannot ensure human growth, creativity, and community. Rather than simply avoiding limits, mature freedom entails living up to one's best potential, meeting responsibilities toward community and toward others with a sense of purpose and satisfaction. Freedom "fulfilled" is freedom to live productively, with meaning, and in relationship to other people.

Just as "freedom from" a restriction finds completion in "freedom to" do something meaningful, so the festival of Passover initiates a process of liberation that culminates in the festival of Shavuot. Shavuot marks the coming-of-age and responsibility of the Jewish people and celebrates the encounter between God and the Jewish people at Mount Sinai. That moment of divine–human commitment resulted in a formal link between the two, a *brit* ("covenant") that binds God and the Jewish people forever. This *brit* received its first expression in the writings of the Torah, which has formed the core of all subsequent Jewish identity.

Shavuot, then, marks the special relationship between God and the Jews, celebrates the biblical understanding of the Jews as God's "Chosen People," a concept essential to Jewish identity, and one that has been distorted, by both Jews and non-Jews.

What does it mean to be chosen? Chosen does not mean superior, and it does not mean that God loves the Jewish people better than other people: the Bible itself records God's love for all humanity. Being chosen does, however, imply that God loved the Jewish people first. That love is a matter of historical record: Judaism gave birth to two other monotheistic faiths, Christianity and Islam, which have spread a commitment to biblical values and knowledge through much of the world.

"To be chosen" is really a grammatical fragment: a person is never simply chosen, but always chosen for something. When we say that the Jews are chosen, we mean that we were selected to embody the practices and values of Judaism as expressed in the Torah and subsequent Jewish writings. God chose us to be a role model—to demonstrate that a society of people dedicated to ritual profundity, moral rigor, and compassionate action could profoundly shape the world. Jews were chosen to live Torah, nothing more and nothing less. In the words of the siddur (the daily, Sabbath, and festival prayer book), "You have chosen us from among all peoples by giving us Your Torah." To the extent that we make the practices and values of the Torah real in our daily lives and in our communal priorities, we in turn choose God. The Torah is given anew each time we allow it to live through our deeds. To live Torah is far more than an affirmation of ritual commitments, although it certainly includes that. Living Torah means caring for the widow and orphan as an expression of religious obligation. It means loving the stranger as oneself, honoring our parents, feeding the hungry, preventing the blind from stumbling, and a whole host of ethical commitments that elevate human relationship and human caring to a pedestal of justice—the truest expression of covenantal love.

Shavuot is thus a recommitment to our founding purpose. Each year, we remember why there is a Jewish people, why there is Judaism. On this festival, we celebrate in wonder—as did our ancestors—the fact that God chose our people to live the mitzvot; and we renew our commitment to walk in God's ways and to help each other along the path.

·◆— Shavuot —◆·
Alternative Meditation

The Covenant that Binds God[101]

by Irving Greenberg

Many people—some formally religious and some not—agree that an infinite God or power is the source of this vast universe. But some of them are bothered by the Jewish claim that this Divine Being has chosen the Jews to serve as a special vehicle. (As the old anti-Semitic doggerel puts it, "How odd / of God / to choose / the Jews.") Similarly, Judaism's daughter religions, Christianity and Islam, agree that God binds humans to God's covenant. However, theologians of the other monotheistic religions find it somewhat hard to accept Judaism's affirmation that God is not merely the source of the Torah, but is also bound by it. Opponents argue that such a statement is incredibility piled on top of paradox. Would an infinite, universal, all-powerful One care enough to intervene in "trivial" human concerns? Would that Being then be held to the terms of that intervention? Yes, says the Bible and later Jewish tradition.

It all stems from the biblical assertion that the human is in the image of God. Like God, humans are endowed with freedom, power, and consciousness. According to Scriptures, God allows for these human qualities. (In biblical language: Adam and Eve sin but are not put to death. Then, after the flood, God self-limits in the first covenant and promises never again to destroy the earth with a deluge.) This means that the process of exercising human freedom, including the doing of evil, is accepted. Perfection may come more slowly, but henceforth it will come only in a partnership—a covenant—of humans and God. In this covenant, the human will not be overwhelmed and forced to do good.

If goodness will not be imposed by power, then the human must be educated toward perfection. The rabbis conceive of God as teacher and pedagogue—teaching Torah to Israel and to the world. This also explains why, in the words of Ethics of the Fathers (chapter 6, Mishnah 2), "The only truly free person is one who studies Torah."[102]

As teacher, God offers a personal model for human behavior. The imitation of God is the basis for ethics. Parents, however warm or spontaneous, cannot enable children to grow unless the parents are prepared to bind themselves—to be available in some committed, dependable way. To teach successfully, teachers must offer a reliable and consistent model. Then God, as parent and teacher, must bind God's own self to humans.

From this understanding of the divine commitment in the covenant stems Abraham's incredible challenge when God seeks to destroy Sodom, "You dare not! Shall the Judge of all the earth not do justice?" (Genesis 18:25). Out of this comes the Jewish tradition of a *din torah mit'n Ribbono Shel Olam*—a trial of God. From Moses to Jeremiah and Lamentations through Levi Yitzchak of Berditchev and Elie Wiesel in our time, Jewish religious life has brought forth people who do not fear arraigning even God when there is injustice.

The binding of God in the covenant is the guarantor that redemption is the true fate of humankind. Reality itself does not always seem to operate to ensure the triumph of good. Ultimately, then, it is God's promise that justifies hope. This is the irony and paradox of the "guarantee": It is built on nothing more substantial than the word of God. What could be more ephemeral than a word, especially when the promise of redemption may point to an event hundreds or even thousands of years away? Yet Jews trusted, waited, and worked. The Torah is no easy, ironclad guarantee against fate or suffering, yet it has outlasted empires. The Jews' testimony is that the covenant will outlast even those societies and cultures that deny its existence. On the other hand, the ethics of asking people to depend on God's word implies that God will truly bind God's own self to keep that promise.

Therefore, Shavuot is not a coronation ceremony. On Rosh Hashanah, Jews blow the shofar and crown the Lord as ruler of the universe. Shavuot is a more "democratic" holiday. It remembers those who trekked to Sinai to receive the Torah. It celebrates the God who "descended upon the mountain" and bound the divine self permanently to the Jewish people. A ruler issues decrees of life and death. A covenant rests upon "free negotiations, mutual assumption of duties, and full recognition of the equal rights of both parties."[103] God also becomes a partner in this covenantal community. God joins in human community and shares in its covenantal existence. As Joseph B. Soloveitchik points out, the whole concept of God suffering along with humanity ("I [God] shall be with him in trouble" [Psalm 91:5]) "can only be understood within the perspective of the covenantal community that involves God in the destiny of his fellow members."[104]

So Shavuot is the holiday of partnership. The Divine, out of unbounded love, voluntarily puts aside unbounded power; this equalizes the two partners. This idea of partnership has had an immeasurably positive impact on human history even beyond religion. Covenant became the source of morality and ethics, moving humanity away from magical and ritual/mechanical concepts of divine-human interaction. Concern for social justice, compassion for human suffering, and the demand that religious people serve other humans have all flowed from this idea.

PART 5

Tisha b'Av

Alas!
Lonely sits the city
Once great with people!
She that was great among nations
Is become like a widow;
The princess among states
Is become a thrall.

—Lamentations 1:1

To Survive and Thrive

A LTHOUGH SOME POLITICALLY motivated extremists deliberately choose to deny the Holocaust, generally speaking, the Western world has provided information and promoted awareness of this historical obscenity, the tragedy and horror that befell the Jewish people. At the same time, historians tend to ignore the thousands of years of Jewish history, riddled with terrible subjugation, that preceded the Holocaust. As 20th-century scholar and author Milton Steinberg suggests, there seems to be a "conspiracy of silence on the part of historians" regarding Jewish history.[1] In fact, the tragedy-saturated history of the Jews would be quite evident by taking a world map and a time line and then plotting all of the Jewish migrations and resettlements that were caused by persecutions over the past millennia. The result would resemble some sort of wild, geometric pattern full of loops and zigzags.

The Jewish people, however, were not always the uninvited houseguests of European nobility, forced to constantly move. They were not always the merely tolerated infidels of the Arabian peninsula. They were not always the local representatives of the Antichrist, who, because of their otherness, could be useful as moneylenders and tax collectors. Indeed, it is easy to forget that centuries before Christianity and its powerful popes or before Islam and its commanding sheikhs and imams, Jews occupied their own land, under their own political and religious leadership. At that time, they were mostly an agrarian people who were both blessed and cursed to live on a small strip of land, which turned out to be the triangular Fertile Crescent bridging Europe, Africa, and Asia.

The historical turning point for the Jews was a date on the Hebrew calendar, Tisha b'Av (the 9th day of Av, a month that corresponds to July–August) in the year 70 C.E., when the Romans laid waste to Jerusalem, destroyed the Temple, murdered or enslaved Jews, and sent many into exile. The Jewish nation had known homelessness before. When the Babylonians destroyed the First Temple in the early 6th century B.C.E. (also on Tisha b'Av), most of the Israelites were sent immediately into exile, principally to one place, Babylonia. But after the Persian Empire overthrew the Babylonians about 50 years later, Cyrus the Great gave the Jews permission to return to their native land, and more than 40,000 are said to have done so. The Roman conquest of Jerusalem was something entirely different. At that moment, the Jews took on the identity of itinerant aliens, a status that would last for 2,000 years. In 70 C.E., with the Romans dismantling the center of world Jewry, the Jews were thrust out into the vast Roman Empire, where burgeoning socioeconomic diversity and new trade routes pushed them into many different places. Despite the destruction that occurred on Tisha b'Av, which ultimately allowed for further persecutions, Jews have prided themselves on their ability to survive and even to advance in the Diaspora. Each year, while commemorating the pain that has its roots in 70 C.E., we remember as well that the rebirth of Israel is our historical destiny.

The Traditional Fasts

There are six statutory, public fasts in the Jewish calendar. The only one clearly commanded in the Torah is Yom Kippur, generally regarded as the holiest day of the year. The Fast of Esther (right before the holiday of Purim) is alluded to in the Book of Esther, but made mandatory in the Rabbinic era. The other four fasts are all associated with the destruction of Jerusalem and the Temple and, consequently, loss of national integrity for the Jewish state. All four are derived from a verse in the biblical Book of Zechariah that discusses the Messianic Age:[2]

> *Thus said the* LORD *of Hosts: The fast of the fourth month* [Shivah-Asar b'Tammuz, *the 17th of Tammuz*], *the fast of the fifth month* [Tisha b'Av], *the fast of the seventh month* [Tzom Gedaliah, *Fast of Gedaliah*], *and the fast of the tenth month* [Asarah b'Tevet, *the 10th of Tevet*] *shall become occasions for joy and gladness, happy festivals for the House of Judah; but you must love honesty and integrity.*
>
> —Zechariah 8:19

Shivah-Asar b'Tammuz (literally, "17th of Tammuz") commemorates five catastrophes concerning the First Temple. The day involves a minor fast—from sunrise to sunset, rather than sunset to sunset. The Mishnah recounts all five of the catastrophes:

*On the Seventeenth of Tammuz the tablets [containing the Ten Commandments]
were broken; the daily sacrifice was discontinued; the walls of Jerusalem were
breached [leading to the destruction of the First Temple]; Apustamus, a Greek officer,
burned a Torah scroll; and an idol was erected in the sanctuary of the Temple.*

—Mishnah, *Ta'anit* 4:6

Tisha b'Av (literally, "9th of Av") is a major 25-hour[3] fast commemorating five grave
tragedies that befell the Jewish people. Again, the Mishnah is our primary source:

*On the Ninth of Av it was decreed that the generation of the desert would not enter
the Land of Israel [Num. 14:29–38]; the First Temple was destroyed; The
Second Temple was destroyed; Betar, the last Jewish stronghold after the destruction
of Jerusalem, was conquered; and Jerusalem was plowed under [136 C.E.].*

—Mishnah, *Ta'anit* 4:6

Tzom Gedalyah (Fast of Gedalyah) is held on the day after the two days of Rosh
Hashanah and thus falls on the 3rd of Tishrei. After the Babylonian king
Nebuchadnezzar had destroyed the First Temple in Jerusalem, he appointed Gedalyah
ben Achikam, a righteous Jew, as governor over the Jews who were not exiled. But
Gedalyah was murdered by another Jew, who had been provoked into jealousy by a
neighboring king. The assassination destroyed any hope for Jewish self-government
and caused the remaining Jews to flee. We commemorate this day with a minor fast.

Asarah be-Tevet (literally, "10th of Tevet") commemorates the Babylonian siege of
Jerusalem in 586 B.C.E., which led to the subsequent capture and destruction of the
First Temple.[4] It is a minor fast day.

With a Heavy Heart

Three weeks elapse between the 17th of Tammuz (Shivah-Asar b'Tammuz) and
the 9th of Av (Tisha b'Av). Jews observe this time as a period of mourning

during which the holding of weddings and other joyous celebrations is customarily avoided.[5] On each Shabbat, one of the special "Haftarot (prophetic readings) of Admonition" is recited.[6] The string of 21 days links the beginning of calamity when the troops of King Nebuchadnezzar breached the walls of Jerusalem (an action that led to the destruction of First Temple) to the culmination of calamity—the date of destruction for each Temple. The time period is referred to as *bein ha-metzarim* (literally, "in the narrow places" or "between the straits"), derived from the verse in Lamentations, "All her pursuers overtook her in the narrow places" (1:3).[7] On the 1st of Av, the somber mood increases. The Mishnah states: "When Av enters, gladness must be diminished."[8]

During the final nine days of the three-week period, eating meat and drinking wine are prohibited (except on Shabbat). In addition, a range of stringencies are customary, which include restraints on cutting hair, bathing, and wearing of freshly laundered clothes.[9] These restrictions vary according to the stream of Judaism and to a person's familial background (whether Ashkenazic or Sephardic). Tisha b'Av itself, the culmination of the mournful three-week period, is generally understood to be the saddest day of the Jewish year, memorializing the destruction of the First and Second Temples. The Rabbis teach that the day was preordained by God as a day of mourning for the Jewish people. The declaration comes from an event recounted in the Book of Numbers. The Israelites have left Egypt and are sojourning in the desert. At God's direction, Moses sends an advance party to analyze the situation in the Land of Israel. When the scouts return, they report on a fertile land but one with formidable enemies and imply that it would be impossible for the Israelites to succeed.[10] This sin—a lack of faith in God—causes God to say that this generation of adult Israelites[11] is barred from entering the land. The Talmud provides God's response to the weeping of the Israelites, so easily discouraged and shaken from their faith by the spies' pessimistic report: "God said to them, 'You wept for no reason, and so I will set this day [Tisha b'Av] for you as a time of weeping throughout all the generations.'"[12]

Accordingly, tragedy after tragedy came down upon the Jews on Tisha b'Av, or at the least very close to that date. In the Bible, 2 Kings states that the First Temple was burned on the 7th of Av (25:8–9), and Jeremiah says the date was the 10th of Av (52:12). The Talmud, however, distinctly cites the 9th of Av as the day for the catastrophe, as well as many subsequent tragic events. History has recorded others. Among the most prominent are events on or noticeably close to Tisha b'Av in the following years:

- **1290.** King Edward I issued the edict expelling all the Jews from England;

- **1492.** King Ferdinand set Tisha b'Av as the final date by which all Jews would be expelled from Spain;

- **1914.** Great Britain and Russia declared war on Germany, and the unresolved issues of World War I ultimately led to World War II and the Holocaust;

- **1942.** The Treblinka concentration camp received and began to exterminate the first of 245,000 Jewish deportees from the Warsaw Ghetto;

- **1994.** The AMIA (Asociación Murual Israelita Argentina) building in Buenos Aires was bombed by unknown perpetrators—86 people died and 300 were wounded.[13]

Fasting and the Observance of Tisha b'Av

Tisha b'Av stands out as a unique fast day. On the one hand, work is permitted, as it is with most other public fasts. On the other hand, it shares many of the stringencies of the holy day of Yom Kippur, which go beyond fasting: no bathing or use of soaps, oils, and perfumes; no wearing leather shoes; and no engaging in marital relations.[14] These physical abstentions are regarded as a means for spiritual focus, to meditate on the meaning of the day and examine one's own sins.

The rules about fasting differ from those of Yom Kippur. On Tisha b'Av, a sick person is permitted to forgo fasting,[15] while on Yom Kippur, fasting is required unless it would be life-threatening. Tisha b'Av has an added stringency, however, beyond those of Yom Kippur. It is based on the verse in Psalms, "The precepts of the LORD are just, rejoicing the heart" (19:9). From this, the Rabbis interpreted that studying Torah brings joy; and, for Tisha b'Av, they prohibited studying sacred literature, with two exceptions: the Book of Job and parts of Rabbinic literature that tell of the destruction of Jerusalem.[16]

The fast of Tisha b'Av is preceded by a meal. Called *se'udah ha-mafseket* (the meal of separation), it actually begins the mourning process. We serve simple foods such as eggs; an egg symbolizes the circle of life. We specifically do not eat meat nor drink wine, activities associated with celebration.[17] Once the sun has set and Tisha b'Av officially begins, Jews gather to pray the evening service and chant sorrowful hymns called *kinot* about the destruction of the Temple.[18] After we finish the *Amidah*, the central prayer of every service that is recited silently while standing, we dim the lights and sit on the floor. Candles are lit for illumination during the chanting of Eikhah— the Book of Lamentations.[19] The melody is uniquely melancholy. In fact, the mood of the entire evening is subdued, appropriate to a house of mourning, where we do not express greetings to friends or engage in frivolous conversations.[20]

The next day, at morning prayers, we refrain from wearing *tallitot* and tefillin (prayer shawls and phylacteries), because they are interpreted as "beautifying ornaments" inappropriate for the mood of lament,[21] and we recite more *kinot*. By the afternoon, the sad mood of the day slowly transitions into one of consolation and comfort. This shift is based on the idea that destruction and sorrow should be followed by deliverance and salvation; indeed, one tradition maintains that the Messiah will be born on a Tisha b'Av and will become known[22] as the Messiah also on a Tisha b'Av.[23] Therefore, once we have completed half of the day, we are already moving toward redemption. During the afternoon prayer service, we may don *tallitot* and tefillin.[24] Furthermore, just as we read the *Haftarot* of Admonition during the weeks leading up to Tisha b'Av, once it is over, we read one of the seven *Haftarot* of Consolation each Shabbat until Rosh Hashanah.[25] Tisha b'Av is the turning point from despair into hope.

Eikhah

Eikhah (literally, "Alas"), the Book of Lamentations, is found in Kethuvim (The Writings), the third section of the Hebrew Bible. The Talmud refers to it as Kinot, meaning "Dirges" or "Elegies," a name that describes its contents: a collection of five poetic laments. Each specifically bemoans the Babylonians' destruction of the First Temple in 586 B.C.E. Yet, all told, with vivid imagery and emotional expressiveness, Eikhah evokes the collective, eternal sigh of anguish expressed by the Jewish people.

▲ ▲ ▲ ▲ ▲ ▲ ▲ ◆ ▲ ▲ ▲ ▲ ▲ ▲

Eikhah is filled with sorrowful responses to the lonely, desperate experience of a Jerusalem in ruins. Traditionally, the book is ascribed to the prophet Jeremiah based on the verse, "Jeremiah composed laments for Josiah … as is done to this day; they became customary in Israel and were incorporated into the laments" (2 Chron. 35:25).[26] True, Jeremiah was the prevailing prophet at the time of the Babylonian siege and conquest of Jerusalem. But in his epynonomous book, found in Nevi'im (The Prophets, the second part of the Bible), Jeremiah foresees the destruction of the city, which he deems warranted because of the spiritual and political failings of Judah.[27] In contrast, the author of Eikhah clearly expresses frustration about what has happened and regards God's punishment as having been especially severe.[28] This comparitive analysis has led some scholars to believe that it is impossible to establish the authorship of Eikhah and that the book is probably a collection of laments compiled shortly after the ruination of Jerusalem.

A Song of Despair

My eyes are spent
with tears,
My heart is in tumult,
My being melts away
Over the ruin of
my poor people,
As babes and
sucklings languish
In the squares of the city.
They keep asking
their mothers,
"Where is the
bread and wine?"
As they languish
like battle-wounded
In the squares of the town,
As their life runs out
In their mothers' bosoms.
—Lamentations 2:11–12

The poetry of Eikhah may be the most complex found in the Bible. It uses rare words and grammatical structures as well as abrupt shifts in thematic order. The first four chapters are alphabetical acrostics in which the verses begin with successive letters of the Hebrew alphabet (chapter 3 is a triple acrostic). This poetic device is not uncommon in the Bible or in Jewish liturgy (psalms 119 and 145, for example). Although the fifth and final chapter is not an acrostic, it is made up of 22 single-line stanzas, most likely representing the 22 letters of the Hebrew alphabet. Using the alphabet this way, the poet symbolically expresses his or her emotions in numerous ways, touching on everything "from *alef* to *tav*," or "A to Z," as the English expression would have it. To the poet, these letters are the building blocks of all verbal expression.

Eikhah is typically not studied or extensively discussed throughout the year, which makes our once-a-year encounter with it even more jarring and poignant. We slowly enter the synagogue without welcome on that one dark night of Tisha b'Av; we slump down and uncomfortably set our fasting bodies on the cold floor; we open the pages of the crying poet by candlelight, the words alive in tears; and we wrench our hearts with the phrases that resonate historically with much of the Jewish experience.

Observance Since Independence

Many Jews regard the establishment of the State of Israel in 1948 as a divine event that symbolizes the beginning of Jewish salvation. They wonder: Should the laws about Tish b'Av, the observance of the destruction of the ancient Jewish kingdom, be amended to recognize current events? For them, the answers vary. Those who are in the more Orthodox streams of Judaism retain the traditional, sunset-to-sunset customs. They reason that the Temple has not yet been reestablished, the disaporic exile has not ended, and the suffering of the past is still a weight that we feel. Full mourning practices are appropriate. In the more liberal streams of Judaism, however, authorities are divided on this issue. One school of thought suggests that the full day of fasting is unnecessary and the practice should conclude at midday. This school argues that the establishment of the State of Israel was a celebratory turning point in history. Thus an entire day of mourning would slight the significance of the nation that exists today. The other school of thought follows practices more similar to the Orthodox, albeit for different reasons. It argues that the traditional, complete fast should be upheld because the State of Israel, although a homeland for Jews, has yet to become truly secure or know lasting peace. In fact, according to this perspective, not only should Tisha b'Av remain in its traditional form but the other minor fasts should be compulsory for the same reason.

·✦—Tisha b'Av —✦·
Pathways Through the Sources

Jerusalem Talmud
Five Nights in a Grave

Tisha b'Av marks a change in the flow of the Jewish year. According to tradition, God ordained this day as one of destruction and suffering, based upon the Israelites' transgression in the desert: They believed the report of 10 spies sent to scout Canaan and thus showed lack of faith in God.[29] Once Tisha b'Av has passed, the mood gradually becomes more hopeful and comforting, a reestablishment of the relationship with God—beginning with Tu b'Av (a minor holiday six days later, on the 15th of Av) and spreading into the High Holy Days in the fall.

The following legend from the Jerusalem Talmud adds detail to what we know of the biblical experience that occurred during the time in the wilderness. It describes the sort of trepidation and pain associated with Tisha b'Av and the subsequent joy of the people who were fortunate enough to survive the events of that date. Today, such experiences are symbolized in our ritual observances.

> During all the years that Israel was in the wilderness, on the eve of every ninth of Av, Moses sent a herald throughout the camp to proclaim, "Go out and dig graves!" and the people went out and dug graves, in which they spent the night. In the morning, the herald went out and announced, "Let those who are still alive separate from the dead!" The living then stood up and found themselves some fifteen thousand short. [And so it continued year after year this way] until Israel was sixty myriads short. In the last of the forty years, they did the same thing, and upon finding that they were still alive, said: Perhaps we have erred in calculating the new moon [and have the wrong date for Tisha b'Av]. So, to make sure [that they had the right date], they did the same thing the night of the tenth, each one spending it in the grave he had dug. In the morning, all of them again stood up alive. Then, to make quite sure, they did the same thing the night of the eleventh, twelfth, thirteenth, fourteenth, and fifteenth of the month. Finally, when they saw that not one of them had died, they said: It appears that the Holy One has removed the harsh decree from over us. They declared that day

a festival. Accordingly, the sages taught: Israel had no days more festive than the fifteenth of Av and the Day of Atonement.[30]
—Jerusalem Talmud, *Ta'anit* 4:10, 69c

Midrash Rabbah
A Song out of the Rubble

The sages of the Rabbinic tradition repeatedly ask why God would allow the Temple and Jerusalem to be destroyed. The most common response references some fault of the Jews. But even those who believe that the destruction was punishment for sins committed do not see God as having completely abandoned the Jewish people. They see God as loving and characterized by boundless mercy, proven by the continuing existence of the Jews. The special covenant and relationship with God, forming a bond that God treasures, may be just as strong now as at any other time, even though the Jews are without the Temple.

Lamentations Rabbah is one of the volumes within *Midrash Rabbah* (Great Midrash), a series that expounds upon and further illustrates each book of the Torah as well as the five historical tales called *megillot* that are part of the Kethuvim section of the Bible.

> *A psalm [song] of Asaph.*
> *O God, heathens have entered Your domain, defiled Your holy temple, and turned Jerusalem into ruins* (Ps. 79:1).

> The verse should have said "A weeping of Asaph," "A sighing of Asaph," "A lament of Asaph." Why does it say "A psalm of Asaph"?

> This can be compared to a king who built a wedding canopy for his son, and had it beautifully plastered, inlaid and decorated. Then this son strayed off to an evil life. So the king came to the canopy, tore down the tapestries and broke the poles. Upon which the prince's tutor took a flute and began to play. Those who saw him, asked, "The king has overturned the canopy of his son, and you sing?" He replied, "I sing because the king vented his anger on the wedding canopy, and not upon his son."

> The same was said of Asaph, "God destroyed the Temple and Sanctuary, and you sing?" He replied, "I sing because God vented His wrath upon wood and stone, and did not vent His wrath upon Israel."
> —*Midrash Rabbah, Lamentations Rabbah* 4:15

Avot de-Rabbi Natan
The Heart of the World

In the Jewish tradition, Jerusalem is the epicenter of the world both physically and spiritually. It represents all of the most important virtues and principles upon which the entire world rests. For Jews, one might say: As Jerusalem goes, so goes the rest of the world.

Jerusalem embodies not only the positive attributes of the world, but also the suffering. This negative attribute deepens the symbolism of Jerusalem as the spiritual pulse of the world. It is as if the city and its people are tapped into an artery that leads directly to God's heart. Indeed, whether they live in the city itself or elsewhere in the country or in the Diaspora, Jews have a finger on the pulse of Jerusalem obtained by following the news, making pilgrimages, and practicing the holidays in accordance with the Hebrew calendar.

Many of us can attest to the truth of the following Rabbinic teaching. It comes from a book that is considered to be the homiletic companion to the better-known Pirkei Avot (literally, "Chapters of the Fathers"). Most scholars believe that *Avot de-Rabbi Natan* (literally, "Fathers of, or according to, Rabbi Nathan") was compiled sometime between 700 and 900 C.E.

> There are ten portions of beauty in the world:
> Nine in Jerusalem, one in the rest of the world.
> There are ten portions of suffering in the world:
> Nine in Jerusalem, one in the rest of the world.
> There are ten portions of wisdom in the world:
> Nine in Jerusalem, one in the rest of the world.
> There are ten portions of Torah in the world:
> Nine in Jerusalem, one in the rest of the world.[31]
> —*Avot de-Rabbi Natan*

Pirke de-Rabbi Eliezer
Full Circle

One of the deepest teachings in the Jewish tradition, especially Jewish mysticism, is that for a creation to happen there must be a prior destruction. In other words, space—whether it is physical or spiritual—must be opened for the new creation to grow. From this perspective, Judaism claims that the Messiah will come on Tisha b'Av, a day of destruction. Thus God planted the seed of the Messiah when the destruction happened; and we will see the world come full circle on that very day, when the seed blossoms and fulfills its intended purpose.

Modern scholars believe that *Pirke de-Rabbi Eliezer* (literally, "The Chapters of Rabbi Eliezer"), a book of narrative midrash or exposition on biblical stories, was likely written in the Land of Israel in the 8th century C.E.

> Abbaye said: "The Messiah will come only on the ninth of Av, which is set apart as our time for mourning, but which the Holy One will turn into a festive day, as is said, *They shall never languish again*" (Jer. 31:12).[32]
> —*Pirke de-Rabbi Eliezer* 28:3

The Zohar
Wrenched at the Hip

The Zohar (literally, "Illumination") is the central text of Jewish mysticism, which adheres to the premise that the greatest secrets lie hidden within the seemingly slightest details. In this case, the origin of Tisha b'Av as a preordained day for destruction can be found in the moment when the "Children of Jacob" become the "People of Israel." This collective identity comes from the alternate name of Jacob, who wrestled with an angel and was then given—by God—the name Israel ("he who wrestles with God"). The angel is understood by the Zohar to be Satan[33] (literally, "Opponent" or "Accuser") and is identified by the characteristics of being overly strict and judgmental. With this encounter between Jacob and the angel, the imprint of Tisha b'Av is made. The day acts as a sort of yearly reminder of our uniquely Jewish, spiritual imperfections.

> A person has 248 limbs corresponding to the 248 positive commandments [for which] the Torah requires [our taking] action to fulfill. These also correspond to the 248 angels that the *Shekhinah* clothes herself in. The names of these angels are like the name of their Master.

> A person also has 365 sinews and these correspond to the 365 negative commandments that one should not do, and corresponding to this are the 365 days of the year. And here we see that Tisha b'Av is one of these days and its corresponding angel is Satan [Samael, literally, "the poison of God"] who is one of the 365 angels.

This is the reason the Torah says, *The children of Israel to this day do not eat the thigh muscle that is on the socket of the hip, since Jacob's hip was wrenched at the thigh muscle* [by the angel Samael] (Gen. 32:33). [Note: The Hebrew for this sentence begins *Al ken lo yokhlu b'nei yisrael et gid ha-nasheh …*, but *et* has no equivalent in English and therefore no translation.]

The word *et* [*alef, tav*] comes to include the Tisha b'Av on which there is no eating [*lo yokhlu*]or drinking. [The text hints at this idea, because *et* is spelled *alef-tav*, and the initials of Tisha b'Av are the same letters in reverse, *tav-alef*].

On this day the power of Samael is increased, and the attribute of *din* (strict justice) was decreed upon us [causing a whole generation to die in the desert after they believed the report of the spies] and the Temple was destroyed. And so it is that anyone who eats on Tisha b'Av is considered as though he eats of the sciatic nerve.[34]
—The Zohar

Milton Steinberg
Ready for Exile

Tisha b'Av recalls the destruction of the physical center of Jewish spirituality and the subsequent dispersion of the Israelites. And yet, through thousands of years laden with catastrophe, the Jews as a people have survived. It may be impossible to totally discern how and why, yet we know there are aspects of Judaism that preserve Jewish identity no matter the place and time. Perhaps it was the wisdom and efforts of the early sages that provided Jews with the tools for survival, offering hope and inspiration even in the most despairing moments.

In this excerpt from *The Making of the Modern Jew: From the Second Temple to the State of Israel*, originally published in 1934, philosopher and author Rabbi Milton Steinberg (1903–1950, United States) discusses how Judaism has coped throughout history with the destruction of the Temple and with the subsequent Diaspora.

Time was when its [Israel's] existence was as normal as that of any other people. It occupied its own land, lived its own life and suffered vicissitudes of fortune such as inevitably befall any nation. It was unique only in that it had developed an individual culture and subscribed to an unusual theology and ethic. The crisis in its career, the shift from normality to eccentricity, began in 70 C.E. when, after the fall of Jerusalem, large bodies of Jews were transplanted to all parts of the Roman Empire.

History has played many a cruel trick on the Jew. It did him only one favor—it allowed him to prepare for his homelessness. By the time the eviction from Palestine was under way, the Jew had already evolved a technique of living as an unwelcome guest in other men's homes. Early in his history, he had become a skilled and inveterate alien .... For several centuries before and after the collapse of the Jewish state, Jewish scholars were engaged in this process of interpreting, expounding, amending and improving the Law of Moses .... By the time of the dispersion, this body of tradition was already in a highly developed form, the Jewish way of life under its influence had taken on definite, authoritative shape. The Jew carried from Palestine not only the Bible, but an interpretation of it which embraced a corpus of civil law, a sharply fixed ritual for synagogue and home, a clearly defined morality, and definitive forms of regulating every phase of life.[35]
—Milton Steinberg

·✦— Tisha b'Av —✦·
Interpretations of a Sacred Text

The text studied in these pages is from the first of the two Books of Kings. These books are found in a portion of the Bible called *Nevi'im Rishonim* (Former, or First, Prophets), which covers the history of the Israelites from their crossing the Jordan River into the Land of Israel until their exile into Babylonia after the destruction of the First Temple. In First Book of Kings, the narrative begins with the death of King David and focuses primarily upon the rule of Solomon and the subsequent civil war between his sons Rehoboam and Jeroboam.

THE THREE LEVELS
Peshat: simple, literal meaning
Derash: historical, rabbinical inquiry
Making It Personal: contemporary analysis and application

Heaven on Earth

When Solomon had finished building the House of the LORD and the royal palace and everything that Solomon had set his heart on constructing .... The LORD said to him, "[I] consecrate this House which you have built and I set my name there forever. My eyes and My heart shall ever be there.... [But] if you and your descendants turn away from Me and do not keep the commandments [and] the laws which I have set before you, and go and serve other gods and worship, then I will sweep Israel off the land which I gave them; I will reject the House which I have consecrated to My name .... And when they ask, 'Why did the LORD do thus to the land and to this House?' they shall be told, 'It is because they forsook the LORD their God who freed them from the land of Egypt, and they embraced other gods and worshiped them and served them; therefore the Lord has brought all this calamity upon them.'"
—I Kings 9:1–9

Peshat

When people ask why the Temple was destroyed, or why any other calamity has occurred, the classical answer is, "It was an act of divine justice." In other words, the Jews must endure exile and all the suffering that exile brings, because they are being punished for their sins. This biblical text shows that such a theological response is embedded in the Jewish mind-set; it is meant to inspire us to follow God's will in hope that doing so will lead to future redemption.

Derash

Rabbinic literature is replete with images of the beauty of Jerusalem and the Temple. The Talmud, compiled after the Roman conquest of Jersusalem and the destruction of the Second Temple in 70 C.E., clearly intends its readers to understand just what they missed. It says, "He who has not seen Jerusalem in her splendor has never seen a desirable city in his life. He who has not seen the Temple in its full construction has never seen a glorious building in his life."[36]

By portraying Jerusalem in such impressive terms, the Rabbis are not merely describing it as an ideal earthly capital. They are describing it as God's kingdom, a kingdom truly imbued with the sacred spirit of heaven.

This image is not meant to evoke a sense of mere guilt, but rather to motivate us to behave in a way that will restore God's kingdom on earth. In a sense, as we are punished and exiled, so is God. We bear the responsibility of having free will, and we must make our choices correctly. The Talmud, in tractate *Yoma,* seeks to convey moral lessons learned from the destruction of the Temple:

> Why was the First Temple destroyed? Because of three evil things that prevailed there: idolatry, immorality [illicit relations], and bloodshed …. But why was the Second Temple destroyed …? Because baseless hatred became rampant, which teaches you that baseless hatred is as grave as the three sins of idolatry, immorality, and bloodshed.[37]

Making It Personal

Perhaps the most profound teaching the Talmud shares about the destruction of the Temple comes in the talmudic tractate *Bava Metzia*[38] (literally, "Middle Gate") 30b:

> For Rabbi Yochanan* said, "Jerusalem was destroyed only because they gave judgments only in accordance with Torah law." Were they supposed to judge in accordance with untrained arbitrators! Rather say, "because they based their judgments strictly upon Torah law, and they did not go *lifnim mishurat ha-din* [beyond the letter of the law]."

Accordingly, for us to truly fulfill God's will we must go beyond the technical, written word of law; we must see and judge each other as complete, multifaceted individuals. We hope that God sees us in this way, which is also the way in which we recognize the divine image in one another. If we look upon each other with God's eyes and see beneath the surface, we will have the power to create heaven on earth.

---

* Rabbi Yochanan (c. 250–290 C.E.) was one of the leading sages of the Jerusalem Talmud and head of the renowned academy in Tiberias, in northern Israel.

·◆—Tisha b'Av —◆·
Significance of the Holiday: Some Modern Perspectives

The Place of Remembrance
by Michael Berenbaum

> By the rivers of Babylon,
> there we sat,
> sat and wept,
> as we thought of Zion
> —Psalms 137:1

With these words, the Psalmist reminds us that the place from which we remember an event shapes how the event is remembered. Place does this, even more than time.

We weep for different reasons. There are tears of sorrow, tears of joy, tears of exultation, and tears of frustration.

So permit me to grapple with Tisha b'Av and its contemporary meanings by recalling place and remembering the different tears that I shed as I remembered Zion, on what had been traditionally regarded as the saddest day in the Jewish calendar.

TISHA B'AV 5718 (1958), CONNECTICUT

Like many American Jews of my generation, my first serious encounter with Tisha b'Av came at summer camp, in my case Camp Ramah.[39] Because of the peculiarities of the Jewish calendar, the only holiday that occurs in the camping season is Tisha b'Av, and thus it becomes a centerpiece of the summer. There were many hours of preparation during the three weeks of mourning between the 17th of Tammuz and the 9th of Av. We were taught the laws of the holiday; and when we reached the nine days just before Tisha b'Av, our sense of enjoyment was diminished ever so slightly. Our classes and the new melodies we learned shaped our consciousness of the anguished moments in Jewish history. And then the evening itself arrived. Shoes were removed for sneakers; the lighting was dimmed and replaced by candles. From the choir came songs of sadness, *Ma'ariv* (the daily, evening prayer service) was recited, followed by chanting of the Book of Lamentations (Eikhah) with its haunting melody and the special trope for the 66 short, crisp verses of chapter 3. Silence was present, rather than chatter; softness rather than the loud voices of children at play. The entire atmosphere in the camp was transformed; and there was little reality from the outside world to intervene, to shatter the mood.

We experienced the rhythms of Tisha b'Av: heavy mourning in the evening; mourning of less intensity in the morning, but with benches still overturned and mourners not wearing tallit and tefillin; and a gradual lifting of the mourning as the day progressed. We were taught to think historically and to see that past, present, and future were related. We were taught to understand that the Jewish people have repeatedly faced defeat, lived in its aftermath (albeit in a diminished and weakened state), and been blessed with enough energy to endure and, ultimately, to be creative again. We were taught the rebukes of Jeremiah in the first part of Isaiah and the consolation of Jeremiah in the second part. We were taught to think about Jerusalem, the city so seemingly distant and not-of-this-earth, and about the Holocaust, 13 years in the past, but still fresh.

Since camp, Tisha b'Av has always loomed large on my calendar. Since camp (which coincided with my bar mitzvah), I have fasted and observed it seriously, although perhaps not with the intensity I experienced in camp. For in camp, the outside world did not interrupt; such was the power of camp and a prime reason for its effectiveness.

TISHA B'AV 5727 (1967), JERUSALEM

I belong to the generation that went to Israel for the 1967 war, the one that lasted only six days. In fact, I left for Jerusalem instead of going to my college graduation. The mood in the United States was bleak and the sense of looming catastrophe overwhelming. We left right before the war began, and we arrived on its second day. On June 7, the third day of the war, I was on a bus headed toward Jerusalem when the driver turned up the volume on the bus's radio. A spokesperson for the Israeli Defense Forces announced: "The Old City is ours." My friends and I had departed from the United States in sadness; in Israel, we experienced a historical exultation unlike any I have ever experienced before or since. On Shavuot, the Kotel (Western Wall) was made accessible to Jews for the first time since December 1947 when the Arab Legion gained control of the Old City.[40] Hundreds of thousands of Jews—from caftan-clad Hasidim to mini-skirted women—arrived as pilgrims and rejoiced to see the site of the destroyed Temple. We exulted in the unfamiliar glow of Jewish triumph, in what we sensed was the reversal of Jewish anguish. We had gone from Auschwitz to Jerusalem in one generation, from defeat to victory—so we thought, so we felt. The sixth day of the Six-Day War was Shabbat. Zalman Shazar, the president of Israel, spoke poetically and masterfully at student services: *Livshi bigdei tifartekh Yerushalayim* ("Wear the clothes of your majesty, Jerusalem").

That year Tisha b'Av felt different. The Book of Lamentations sounded joyous, defiant. Even as we heeded the Jewish laws about mourning, we glowed inwardly. We had experienced the majesty and mysterious attraction of Jerusalem. I paused at one verse (18) in chapter 5:

> Because of Mount Zion, which lies desolate;
> Jackals prowl over it.

I remembered the talmudic tale[41] of Rabbi Akiva and his friends walking by the site of the destroyed Temple. The other rabbis wept while Akiva remained merry. His reasoning? Because the first words of prophecy—the prophecy of rebuke—had been fulfilled, so, too, would the second promise be fulfilled, that of return: "There shall yet be old men and women in the squares of Jerusalem …" (Zech. 8:4).

I laughed as I read that verse. For here were a hundred thousand of the children of Zion, walking amid a thriving city that was no longer desolate, no longer forlorn. How does one speak of the destroyed Jerusalem when in the hills of Judah and the courtyards of Jerusalem the voices of joy and gladness, the voices of the bridegroom and the bride are being heard—when the Jewish people have returned? I fasted half a day; after *Mincha* there was a *seudah*, a meal not of famine but of joy.

TISHA B'AV 5736 (1976), KIEV

In the summer of 1976, I visited the Soviet Union for the first time. Like many Jewish activists of my generation, I was in the Soviet Union to meet with Refuseniks and, for an even more specific purpose, to continue arrangements for a conference on the topic of "Jewish studies" scheduled (clandestinely) for December. The trip was intense. In what may have been an amateurish (or perhaps actually effective) guise, we behaved as tourists during the day—seeing museums and monuments, visiting the sites of Kiev, Leningrad, Moscow, and Tallinn. In the evening we broke away from our group (travel to the Soviet Union in those days was always in groups) to go to phone booths to telephone our contacts. Then we traveled by cab or by subway to meet them, to deliver material, and to offer contact and support. We talked, sang songs together, worked on learning texts, and became friends, family. On Shabbat, we went to synagogue; but we spoke to the Refuseniks outside, not inside, where there were informers. We were in Kiev for Tisha b'Av. We associated Kiev with the slaughter at Babi Yar.[42] A visit to the site on Tisha b'Av was imperative; and there we met Russian Jews who were observing the solemn day by visiting the killing fields. In the words that were spoken that morning, the Jewishness of the victims was unmentioned; the Jewishness of the visitors was also unmentioned, but so apparent. My group had earlier gone to synagogue to recite the *kinot* (lengthy poems of sorrow) during the morning service. I came as any other Jew; and I sat unnoticed, unwelcomed—or so I thought. About three quarters of the way through the reading of *kinot*, I was asked to lead the congregation. Only once I started to read the lamentation did I realize why I had been invited to recite this particular one. It begins, *Tzion halo tishali l'shalom asirayikh,* "Zion, will you not ask of the fate of your captives." For the Russian Jews, the words of the poem's author, Rabbi Yehuda Ha-Levi, were an admonition; for me, they were a personal imperative. In my chanting those words, we all understood each other well.

That afternoon, we flew to St. Petersburg, then under its Communist name of Leningrad, where, because of the long summer days, daylight still prevailed at 10:30 or 11:00 P.M. On Tisha b'Av, the parameters of the length of the fast is based on actual location; and I learned to consider not only whether I had traveled into a different time zone but also the latitude of the city I was visiting. After meeting with Refuseniks, I went to synagogue and donned my tefillin for the afternoon and evening services of *Mincha* and *Ma'ariv.* The old Jews who were present asked if I would speak to them. The only language we had in common was Yiddish, a language that I understood but did not speak. But I did speak. For 30 minutes I managed to say everything that I wanted to say using my extremely limited vocabulary. Proud of my performance, I said with a tinge of apology, "You know, I have never spoken in Yiddish before."

A man in the back of the synagogue nodded his head and said sadly: "We know, we know." Although he was merely expressing his awareness that Yiddish was rapidly disappearing among Jewishly educated and observant American Jews, I was somewhat intimidated by his remarks. I have not spoken Yiddish since.

Tisha b'Av 5739 (1979), Krakow

Three years later, traveling with the President's Commission on the Holocaust, I made my first visit to Auschwitz on the 8th of Av. We had wanted to visit the extermination camp at Auschwitz-Birkenau on Tisha b'Av, but the planes between

Warsaw and Kiev would not cooperate. We simply could not visit Auschwitz on Tisha b'Av, then make a flight to Kiev for a visit we had planned, and manage to be in Moscow, our next stop, for Shabbat. So we decided on a different plan. We would visit Auschwitz on the 8th instead of the 9th of Av. Then we would go from Auschwitz to the city of Krakow, to the Remuh Synagogue, named after Rabbi Moses Isserles[43] (buried in the adjacent cemetery), in time to join the Jews of Krakow for Tisha b'Av services that would begin that night.

Anyone who has been to Auschwitz more than once knows that the first time is the most painful, the most difficult. Walking in Birkenau (the extermination camp within the Auschwitz complex), one is enveloped by the evil that befell the Jewish people. The presence of the killers can be felt—and the magnitude of their crime.

We arrived in synagogue shattered.

Meeting the remaining Jews of Krakow was perhaps even more shattering.

One Jew was blind and one was lame. One was without legs and the other without arms. One seemed mentally disturbed; and another, who was not disturbed, was disturbing to us by the very appearance of normality in the midst of everything. The synagogue smelled, and the books were tattered and not cataloged. It felt like we were arriving after the *Hurban* (literally, "the Destruction"), the fall of the Temple in Jerusalem. The scene was all too appropriate for Tisha b'Av.

That particular evening resonates with me now in a 1979 fable written by Yaffa Eliach,[44] which she included in her 1988 book *Hasidic Tales of the Holocaust*. In it, the character[45] Miles Lerman challenges God to a *din Torah* (literally, "judgment of Torah") to bring God to justice. Lerman, a partisan fighter during the Shoah, lost much of his family in Poland. His mother and sister and her children were murdered at Belzec, and his wife, whom he met after the war, had been imprisoned at Auchwitz-Birkenau. This is his first journey back to Poland, and he is profoundly shaken. He pours out his heart, but the final commentary on his memorable speech is given by an old Jew. "A *din Torah* with God? Here there is no God. God doesn't live here anymore."

For me, the paradox of the evening came in the fifth chapter of Lamentations:

> Remember, O LORD, what has befallen us;
> Behold, and see our disgrace!
> Our heritage has passed to aliens,
> Our homes to strangers.
> We have become orphans, fatherless;
> Our mothers are like widows. …
>
> Gone is the joy of our hearts;
> Our dancing is turned into mourning.
> The crown has fallen from our head; …
>
> Because of this our hearts are sick,
> Because of these our eyes are dimmed:
> Because of Mount Zion, which lies desolate;
> Jackals prowl over it. (verses 1–3, 15–18)

I wondered as the author of Lamentations had:

> Why have your forgotten us utterly,
> Forsaken us for all time? …
>
> For truly, You have rejected us,
> Bitterly raged against us (verses 20, 22).

The tradition requires that one not end with despair but with hope. It mandates that the Book of Lamentations end with a repetition of verse 21:

> Take us back, O LORD, to Yourself,
> And let us come back;
> Renew our days as of old!

That evening there could be no renewal, merely abandonment. I simply could not recite the words of return aloud.

▲   ▲   ▲   ▲   ▲   ▲   ▲   ▲   ◆   ▲   ▲   ▲   ▲   ▲   ▲   ▲

TISHA B'AV IN THE HERE AND NOW

From the place where we are today, how should we approach Tisha b'Av?

First of all, we must mark the day, embrace the day, and find a means to engage the past and to encounter the present and the future. We can read the Book of Lamentations from a new perspective and see that because of the unfolding of events, the ancient text has the capacity to speak to contemporary Jews in ways that the tradition may never have contemplated. Sometimes, by contrasting the pain described in the book with the many blessings Jews enjoy today—especially in Israel and in the United States—we become acutely conscious of and grateful for what has been accomplished. At other times, we think about the days of old, categorized by defeat and catastrophe, exile and anguish; and we see the link to today—to our current fears, suffering, and losses. But always after the 9th of Av comes the 10th; and we struggle to live, to endure, and to overcome our pain in the aftermath of tragedy.

Tu b'Av: Coming Back to Life

by Paul Steinberg

Less than a week after Tisha b'Av, the saddest day of the Jewish year, is Tu b'Av, one of the happiest days of the Jewish year. Tu b'Av (literally, the 15th of Av in the Hebrew calendar) remains a little-known holiday in the Diaspora but is gaining popularity in modern Israel. It was certainly a popular and festive day during the era of the Second Temple. Falling in the heat of August, Tu b'Av was historically the Jewish "Lover's Day," a day when, according to the Mishnah, young people would go out dancing in the vineyards to find romance.[46] Everyone was invited to participate, regardless of social status; and the girls—even the most wealthy—were all wearing white clothes that had been borrowed, so that no one would feel embarrassed about being the one in need.[47] From this particular aspect of the holiday, we learn that one should not judge prospective mates on the basis of beauty or wealth, but on what is in their hearts.

The Rabbinic sages of the Talmud offer a number of reasons for celebrating Tu b'Av.[48] One builds upon the role of the proximate fast day Tisha b'Av, which already marks a transition point on the calendar. By the time we have reached Tisha b'Av, the joyous flavor of Passover has long since shifted into a solemn and sad mood. Tisha b'Av itself embodies sadness as we remember times of destruction and death. Yet once Tisha b'Av passes, we begin to look forward to the sense of renewal that will come in the fall with Rosh Hashanah, the "birthday of the world," a time of hope and relative contentment.

The Rabbis understood Tisha b'Av to be a preordained day of destruction, rooted in the fearful report given by the 10 spies in the Book of Numbers. The spies' lack of faith led to God's punishment: God refused to allow the entire generation that had left Egypt (with the exception of the 11th and 12th spies, Joshua and Caleb, who gave optimistic reports) to enter the Land of Israel. Not until that generation had died off, which would take decades, would their descendants cross the Jordan River. God says, "*In this very wilderness shall your carcasses drop. Of all of you who … have muttered against Me, not one shall enter the land in which I swore to settle you …*" (Num. 14:29–30). *Midrash Rabbah* tells that each Tisha b'Av during the 40 years in the desert, 15,000 Israelites died (¹⁄₄₀ of the 600,000 adult males referenced in the Torah).[49] The Israelites subjected to this decree[50] would actually anticipate this dreadful day by digging their own graves on the 8th of Av and sleeping in them each night from the 9th to the 14th. Should they be among those to die during any of the nights from the 9th through the 14th of Av, their burial would be easier on the survivors because the deceased would already be in their graves. On the 15th of Av (Tu b'Av), the survivors felt confident that the dying was over and they could go home to bed. Thus that day became marked as one of celebration.

Another reason for the tradition of celebration on Tu b'Av goes back to its having been the only day when intertribal marriage was permitted. The biblical books of Numbers and Judges have passages that say an Israelite may only marry an Israelite from within the same tribe.[51] The Rabbis of the Talmud recognized the hardship of this limitation and granted relief on Tu b'Av, making it the one day of the year when the ban was lifted and people could marry outside their own tribes. Later, through various interpretations and inferences, the Rabbis went much further, deciding that this particular ban was intended only for the generation that originally inherited the Land of Israel and not for all Jews in all times.[52] The sages completely repealed the ban, and that action, the Talmud says, was taken on Tu b'Av. From then on, intertribal marriage was permitted on any day that marriage itself was permitted.[53]

A non-Rabbinic rationale for Tu b'Av is found in Nogah Hareuveni's 1980 book, *Nature in Our Biblical Heritage*.[54] She writes that our agrarian ancestors found meaning in the season and date for celebrating Tu b'Av, as do people living today on Israel's reinvigorated land. Around the time of the full moon in early to mid-August, just when Tu b'Av falls, the large, white squill flowers begin to blossom all over Israel. This flower has a special place in Middle Eastern folklore because, Hareuveni writes, its bloom coincides with "the season in which morning mists gather, clouds appear in the sky and once again farmers begin to be concerned with the amount and distribution of rainfall in the coming year." Moreover, it is the time when the olives on the tree begin to fill with oil. Hareuveni writes that white squill flowers emerge from their large bulbs on what the farmers call "olive day." Arab olive growers say that if you take "an olive between your fingers on the day the white squill blossoms, you will be able to squeeze oil from it. Before that there is no oil."[55] Tu b'Av is a natural turning point in the season, although such markers go unnoticed in the Diaspora and in urban areas of Israel.

Hareuveni gives a naturalistic rationale for the description in the Mishnah of the young women wearing white. She makes a symbolic connection to the blossoming of the white squills; and she interprets the "vineyards" where the women danced as being olive groves, which, by virtue of their height and spacing, would offer more privacy and room for dancing than the lowness and density of grapevines.

Hareuveni also offers a seasonal explanation for another comment in the Mishnah, this one based on the comments of Rabban Shimon ben Gamliel,[56] who says that Tu b'Av and Yom Kippur are two of the year's most festive days. What is the connection between these seemingly unrelated holidays? According to Hareuveni, if Tu b'Av marks the opening of the olive season, Yom Kippur, seven weeks later, marks its end. The olives are harvested around the time of Sukkot (the fall harvest festival), which falls just five days after Yom Kippur. Hareuveni says that the Mishnah describes Yom Kippur as a time of joy because the olive crop, which began ripening on Tu b'Av, has flourished. For us today, considering the totally solemn character of Yom Kippur, it is difficult to envision that during the times of the Temple, this day may have had a lighthearted component amid all the otherwise serious elements.

Because Tu b'Av had no significance beyond agriculture and the issue of intertribal marriage, it was forgotten after the destruction of the Second Temple and as the Jews scattered in the Diaspora. Yom Kippur, on the other hand, imbued with the profound elements of communal and personal forgiveness, remained one of the most important days of the Jewish year. Following the establishment of the State of Israel and the tremendous interest in making the land productive again, some people there have developed a renewed interest in Tu b'Av. They have reintroduced the ancient customs, such as wearing white, giving flowers, and dancing; and some even choose Tu b'Av as a wedding day. People continue to look for opportunities to express their spiritual relationship to the land, the land of which they had long been deprived. Whereas Tisha b'Av commemorates the destruction of the Temple and the beginning of the Diaspora—a loss of sovereignty—Tu b'Av represents the reacquisition of the beloved land and the regaining of that sovereignty.

·✦— Tisha b'Av —✦·
An Alternative Meditation

When the Walls Come Down[57]

by Alan Lew

Exactly seven weeks before Rosh Hashanah, we mark the turn toward Teshuvah—repentance or return—with the observance of Tisha B'Av. Tisha b'Av is the beginning of Teshuvah, the point of turning toward this process by turning toward a recognition of our estrangement from God, from ourselves, and from others. Yom Kippur is the culmination of the process that begins on Tisha b'Av, when we acknowledge the darkness, when we let our guard down, when we turn toward the truth.

The natural event connected to Tisha b'Av is the height of summer, the fullness of the year. Six days later, on the fifteenth of Av, the summer actually reaches its peak and begins to decline; the sap in the trees reaches its full strength and begins to turn toward dryness. The days reach their full length and begin to shorten. Fullness and decline are intimately linked. The end of one is the beginning of the other. Conversely the decline and destruction necessarily precede renewal; tearing down is necessary before rebuilding is possible. And all these things—fullness, decline, destruction, renewal, tearing down, rebuilding—are actually part of the same process, points on a single continuum, consecutive segments of a never-ending circle.

The time between Tisha b'Av and Yom Kippur, this great seven-week time of turning, is the time between the destruction of Jerusalem—the crumbling of the walls of the Great Temple—and our own moral and spiritual reconstruction. The year has been building itself up, and now it begins to let go—the natural cycle of the cosmos, the rise and fall, the impermanence and the continuity, all express themselves in this turning. The walls come down and suddenly we can see, suddenly we recognize the nature of our estrangement from God, and this recognition is the beginning of our reconciliation. We can see the image of the falling Temple—the burning house—that Tisha b'Av urges upon us so forcefully, precisely in this light.

One of the extraordinary things about the Torah is the amount of time and space it devotes to the physical details of the sanctuary in the wilderness, the Great Tabernacle, the prototype for the Great Temple of Jerusalem. Almost half the Book of Exodus—the last five weekly Torah portions of this book—is given over to a minute and repetitive description of this structure. This schema is repeated as the Children of Israel gather the necessary materials to build it, then repeated as they begin to execute the design, and then finally repeated one more time as the erection of the Tabernacle is completed. The classical commentators, who are rarely at a loss for words, make a few forced symbolic interpretations of these structural details and then fall silent as they are repeated over and over. Page after page goes by without any commentary at all, a happenstance replicated nowhere else in the Torah. The point seems to be that the Torah is neither trying to teach nor to tell us anything. Rather, it seems interested in simply engraving the image of the Tabernacle in our psyches, as if it were spiritually important to have this image there; as if there were something in the structure of the Tabernacle we need to impose on our own inner structure, as if we need to bring our own inner life into harmony with this design.

It has occurred to me in recent years that the Jewish calendar year does the same thing with another image, and that is the image of the fall of the Temple. It does this through a series of public fasts. On the fifteenth of Tevet, [a month] which falls in late November and December, we fast in memory of the beginning of the siege of Jerusalem. On the seventeenth of Tammuz, a midsummer month, we fast in memory of the breaching of the walls of the city of Jerusalem, toward the end of this siege. Exactly three weeks later, on the ninth of Av (Tisha B'Av), we observe a major fast— the longest and most difficult fast of the year—to remember the fall of Jerusalem and the destruction of the Temple. Then, seven weeks later, and one day after Rosh Hashanah, we observe the Fast of Gedalyah. Gedalyah was the Jewish governor who presided over Israel after it had been conquered by the Babylonians. He was assassinated by Jewish zealots—disgruntled Jewish monarchists—and after his death, the Jews were cleaned out of the land of Israel and shipped off to a Babylonian exile. So the Fast of Gedalyah marks the beginning of the Jewish Diaspora—the exile.

This image, this series of fasts, tells our bodies and our souls the story of the encroachment of emptiness: the story of impermanence. There was a Great Temple, a great nation with its capital in Jerusalem, but even such seemingly unshakable institutions as these slipped away into the mists of history. Yet even while it stood, the Great Temple was a structure that was centered around emptiness. The Holy of Holies, the Sacred Center upon which all the elaborate structural elegance of the Temple served to focus, was primarily a vacated space. It was defined that way in the Torah. The Holy of Holies was the space no one could enter except the high priest, and even he could only enter for a few moments on

Yom Kippur. If anyone else entered this place, or if the high priest entered on any other day, the charged emptiness at the Sacred Center, the powerful nothingness there, would break out on him and overwhelm him, and he would die. So Yom Kippur is, among other things, the day we enter the vacated space, even if only by proxy, the day we experience the charged emptiness at the Sacred Center.

On Tisha b'Av it is as if this emptiness has broken loose from its bounds and swallowed everything up. The Temple burns. The emptiness once confined to the center of the Temple now characterizes it completely.

This image touches us deeply because we are always under siege, and we are held there by our attempts to hold off the emptiness we intuit at the center of our lives. In *The Denial of Death*, Ernest Becker observed that while all sentient beings die, we humans are the only ones who know that we will die. All of our lives, according to Becker, are an accommodation to this dreaded intelligence. Terrified of this emptiness, seeing it as utter negation, we fill our lives with stuff. Against the ultimate negation, we strive for success. Against the hard information that we came from nothing and end there as well, against the resulting suspicion that we might, in fact, be nothing all the while, we struggle mightily to construct an identity, but we're never quite persuaded by it. Some deep instincts keep whispering to us that it isn't real, and the walls keep falling down, and then the city finally collapses, and the idenity we have been laboring so desperately to shore up collapses along with it. . . .

We spend a great deal of time and energy propping up our identity, an identity we realize at bottom is really a construct. So it is that we are always living at some distance from ourselves. We live in a fearful state of siege, trying to prop up an identity that keeps crumbling, that we secretly intuit to be empty. Then Tisha b'Av comes and the walls begin to crumble, and then the entire city collapses. But something persists—something fundamentally nameless and empty, something that remains when all else has fallen away.

Something remained when the Temple was destroyed two thousand years ago. This was perhaps the most significant turning point in Jewish history. Judaism continued without the Temple, an inconceivable possibility at the time. But the truth is that if the Temple had never been destroyed, the renewal Judaism needed so badly could never have taken place. If the walls of the Temple had never fallen down, the fundamental spiritual impulse of Judaism—the powerful emptiness at its core—may very well have been smothered. . . .

Life bets that we won't be willing to endure the suffering it requires. Life bets that we will try to shut out the suffering, and so shut out life in the bargain. Tisha B'Av slides up to us, whispering conspiratorially with a racing form over its mouth. Tisha b'Av has a hot tip for us: Take the suffering. Take the loss. Turn toward it. Embrace it. Let the walls come down....

What might we see as a result? What wellspring would suddenly become apparent to us? What pattern would we see ourselves repeating? What larger gesture would we see about to complete itself in our lives? What do we need to embrace?

The walls of our soul begin to crumble and the first glimmerings of transformation—of Teshuvah—begin to seep in. We turn and stop looking from beyond ourselves. We stop defending ourselves. We stop blaming bad luck and circumstances and other people for our difficulties. We turn in and let the walls fall.

Our suffering, the unresolved element of our lives, is also from God. It is the instrument by which we are carried back to God, not something to be defended against, but rather to be embraced. And this embrace begins here on Tisha B'Av, seven weeks before Rosh Hashanah, so that by the Ten Days of Teshuvah, we are ready for transformation. We can enter the present moment of our lives and consciously alter that moment. We can end our exile.

We can step outside our walls and feel the full force of the great tidal pulls on our body and our soul; sun and moon, inhale and exhale, life and death, the walls building up and the walls crumbling down again.

PART 6

Guidance along the Way

Study it and review it: You will find everything in it.
Scrutinize it, grow old and gray in it, do not depart from it:
There is no better portion in life than this.

—Mishnah, *Avot* 5:24

The Spirit of Learning

WESTERN SOCIETY HAS DEVELOPED a philosophy of education built on practical and pragmatic principles. Academic success is viewed as the most direct route to financial success; that is to say, acceptance to a good school translates into the acquisition of a good (meaning lucrative) job. Scholarship also often leads to specialization and thus marketability. Moreover, according to this view, such academic success may even lead to social success, through experience in certain kinds of conversation and practice in gaining acceptance from different interest groups, particularly the upper class. Indeed, "networking" is now a well-known word, even a highly regarded talent. Statistical evidence undoubtedly exists to support the claims of this educational philosophy—a success system that has Jews among its chief beneficiaries, especially in the United States. Judaism, however—it is good to remember—has constructed its educational philosophy on the grounds of what is less measurable than the rewards found in the secular world, that is, the rewards of spiritual success.

The spiritual significance of education in Judaism, particularly the study of Torah and of Rabbinic texts, developed after the destruction of Jerusalem and the Temple in 70 C.E. Until then, sacrifices in the Temple were understood to be the most direct and efficient manner of reaching out to God. The Temple served as the mechanism Jews used to communicate gratitude and hope, and to confess guilt. It was a place where participation and the expression of devotion enabled Jews to reflect upon their own communal and personal lives. The experience of the Temple lent them a tangible representation of both their spiritual and moral disposition. Once the building was laid to ruins, the Rabbinic sages were compelled to ensure Jewish survival by cultivating an equivalent alternative. Whether conceived by an act of divine providence or by one of human invention, the new practices of study and scholarship became the path away from the despair about what had happened—a path that led to a renewed relationship with God. In the end, as the Talmud tells us, these new traditions were even more valuable than sacrifices![1]

The Rabbis saturated their literature with the importance of study. Study became such a core value that one's entire spiritual destiny rested upon it.[2] The condition of the soul itself, whether of the rich or the poor, the young or the old, the infirm or the well, came to depend upon scholarly dedication.[3] Furthermore, the Rabbis encouraged Jews to integrate scholarship into their social structure, such that a resident scholar and a schoolhouse were among the hallmarks of a viable Jewish community.[4] Eventually Jewish scholarship, especially when conducted with no intention of material reward, became the preeminent path to encountering the Divine and fulfilling God's intention for the Jewish people.[5] Rabbi Yochanan ben Zakkai, a survivor of the 70 C.E. destruction of the Temple and the founder of the new academy in Yavneh[6] (near the Mediterranean Coast) put it succinctly in one of his favorite teachings: "If you have studied much Torah, take no special credit for it, since you were created for this very purpose."[7]

However, we must ask what the Rabbis meant by this idea. How is study a way to commune with the Divine? Why is the study of Torah (meaning all Jewish law and learning) greater than all of the other mitzvot (commandments) put together? What is it exactly about study that offers us such spiritual growth?

Study is meant to inspire questions. Learning has the power to stir something deep within us, something that is already there, percolating and waiting to rise to the top. We each have an unquenchable fire within us, and it is from the sparks of that fire that questions are born, grow, and then ascend to our consciousness, messengers to the intellect from the soul. There is, after all, a satisfaction gained from "coming up" with a good question; we are affirmed by acknowledging that fire within, that fire that burns but does not consume.

When we identify a question that comes from within, we are motivated to seek out the answer. The terms *midrash* and *derash* (from the Hebrew root *dalet.resh.shin.*, meaning "to search") arise from this place. What are we seeking? Truth. And if we discover something in our search, even if it is not the complete answer—just a kernel of truth that we can carry with us—there is no better affirmation of the spirit. We are imbued with a greater sense of self, more self-esteem and self-knowledge. This seeking and finding does not lead to overconfidence and pridefulness, but to a course of personal healing and growth. Once this learning process is complete, we are given a newfound appreciation for life and all of its complexities.

In their immense wisdom, the Rabbis realized that study provokes questions, which are fuel for the development and evolution of the spirit. And questions are the most tangible way of evaluating whether or not we care about something. Not asking questions is a sign that we do not care, and not caring is a sign of the decay of the soul.

Torah and Rabbinic literature abound in questions. There are so many questions to be asked that we are able to generate new ones with each encounter. Because the subject of these texts is life and the human purpose on earth, the possibility of discovery is endless and, in fact, often requires study of other disciplines, such as history, science, and philosophy for arriving at the truth.

The scholars and sages from 70 C.E. to the present day—the devoted teachers who inherited, advanced, and transmitted Judaism—have prominent voices and respect in our tradition because they raised good questions. They are our luminaries, lucid in their thought; they took their questions seriously, sought out answers, and posited them responsibly.

The Torah as the "tree of life" and the Rabbinic expositions as the "garden" that surrounds it, bind the Jewish people together from the ends of the earth. In our lifelong commitment to study, we unearth our spiritual history, while, at the same time, we explore our spiritual destiny. The study of our tradition stokes the internal fire within each of us, which extends all the way to heaven and also touches every Jew who has ever been and who ever will be. In this way, we congregate at Sinai over and over again throughout time.

Exploring Traditional Sources

Judaism is a religious tradition that is text centered—it places great value on the study of texts and their commentaries. It asserts a fundamental assumption that the text offers us something inherently beneficial, and as recipients, we are welcome to not simply read the text but to interact with it. There is something both humbling and empowering about such an assumption, as the following teaching from the Mishnah expresses:

Rabbi Meir[8] taught: Whoever engages in the study of Torah for its own sake (Torah lishmah) *achieves a host of merits; moreover, it was worth creating the world for his sake alone .... Torah clothes him with humility and reverence, it equips him to be righteous, saintly, upright, and faithful .... It endows him with sovereignty, with authority, with power of keen judgment ....*[9]

On the one hand, when studying texts, we are humble in our acceptance of the notion that there is something for us to gain from and learn. In addition, the ideal form of study is described by Rabbi Meir as being "for its own sake" and not for any self-aggrandizement or reward; in fact, the Mishnah implies that the goal of study is only to become more humble. On the other hand, the emphasis on the study of texts empowers the intellect. Through knowledge we gain confidence and a sense of authority—a likely result of recognizing our own self-worth through the process of the study itself. Beyond those two experiences, the gaining of humility and of authority, the study of texts is inherently inspirational. It requires the best of our efforts—interpretive and critical—to unearth the true beauty and significance of the text.

The study of texts is therefore a balancing act—gaining knowledge and merit without becoming bigheaded, always knowing there is another text to learn (and a person who knows more than we do). No matter how high our academic standing, it is assumed that a text contains something new and useful, if we only dig deeply enough, or if we have the right teacher to guide us through the layers. In Judaism we find there are innumerable resources from whom to learn and texts from which we can draw intellectual and spiritual enrichment. Our teachers are the famous and lesser-known sages, rabbis, and scholars of the past, as well as the contemporary educational and spiritual leaders who heighten and deepen our understanding.

Abarbanel, Don Yitzchak

(b. 1437–d. 1508, Portugal, Spain, and Italy) One of the great Bible commentators and philosophers. A very influential political leader, Abarbanel served as treasurer for King Alfonso V of Portugal and later as minister of finance for Ferdinand and Isabella of Spain. Despite his strong influence upon the monarchy, he could not prevent the onset of the Spanish Inquisition and the expulsion of Jews in 1492. He fled to Italy where he continued to write commentaries on *Avot*, the Passover haggadah, and Maimonides' *Guide of the Perplexed*. His work helped strengthen the spirits of the exiled Jews.

Apocrypha

(literally, "Hidden Writings" in Greek) A collection of books that is part of Jerome's Vulgate translation of the Christian Bible but not part of the Hebrew Bible (TANAKH). All 15 books are now canonized except for Prayer of Manasseh and I and 2 Esdras, which are a part of the Christian Bible appendix. The Apocrypha was a part of the Greek Bible used by Jews in Egypt, and today scholars question why these books did not become part of the TANAKH. Most scholars say that they were written too late to be included and that 2 Maccabees and Wisdom of Solomon were composed in Greek rather than Hebrew. Among the titles included in the Apocrypha are I Maccabees, Ben Sira, Tobit, Judith, Baruch, Susanna, and Bel and the Dragon.

Arukh Ha-Shulchan

(literally, "Laying the Table") A comprehensive code of Jewish law compiled by Rabbi Yechiel Michel Halevi Epstein (b. 1835–d. 1905, Russia). This code attempts to update the Shulchan Arukh (literally, "Set Table") by Joseph Karo and claims to be the final authority on many customs.

Avot de-Rabbi Natan

(literally, "Chapters of Rabbi Nathan") A collection of Rabbinic material considered to be the homiletic companion to the Mishnah's Pirkei Avot (literally, "Chapters of the Fathers"). Rabbi Natan lived in the 2nd century C.E., a generation before the development of the Mishnah and is, therefore, not likely the author, although his name does appear in the opening chapter. Most scholars believe the collection was compiled between 700 and 900 C.E. It is generally located at the back of the tractate *Nezikin* (literally, "Damages") in the Talmud, among what is known as the minor (extracanonical) tractates. *Avot de-Rabbi Natan* consists largely of maxims, with long commentaries, that give advice on life, including common courtesy and the proper approach to Torah study. In 1887, Solomon Schechter (b. 1847–d. 1915, Romania, England, and United States) published the first-ever critical edition of a Rabbinic work, wherein he proposed the existence of two distinct, though similar, versions of this text, designated as Version A and Version B. The two versions offer different perspectives on certain stories and sayings, and each includes material not found in the other. Other scholars, who later found additional manuscripts, have suggested that more than two versions of *Avot de-Rabbi Natan* may exist.

Bible See TANAKH.

Buber, Martin

(b. 1878–d. 1965, Austria) Renowned religious philosopher. His translations and organization of Hasidic parables and anecdotes, such as *The Legend of the Baal Shem Tov*, *The Tales of Rabbi Nachman*, and *Tales of the Hasidim*, helped introduce the Western world to Eastern European Jewry. His greatest philosophical discourse is the book *I and Thou*.

Buber, Solomon

(b. 1827–d. 1906, Russia) Scholar, editor, independent researcher, bank employee, and philanthropist. He lived in Lemberg, now Lviv, in Ukraine. Buber was particularly interested in midrash, to which he devoted a very high level of systematic research.

Chaye Adam

A commentary written by Rabbi Avraham Danzig (b. 1748–d. 1820, Poland) on *Orach Chayyim* (matters of daily Jewish life) of the Shulchan Arukh. Danzig is also famous for his commentary on the laws of kashrut from *Yoreh De'ah* of the Shulchan Arukh, called *Chokhmat Adam*.

Gemara

Usually referred to as the Talmud, even though this description is technically erroneous. Written in Aramaic, the Gemara (literally, "Learning") is the discussion of and commentary on the laws of the Mishnah by the Rabbinic sages of the 2nd through 5th centuries C.E., who are known as *amoraim*. In their explanation and elucidation of the Mishnah, the *amoraim* draw from other sources including the Midrash, the Tosefta, and postbiblical works (e.g., *Ben Sira*, a.k.a. *Ecclesiasticus*). Two 5th-century Babylonian sages, Ravina and Rav Ashi, have traditionally been given credit for finalizing the Gemara; modern scholars believe that it did not reach its present form until the end of the 7th century.

Guide of the Perplexed See Maimonides.

Hartman, David

(b. 1931, United States and Israel) Founder and director of the Shalom Hartman Institute in Jerusalem, which conducts research into the study and teaching of classical Jewish sources and contemporary issues of Israeli society, Jewish life, and religious pluralism. Ordained by Yeshiva University in New York City, Hartman is a leading philosopher and internationally renowned author. He is a two-time recipient of the National Jewish Book Award, which he won for *A Living Covenant: The Innovative Spirit in Traditional Judaism* and for *Maimonides: Torah and Philosophic Quest*. His other publications include *A Heart of Many Rooms: Celebrating the Many Voices within Judaism*; *Israelis and the Jewish Tradition: An Ancient People Debating Its Future*; and *Love and Terror in the God Encounter: The Theological Legacy of Joseph B. Soloveitchik*. He was a professor of Jewish thought for more than two decades at Hebrew University of Jerusalem and has served as an advisor to Israel's minister of education and several of its prime ministers.

Heschel, Abraham Joshua

(b. 1907–d. 1972, Poland, Germany, and United States) One of the most prominent and most widely quoted Jewish religious philosophers in the modern era. Born in Warsaw, he was descended from Hasidic dynasties on both sides of his family. He studied Talmud in the school for *Wissenschaft des Judentums* (Science of Judaism) in Germany and philosophy at Berlin University. With the rise of Nazism, he was brought to the United States as a teacher by the Hebrew Union College. Later he was a professor of Jewish ethics and mysticism at the Jewish Theological Seminary. He is known for having been extremely active in the civil rights movement and for having served as a leader in the Jewish–Christian interfaith movement. His best-known books are on theology and include *The Sabbath*, *God in Search of Man*, and *Man Is Not Alone*.

Hirsch, Samson Raphael

(b. 1808–d. 1888, Germany) The father of contemporary Orthodox Judaism and one of the preeminent rabbis, preachers, and philosophers in Jewish history. His writings often reflect his strong opposition to the current of Reform Judaism and modernization that swept through Western Europe, especially Germany, during his lifetime.

Ibn Ezra, Avraham

(b. 1089–d. 1164, Spain) A poet, grammarian, and astronomer, known best for his commentary on most of the Tanakh. His commentary is unique in its grammatical analysis and independent ideas. After his son converted to Islam in 1140, Ibn Ezra went into self-chosen exile, traveling through North Africa and Europe.

Isserles, Moses

(b. circa 1525–d. 1572, Poland) One of the outstanding *posekim* (rabbinical descisors).

He was an authority on Kabbalah, philosophy, astronomy, and history. Among his best-known work is the *Mapa* (see Shulchan Arukh) and *Darkhei Moshe*, his commentary on the *Tur.* Isserles was called Rema or Rama, two acronyms of his name.

Jerusalem Talmud See Talmud.

Jubilees

A book in the postbiblical Jewish literature known as the Pseudepigrapha. It retells and expands upon much of Genesis and Exodus and falsely claims to be the hidden revelation of Moses. (However, the ancient community at Qumran, where the Dead Sea Scrolls were found, considered it to be authoritative.) The book is called "Jubilees" because of its concern with cycles of time.

Karo, Joseph See Shulchan Arukh.

Kethuvim

(literally, "Writings") The third of the three sections of the TANAKH. It was the last to be canonized and consists of Psalms, Proverbs, Job, The Song of Songs, Ruth, Lamentations, Ecclesiastes, Esther, Daniel, Ezra, Nehemiah, 1 Chronicles, and 2 Chronicles. It is also known by its Greek rendering, "Hagiographa," or as "The Writings."

Kitzur Shulchan Arukh

An abridgement (*kitzur*) of Joseph Karo's *Shulchan Arukh* by Solomon Ganzfried (b. 1804–d. 1886, Hungary). Ganzfried was a firm traditionalist who fought to preserve traditional observance amid the rapid changes of modernity. In this abridgement, Ganzfried tended to select the most stringent views and eliminate minority or alternative opinions on Jewish law.

Klein, Isaac

(b. 1905–d. 1979, Hungary and United States) Author of *A Guide to Jewish Religious Practice,* one of the most popular and expansive books of customs and observances written in English. Rabbi Klein's work is considered authoritative by the Modern Orthodox, Conservative, and Reform streams of Judaism.

Leibowitz, Nehama

(b. 1905–d. 1997, Livonia and Israel) An esteemed and adored teacher, educated in Berlin, who taught for many years at the Mizrachi Women Teachers Seminary of Tel Aviv University and numerous other schools. In 1942, she began to distribute stenciled pages of questions on the weekly Torah portion to anyone who requested them. These *dapim* (pages) appealed to all sectors of Israeli society and were translated into many languages, reaching worldwide audiences. Recipients would answer the questions and send the pages back to Leibowitz for her red-pencil review—and more questions. The pages were eventually collected and published as *Studies in the Weekly Sidra* and *Studies in Genesis* (with similar volumes for the other books of the Torah). Leibowitz, who lived very modestly and preferred the simple title of "Nehama" to "professor," was a frequent radio commentator. In 1956, the nation awarded her the Israel Prize for Education for her work in furthering understanding and love of Torah. She is recognized as one of the leading Jewish educators of the 20th century, and as a role model for Orthodox women who are scholars and teachers. Nehama was the sister of noted philosopher Yeshayahu Leibowitz.

Levinas, Emmanuel

(b. 1906–d. 1996, Lithuania and France) Professor of philosophy at various French universities from 1961 to 1979, including the Sorbonne. Earlier, he had served as director of the École Normale Israélite Orientale, a school established by the French Jewish community to train teachers for its schools in the Mediterranean basin. By the late 1920s, Levinas, who as a youth in Lithuania received a Jewish education, had moved to France and become a scholar of secular German philosophers Edmund Husserl (a Jewish convert to Christianity) and Martin Heidegger (who would later join the Nazi Party). During World War II, Levinas's family in Lithuania was murdered by the Nazis, and Levinas himself, as a captured French soldier, was imprisoned in a German prisoner-of-war camp. He became disillusioned by Nazi Germany and its strict universalism, a philosophy he had previously endorsed. He came to believe that the uniqueness of Judaism was necessary for the welfare of the world, and he devoted much of his thought to the relationship between Jews and non-Jews. Among his significant works translated into English are *Ethics and Infinity*; *Nine Talmudic Readings*; and *Difficult Freedom: Essays on Judaism*.

Levush

A collection of laws and customs, including elements of the *Tur* and the Shulchan Arukh, by Rabbi Mordecai ben Avraham Jaffe, also known as Baal Ha-Levush (b. circa 1535–d. 1612, Prague). A very popular, authoritative source that gives the rationale for many of the customs, it was referred to frequently by the scholars who came after him. This work can be found in the back of many traditional volumes of the *Tur*.

Luria, Isaac Ashkenazi

(b. 1534–d. 1572, Israel) Renowned teacher of Kabbalah and *halakhah*. Born in Jerusalem, he grew up in Egypt and later settled in Tzfat, a city in northern Israel. His teachings inspired a school of thought; and although Luria himself really did not write much, his followers produced volumes of material representing his teachings. "Lurianic Kabbalah" basically teaches that the purpose of Creation is to have the community and each individual heal the world (*tikun olam*, literally, "fixing the world"), thus gradually reuniting and perfecting the heavenly realms, as well as humanity.

Luzzatto, Moses Chaim

(b. 1707–d. 1747, Italy, Holland, and Israel) A leading mystic and kabbalist who headed a secret messianic order. Known by the acronym Ramchal, Luzzatto authored several kabbalistic writings including popular volumes, such as *Mesillat Yesharim*, *Migdal Oz*, and *Derekh Hashem*. He was a leading supporter of Shabbetai Tzvi (the most famous false Messiah) and was, therefore, exiled by the Italian rabbinical court. He and his family all died of the plague in Acre.

Magen Avraham

A popular commentary to the *Orach Chayyim* section of the Shulchan Arukh, which seeks to harmonize differences between Moses Isserles and Joseph Karo, as well as uphold the authority of the Shulchan Arukh over the *Tur*. It was written by Rabbi Avraham Abele Gombiner (b. circa 1637–d. circa 1683, Poland).

Maharil

(b. circa 1360–d. 1427, Austria) Rabbi Jacob Ha-Levi of Moelin, sometimes referred to as the "Father of Ashkenazic Customs." He wrote his compendium on the yearly customs of Ashkenazic Jewry, called *Minhagei Maharil*. He is widely quoted by many Ashkenazic codifiers, including Moses Issereles. Maharil is an acronym for "Our teacher, the Rabbi Israel Levi." (The patriarch Jacob was known by the name Israel.)

Maimonides

(b. 1135–d. 1204, Spain and Egypt) Rabbi Moses ben Maimon, a physician and possibly the greatest Jewish thinker of all time. He wrote many important works, including legal codes and philosophical expositions. Among them are the *Mishneh Torah*, the first written Jewish legal code, which is composed in remarkably clear Hebrew, and the *Guide of the Perplexed* (*Moreh Nevukhim*), a philosophical work showing a tremendous influence of Aristotelian influence, which interprets the Torah with the objective of eliminating apparent contradictions with philosophy. Maimonides is also known by the acronymn Rambam.

Mei Ha-Shiloach

A commentary and kabbalistic exposition on the Bible; also the commonly used name of its author, Rabbi Mordechai Yosef Leiner of Isbitza (b. 1800–d. 1854, Poland). Rabbi Leiner was part of a Hasidic dynasty; his son and grandson succeeded him as its leaders. Study of *Mei Ha-Shiloach* recently gained popularity through Rabbi Shlomo Carlebach and through Carlebach's student Betsalel Philip Edwards, who made an English translation called *Living Waters.*

Midrash

(literally, "Elucidation" or "Exposition") A body of work that combines the theological, homiletical, and ethical lore of the Rabbis in the Land of Israel from the 3rd through 10th centuries C.E. The word "midrash" is derived from the Hebrew root *dalet.resh.shin.* (*lidrosh*), meaning "to search for," which denotes searching out and discovering other meanings and information from Scripture.

Midrash Rabbah

An important series of books that expounds upon and further illustrates each book of the Torah, as well as the *megillot* (five historical tales that are part of the biblical book called The Writings): The Song of Songs, Ruth, Esther, Ecclesiastes, and Lamentations. Each volume is identified by the name of the corresponding book from the Bible, followed by the word *Rabbah* ("Great"), for example, *Exodus Rabbah* and *Song of Songs Rabbah*. As a series, these works were edited and redacted between the 5th and 10th centuries C.E. Final touches to *Numbers Rabbah* and *Esther Rabbah* were made as late as the 13th century. *Genesis Rabbah*, the oldest (425 C.E.) of the series, includes material from the Apocrypha, Philo, and Josephus.

Mishnah

(literally, "Teaching") The first compilation of the Oral Law and the foundational text for the Talmud and for the Rabbinic tradition. Most scholars attribute it to Rabbi Yehudah Ha-Nasi (Rabbi Judah the Patriarch, who lived in Judea under control of the Roman Empire) and date its final editing to circa 200 C.E. There are six "orders," or volumes, of the Mishnah categorized by different areas of Jewish law: *Zera'im* (laws governing agriculture and farm products); *Mo'ed* (laws relating to seasons and holidays); *Nashim* (laws relating to women and family life and to marriage and divorce); *Nezikim* (summaries of Jewish civil and criminal law); *Kodashim* (laws relating to holiness in matters of sacrifices and ritual slaughter); and *Toharot* (laws about purity). The word "Mishnah" is derived from the three-letter Hebrew root *shin.nun.heh.*, "to repeat," which indicates the primary method for learning and oral study at that time.

Mishnah Berurah

(literally, "The Clarified Teaching") One of the most authoritative commentaries on the part of the Shulchan Arukh that is devoted to everyday Jewish life, *Orach Chayyim* (literally, "Path of Life"). It was written by Rabbi Yisrael Meir Ha-Kohen (b. 1838–d. 1933, Poland), who is known widely by the name of his first book, *Chofetz Chaim* (literally, "Seeks or Desires Life"), which primarily deals with the laws of *lashon ha-ra* or guarding one's speech.

Mishneh Torah See Maimonides.

Nachmanides

(b. 1194–d. 1270, Spain and Israel) Rabbi Moses ben Nachman, a physician and one of the most important scholars in Jewish history. He is most well known for his commentary on the Torah, but he was also an important halakhist, kabbalist, and poet. Between 1263 and 1265, he represented Spanish Jewry in an official debate between Christians and Jews about religious truths. Victorious in his aggressive refutations of Christianity, he recorded the points of the debate in *Sefer Ha-Vikkuach* (literally, "The Book of the Dispute"), a publication that led to a papal warrant for his arrest; he escaped to Israel. Nachmanides is also known by the acronym Ramban.

Naftali Tzevi Judah Berlin

(b. 1817–d. 1893, Russia) Head of the renowned Volozhin Yeshiva, a position he held for nearly four decades, and a strong supporter of resettlement of the Land of Israel.

Commonly known as the Natziv, an acronym for his name, Rabbi Berlin was descended from a line of talmudic scholars, and his first and second wives were each from an esteemed rabbinical family. His approach to Torah study was traditional, striving to go back to the earliest sources, and thus it differed from the style of deep analysis prevalent in the 19th century. The Natziv's most famous work is a commentary on the Torah known as *Ha-Amek Davar* (literally, "The Depth of the Word").

Nevi'im

(literally, "Prophets") The second of the three parts of the TANAKH. It is often further divided into its first set of books, *Nevi'im Rishonim* (Former, or First, Prophets), which are primarily historical in nature, and its second set, *Nevi'im Acharonim* (Latter Prophets), which are the speeches of the prophets whose names they bear. One or two chapters from Nevi'im, which is sometimes titled in translation as "The Prophets," are read each Sabbath and on most holidays. Called *haftarot* (plural of haftarah), they each have particular relevance to the Torah reading for that day.

Or Ha-Chaim

(b. 1696–d. 1743, Morocco and Israel) Rabbi Chaim ben Attar, who was known by the name of his most well-known work. *Or Ha-Chaim* (literally, "The Light of Life"), a very popular commentary on the Torah. He became quite renowned in the Hasidic world and is often referred to as "The Holy" because many believed he could perform miracles.

Pesikta de-Rav Kahana and *Pesikta Rabbati*

Two versions of Palestinian midrashim written about parts of the TANAKH: The Five Books of Moses and The Prophets. (*Pesikta* means "section" in Aramaic.) *Pesikta de-Rav Kahana* was probably completed by the 5th century C.E., while the *Pesikta Rabbati*—a later version that draws upon the former—was completed after the 9th century and includes glosses from the 13th century. A critical edition of the work was translated into English by William G. Braude in 1968.[10]

Philo

A Hellenistic Jewish philosopher (b. circa 20 B.C.E.—d. 50 C.E.) who lived in Alexandria, Egypt. Although not much is known about Philo's life, his extensive writings have provided great insight into the historical situation of the Jews in Alexandria, especially Roman oppression against them. Philo's most important contributions are his philosophical treatises and interpretations of the Torah. Philo was clearly influenced by Platonic philosophy, as he often wrote of transcendent beauty and virtue, as well as the ultimate reality of the soul. He also interpreted the patriarchs in the Torah as archetypes for relating to God and that Jewish law is the supreme system of symbolic meaning. Philo's influence extends to Christianity as well as Judaism.

Pirke de-Rabbi Eliezer

(literally, "The Chapters of Rabbi Eliezer") Narrative midrash, or exposition, on biblical stories, falsely attributed to the 2nd-century sage Eliezer ben Hyrcanus. Modern scholars claim that this work was probably written in the Land of Israel in the 8th century. The work furthered Rabbinic thought and is the basis for many customs. (See Pseudepigrapha.)

Prophets See Nevi'im.

Pseudepigrapha

A post-biblical (circa 200 B.C.E.–200 C.E.) collection of works, literally named "False (from *pseudo*) Writings (from *graph*)." These books were falsely attributed to ancient heroes to gain in authenticity and authority and possibly to coerce biblical canonization. Nonetheless, these works are highly significant for Jews and Christians. Examples of the Pseudepigrapha are Jubilees, 1 Enoch, 2 Enoch, Life of Adam and Eve, and Joseph and Asenath.

Rabbenu Nissim

(b. circa 1315–d. 1375, Spain) Rabbi Nissim ben Reuven Gerondi, a great talmudist, *rosh yeshivah* (head of a Jewish school of higher learning), and court physician. Rabbenu (literally, "Our Rabbi") Nissim is best known for his discourse on Judaism called *Derashot* (loosely, "Interpretations") and for his commentary on the Rif's *Sefer Ha-Halakhot* (The Book of Laws). He is also referred to by the acronym of his name, Ran.

Rambam See Maimonides.

Rashi

(b. 1040–d. 1105, France) Hebrew acronym for Rabbi Shlomo ben Yitzchak, generally regarded as the greatest commentator on both the Torah and the Talmud.

Without his explanations, both would be much more difficult to understand. His commentary on the Torah was the first book to be printed in Hebrew; the semicursive typeface, which the printer created to distinguish the explanations from the biblical text, is called "Rashi script" and is still used today.

Rif

Hebrew acronym for Rabbi Yitzchak Alfasi (b. 1013–d. 1103, Morocco), one of the most influential authorities on Jewish law. His work *Sefer Ha-Halakhot* (The Book of Laws) is generally included in the back of traditional volumes of the Talmud and served as a primary source for other notable codifiers of *halakhah*, such as Maimonides, Jacob ben Asher, and Joseph Karo.

Rosenzweig, Franz

(b. 1886–d. 1929) Influential Jewish-German philosopher who grew up in a minimally observant family. In 1913, while a philosophy student at the University of Leipzig, he decided to convert to Christianity; but he wanted to enter the Church from the perspective of a Jew. Attending High Holiday services, Rosenzweig discovered that Judaism was not a relic of the past, but rather a living faith. He reversed his conversion plan, resolved his Jewish identity and religiosity, began studying the sources of Judaism, and became a student of philosopher Hermann Cohen. Rosenzweig established a friendship with philosopher Martin Buber, despite significant differences in political opinion, and they collaborated on a translation of the Torah from Hebrew to German. After serving in World War I, Rosenzweig assumed leadership of Das Freie Jüdische Lehrhaus (literally, "The Free House of Jewish Teaching"),[11] for people of various ideologies who were trying to find their way back to Judaism in the midst of Western European culture. His major work was *Der Stern der Erlösung* (The Star of Redemption), published in 1923, in which God, the world, and humanity are described as interrelated through a process of creation, revelation, and redemption.

Rosh

Hebrew acronym for Rabbi Asher ben Yechiel (b. circa 1250–d. 1327, Germany and Spain), the leading student of Rabbi Meir of Rothenburg and the father of Jacob ben Asher (author of the *Tur*). He is recognized as one of the top halakhic authorities, and his work *Piskei Ha-Rosh* was one of the primary sources for the *Tur* and for the Shulchan Arukh. His explanations on the Talmud were collected and appear in the back of most traditional volumes of the Talmud.

Sa'adia Ga'on

Sa'adia ben Yosef Al-Fayumi (b. 882–d. 942, Egypt, Israel, and Babylonia), head ("ga'on") of the Academy of Sura in Babylonia and one of the greatest contributors to the Jewish tradition in *halakhah*, liturgy, and philosophical discourse. His siddur (prayer book) is the first known attempt to transcribe the weekly ritual of Jewish prayers for weekdays, the Sabbath, and festivals. The text also contains liturgical poetry by Sa'adia, as well as Arabic-language commentary. His *Emunot ve-De'ot* (The Book of Beliefs and Opinions) was the first medieval classic on Jewish philosophy and is considered his greatest contribution. Influenced by Aristotle and Plato, Sa'adia argues that faith in Judaism and Jewish practice does not contradict reason.

Sefat Emet

A five-volume work (The Language of Truth) that contains some of the most creative and enriching commentaries on the Torah and on the holidays. Written by Rabbi Yehuda Aryeh Leib Alter of Ger (b. 1847–d. 1904, Poland), it is still widely studied. In 1998, parts of it were published in English, translated by Arthur Green.[12]

Sefer Abudraham

(literally, "The Book of Abudraham") A comprehensive commentary on synagogue ritual and prayers, composed by Rabbi David ben Joseph Abudraham (lived 1300s, Spain). Abudraham culls from many sources while explaining the differences between local customs and the calendar.

Sefer Ha-Hinnukh

(literally, "The Book of Education") An anonymous work from the 13th century, intended to be a simple guide to Jewish belief and practice. A 16th-century author attributed it to the talmudist Aaron ben Joseph Ha-Levi (b. 1235–d. 1300, Spain), and this attribution has generally been accepted. *Sefer Ha-Hinnukh* is an enumeration of the 613 mitzvot, arranged according to the order of the Torah portions (*parshiyot*), that includes their halakhic and ethical aspects.

Sefer Ha-Manhig

(literally, "The Guide Book") One of the earliest books on Jewish customs. Written by Rabbi Abraham ben Nathan of Lunel (b. 1155–d. 1215, France), this particular work describes the customs of various Jewish communities, as well as the rationale for their practice.

Sefer Ha-Minhagim

(literally, "The Book of Customs") A highly popular book in its time, it was created by Rabbi Isaac of Tyrnau (b. end of 14th century–d. 15th century, Hungary), It describes the customs (*minhagim*) of different Ashkenazic communities. Moses Isserles, the Ashkenazic authority on *halakhah*, often refers to Tyrnau's work in his additions and comments in the Shulchan Arukh.

Sefer Ha-Toda'ah

(literally, "The Book of Consciousness") A popular 1962 work by Rabbi Abraham Eliyahu Ki Tov (b. 1912–d. 1976, United States) that concentrates on the holidays and seasons and includes halakhic and folkloric material. Published in English as *The Book of Our Heritage: The Jewish Year and Its Days of Significance*.[13]

Sefer Mordechai

(literally, "The Book of Mordechai") A work that discusses halakhic teachings and many customs of Ashkenazic Jewry, written by Rabbi Mordechai ben Hillel (b. circa 1250–d. 1298, Germany). It records many doctrines of the author's principal teacher, Rabbi Meir ben Baruch of Rothenburg, as well as those of the Rif (Rabbi Yitzchak Alfasi). Many subsequent codes quote this work, and it appears in the back of the traditional Talmud.

Sforno, Ovadiah ben Yaakov

(b. 1475–d. 1550, Italy) One of the great Bible commentators and medieval Jewish philosophers, a physician by trade. Sforno's commentary is usually on the plain meaning (*peshat*) of the biblical text and grammar. He also authored a commentary on *Pirkei Avot* (literally, "Chapters of the Sages;" commonly known as *Ethics of the Fathers*) and a philosophical treatise called *Or Ammim* (literally, "Light of Nations").

Shulchan Arukh

(literally, "Set Table") The standard code of Jewish law, first published in 1565. It was compiled by Rabbi Joseph Karo (b. 1488–d. 1575, Spain, Turkey, and Israel). Karo, clearly one of the greatest legal authorities and mystics in Jewish history, followed the style of Jacob ben Asher's *Tur*. He devised the Shulchan Arukh as a key for and synopsis of his own magnificent commentary and elucidation of the *Tur*, known as *Beit Yosef*. The Shulchan Arukh includes the gloss of Rabbi Moses Isserles, also known as Rema (b. circa 1525–d. 1572, Poland), which is titled *Mapa* (literally,

"Tablecloth"). The Shulchan Arukh emphasizes Sephardic customs and practices, while the *Mapa* treats those of the Ashkenazim.

Sifra
(literally, "Book" in Aramaic) Also known as *Torat Kohanim*, a midrash that focuses on the halakhic aspects of the Book of Leviticus. The material comes primarily from the *tannaim* (the Rabbis quoted in the Mishnah). Most scholars believe the final redactor of the work to be a student of Yehudah Ha-Nasi, either Abba Aricha (known as "Rav")[14] or Rabbi Chiya.

Sifrei
(literally, "Books" in Aramaic) Midrash, mostly halakhic in nature, from the school of Rabbi Ishmael that offers verse-by-verse Hebrew exegesis of the biblical books Numbers and Deuteronomy. Parallel works exist from a rival midrashic school (the school of Rabbi Akiva), which are called *Sifrei Zuta* for Numbers; *Mekhilta de-Rabbi Shimon bar Yochai* for Deuteronomy.

Sirkes, Joel
(b. circa 1561–d. 1640) Rabbi of Krakow, Poland, who was known by the acronym Bach, taken from the title of his best-known work, *Bayit Chadash* (literally, "The New House"). It is a commentary on the great halakhic work called *Arba'ah Turim* (literally, "Four Columns," also known as the *Tur*) of Rabbi Jacob ben Asher. Sirkes also authored more than 250 responsa.

Steinberg, Milton
(b. 1903–d. 1950, United States) Philosopher, author, and longtime rabbi of the Park Avenue Synagoue in New York City. Ordained by the Jewish Theological Seminary for Conservative Judaism, he was strongly influenced by Rabbi Mordecai Kaplan, founder of the Reconstructionist movement. *As a Driven Leaf*, Rabbi Steinberg's novel about the lives of the Rabbinic sages living under Greek influence, is among the most important Jewish works of the first half of the 20th century. His other books include *The Making of the Modern Jew, A Partisan Guide to the Jewish Problem, Basic Judaism*, and *Anatomy of Faith*.

Talmud
The central and most important body of Rabbinic literature. Combining the Mishnah and Gemara, the Talmud contains material from the Rabbinic academies

that dates from sometime before the 2nd century C.E. through the 6th century. It includes halakhic and midrashic expositions, wisdom, personal stories, and arguments. There are two versions: (1) the Jerusalem (*Yerushalmi*), or Palestinian, Talmud and (2) the Babylonian (*Bavli*) Talmud. When people speak of the Talmud generically, they are referring to the *Bavli*, as it is more extensive and more widely used. Each has 63 areas of study called tractates (*masechtot*). The Talmud serves as the primary source for all later codes of Jewish law.

Tanakh

An acronym for the three books that make up the cornerstone of Jewish beliefs; Torah (the Five Books of Moses), Nevi'im (The Prophets), and Kethuvim (The Writings). When Jews speak of the Bible, they are referring to the Tanakh.

Tanchuma or *Tanchuma Yelamednu*

A collection of midrashic literature, including large sections from *Midrash Rabbah* and *Pesikta Rabbati*, based on the triennial cycle of Torah readings. Much of it is attributed to the 4th-century Palestinian sage Tanchuma ben Abba, hence the name *Tanchuma*. It is distinguished by the repetition of an opening phrase, *yelamednu rabbenu*, "Let our master teach us." Scholars are unsure of the date for the final version of *Tanchuma*; the first printed edition appeared in approximately 1521. This work is sometimes confused with a different collection of midrashic material called *Tanchuma Buber* published in 1875 by scholar Solomon Buber (b. 1827–d. 1906, Ukraine).

Tanchuma Buber See Solomon Buber.

Tosafot

(literally, "Additions") Additions to and continuations of Rashi's talmudic commentary and the talmudic process in general. They were written between the 12th and 14th centuries in France and Germany by many scholars, including some who were Rashi's grandchildren, for example, Rashbam (Rabbi Samuel ben Meir). An indispensable part of Talmud study, the Tosafot are printed in the margins of each page of Talmud, opposite Rashi's commentary. The phrase "The Tosafot" is used as a group name for the rabbis who wrote these additions.

Tosefta

(literally, "Supplement") A collection of additional teachings and statements by the Rabbinic sages organized in the same arrangement as the Mishnah. Scholars debate whether the Tosefta comprises solely *tannaitic* material (circa 2nd century C.E.) or if it includes material of a later date. Either way, Tosefta is considered authoritative, and much of it is quoted in the Gemara. The Tosefta can usually be found in the back of traditional volumes of the Talmud.

Tur

A book also known as *Arba'ah Turim* (literally, "Four Columns"). It was created by Rabbi Jacob ben Asher (b. circa 1270–d. circa 1340, Germany and Spain), who was known also as the Baal Ha-Turim ("Master of the Columns"). This ambitious work attempts to bridge the gulf between Ashkenazic and Sephardic laws and opinions in force at the time. The legal decisions of great Rabbis are divided into four main topics, called columns, or *turim*. The Baal Ha-Turim emphasizes the work and thought of Maimonides and even more so of the "Rosh" (an acronym for the name of his own father, Rabbenu Asher). Joseph Karo's Shulchan Arukh, the fundamental code of Jewish law, follows the basic structure of the *Tur*.

Writings, The See Kethuvim.

Yalkut Shimoni

An anthology of *midrashim* on all portions of the TANAKH. Rabbi Shimon Ha-Darshan of Frankfurt compiled it in the 13th century as a handbook on religious beliefs for Jews throughout the Diaspora. With *midrashim* culled from 50 different sources, it is very useful for critical analysis.

Yehuda Ha-Levi

(b. 1075–d. 1141, Spain) An important and influential Jewish poet and philosopher who was a physician by profession. His poetry, tending toward the mystical, has been placed in the liturgy (including the *Yamim Nora'im*); but his most famous work is the *Kuzari*, written in Arabic and given a structure similar to a platonic dialogue. The *Kuzari* describes the conversion of the king of the Khazars (a seminomadic people from Central Asia). Ha-Levi uses the dialogue to argue three things: faith is not inconsistent with reason, revelation is superior to reason, and both of the preceding ideas are proven by looking at Jewish history.

Zohar

(literally, "Illumination") A book of mystical commentaries on the TANAKH that mixes together theology, psychology, myth, ancient Gnosticism, and superstition. The objective is to uncover the deepest mysteries of the world—namely, why God created the universe, how God is manifest in the world, and what the forces of life are. Although some accept the claim that the Zohar was authored by Rabbinic sage Shimon bar Yochai (b. and d. 2nd century C.E., Israel) and his saintly contemporaries, most scholars believe it to have been largely written by Moshe De Leon (b. 1240–d. 1305, Spain).

Endnotes

Part 1: Spirituality in Time and Place

1 The Rabbinic tradition claims that the site of the Temple is associated with many profound moments in the Torah, including (1) where Adam, Cain, Abel, and Noah offered sacrifices; (2) the place identified as Mount Moriah (Gen. 22), where God tested Abraham as to whether he would sacrifice Isaac; (3) where Rebecca prayed for children, resulting in her pregnancy with twins Jacob and Esau (Rashi on Gen. 25:21); (4) where Jacob dreamed of the ladder with angels ascending and descending (Gen. 28:10–22); (5) the place on earth closest to heaven (Mishnah, *Yoma* 5:2); and (6) the very point from where God created the rest of the world (B. Talmud, *Yoma* 54b).

2 Exod. 3:1–4:17.

3 *Midrash Rabbah, Numbers Rabbah* 1:7. *See also* similar midrashim about the desert in B. Talmud, *Nedarim* 55a; *Midrash, Mechilta, Ha-Hodesh,* sect. 1; *Yalkut Shimoni, Yitro* 272; *Pesikta de-Rav Kahana* 12.

4 B. Talmud, *Nedarim* 55a.

Part 2: Passover

1 Exod. 12:15,18–20, 13:3,7.

2 In this case, the first day of *hol ha-moed* in Israel is used as the second holy day in the Diaspora. The total number of intermediary days in the Diaspora is thus shortened by one day.

3 Don Well, "Pesach, Civilization and Beer: The Hidden Origins of *Chametz*," *The Jewish Press*, April 28, 2008.

4 Exod. 13:4. Although the Bible mentions months, none of them have the same names used today for the Hebrew months, all of which were established in Babylonian times. The Torah does not specifically say that Aviv (spelled Abib in the JPS Hebrew-English TANAKH) is a month. The correlation between Aviv and the month of Nisan was made by the Rabbis.

5 In the Diaspora, this prayer for dew is routinely included only in Sephardic *siddurim*. Some Ashkenazic *siddurim* offer it as an optional prayer.

6 In the Hebrew language, for reasons of grammar and vocalization, the letter *peh,* for example in the word Pesach, is converted to *feh,* for example in the word *fasachti.*

7 Rabbi Yoshiyah and Rabbi Yonatan are *tannaim* who lived in the Land of Israel.

▲ ▲ ▲ ▲ ▲ ▲ ▲ ▲ ▲ ▲ ▲ ▲ ▲ ▲

8   *Mechilta, Bo* 12:13,23.

9   Josh. 5:2–12. It is unclear who needs to be circumcised. The passage could be referring to those who were not circumcised during the sojourn in the desert, or the passage could be referring to an ancient practice of circumcision before warfare.

10   Ezra 6:19–22.

11   Mishnah, *Hagigah* 1:2–3.

12   *Avot de-Rabbi Natan,* 11a.

13   This is also discussed in 2 Kings 23:21–25, which is part of the haftarah for the second day of Passover.

14   David Mandel, *Who's Who in the Jewish Bible* (Philadelphia: The Jewish Publication Society, 2007), 149.

15   From roughly the 930s to the 720s B.C.E., the Land of Israel was divided into two kingdoms, one in the north called Israel and one in the south called Judah.

16   The LORD spoke to Moses saying: Speak to the Israelite people thus: In the seventh month, on the first day of the month, you shall observe complete rest, a sacred occasion commemorated with loud blasts (Lev. 23:23–24).

17   Tishrei is called *Ethanim* in the Bible.

18   Nachmanides, Exodus 12:2.

19   *Tur*/Shulchan Arukh, *Orach Chayyim* 429:2.

20   Exod. 12:1–20.

21   Ezek. 45:16–46:18.

22   *Tur*/Shulchan Arukh, *Orach Chayyim* 430.

23   The Talmud (*Shabbat* 87b) states, "As to Nisan in which the Israelites departed from Egypt, on the fourteenth they killed their Passover sacrifices, on the fifteenth they went forth, and in the evening [of the 15th] the firstborn were smitten . . . and that day was a Thursday." *See also* Tosafot in B. Talmud, *Shabbat* 87b d"h *V'oto yom hamishi b'Shabbat*; *Tur, Orach Chayyim* 430; see also *Midrash Rabbah, Shemot Rabbah, Bo.*

24   *Arukh Ha-Shulchan* 430:1,4.

25   *Mapa, Orach Chayyim* 430; *Ta'amei Ha-Minhagim*, 205; *see also* Isaac Klein, *A Guide to Jewish Religious Practice* (New York: Jewish Theological Seminary, 1979), 108, where he cites *Shibbolei Ha-Leket*, 205; *see also* Eliyahu Kitov, *The Book of Our Heritage*, vol. 2, (New York: Feldheim, Publishers, 1997), 156.

26   J. Talmud, *Bava Batra* 1:6.

27   *Mapa, Orach Chayyim* 429; *Arukh Ha-Shulchan* 429.

28   B. Talmud, *Pesachim* 99b.

29   Maimonides, *Guide of the Perplexed*, vol. 3, 43. Translation in the *The Guide of the Perplexed*, vol. 2, by Shlomo Pines (Chicago: University of Chicago Press, 1963) 571.

30   *See also* Exod. 12:18–20;13:3,7.

31   B. Talmud, *Pesachim* 21b; Maimonides, *Mishneh Torah, Hilkhot Hametz u'Matzah* 1:2; *Tur*/Shulchan Arukh, *Orach Chayyim* 443:1.

32   Shulchan Arukh, *Orach Chayyim* 459:2; see *Mishnah Berurah* there *se'if katan* 15.

33   *Sefer Ha-Toda'ah*, vol. 2, 107; *The Book of Our Heritage*, vol. 2, trans. Nachman Bulman (New York: Feldheim Publishers, 1997), 538.

34   Philo, *The Special Laws, Book I*, 293–95, trans. F. H. Colson (Cambridge, Mass.: Harvard University Press, 1953), VI, 311–13.

35   B. Talmud, *Pesachim* 6b, 31b.

36   Zohar 2:182.

37   Zohar, *Vayechi* 226b.

38   *Derekh Hashem* 8:1, trans. Aryeh Kaplan (New York: Feldheim Publishers, 1988), 321.

39   *Ha'amek Davar* on Exodus 13:3.

40   B. Talmud, *Pesachim* 35a.

41   Rava was an *amora* born in 270. His yeshiva at Mahuza in Babylonia was an important intellectual center. He died in about 352.

42   Rav Huna was an *amora* of the second generation and head of the academy of Sura, Babylonia. He lived circa 216–297.

43   Rav Ashi was an *amora*. He lived circa 352–427. He reestablished the academy at Sura and was the first editor of the Babylonian Talmud.

44   B. Talmud, *Pesachim* 114b.

45   Maimonides, *Mishneh Torah, Hilkhot Hametz u'Matzah* 5:1; *see also* 6:4.

46   *Sefer Mitzvot Katan*, 222. English translation from Shlomo Yosef Zevin, *The Festivals in Halakhah*, vol. 2 (New York: Mesorah Publications, 1999), 783–84.

47   *Sefer Mordechai* on *Pesachim*, chapter 2, 588.

48   Cited in Beit Yosef, *Orach Chayyim* 453.

49   Beit Yosef, *Orach Chayyim* 453.

50   *Mapa, Orach Chayyim* 453:1; see also *Darkei Moshe, Orach Chayyim* 453.

51   *Besamim Rosh* 348.

52   *Toldot Adam v'Chav*, sec. 5, part 3, p. 41 in Venice edition, reprinted in Jerusalem, 1975. Cited in "A New Look at Peanuts—From the Ground Up" by Ben Zion Bergman in the responsa of the Conservative movement's Committee of Jewish Laws and Standards, January 27, 1986.

53   *Mor u'Ketzia* 453, cited and translated in Zevin, *The Festivals in Halakhah*, vol. 2, 787.

54   In a newspaper editorial, Saul Singer stated that Israelis simply hold by the Sephardic custom. Saul Singer, "Interesting Times: Eat Kitniyot," *The Jerusalem Post*, April 2, 2004. Also, it is a custom among the very traditional for the wife in the marriage to take on her husband's customs (Ashkenazic women who marry Sephardic men usually take on the custom of eating *kitniyot* and certainly allow their children to eat *kitniyot*).

55   David Golinkin, "The Custom to Prohibit the Eating of *Kitniyot* During the Festival of Passover," in *Responsa of the Vaad Halakhah of the Rabbinical Assembly of Israel*, vol. 3, 1989. This responsum appears in complete form in Hebrew with an abbreviated English translation at www.ResponsaForToday.com.

56   For a Reform responum, *see* Central Conference of American Rabbis, www.ccar.org. For a Conservative responsum *see* Bergman, "A New Look at Peanuts." For an Orthodox responsum *see* Rabbi Moshe Feinstein's *Igrot Moshe*, vol. 3, *Orach Chayyim* 63. Note that many Conservative and most Orthodox Ashkenazim tend to ignore the more lenient positions and choose the stricter perspectives.

57   Known also as Yisrael Meir Kagan and popularly known as the Chofetz Chaim (Seeker or Desirer of Life), which was the name of his first book.

58   *Mishnah Berurah* 453, *se'if katan* 7.

59   Abraham Joshua Heschel, *God in Search of Man: A Philosophy of Judaism* (New York: Farrar, Straus and Giroux, 1955), 283.

60   The method depends on the type and design of stovetop and oven.

61   A "day" on the Hebrew calendar runs from sunset to sunset. The word *erev* literally means "evening," but it also refers to the entire Hebrew "day" (an evening through night and on to the next sunset) before Shabbat or a holiday. It does not mean the evening of Shabbat or a holiday itself.

62   Mishnah, *Pesachim* 1:1; Maimonides, *Mishneh Torah, Hilkhot Hametz u'Matzah* 2:3; *Tur*/Shulchan Arukh, *Orach Chayyim* 431:1.

63   Maimonides, *Mishneh Torah, Hilkhot Hametz u'Matzah* 3:3; *Tur*/Shulchan Arukh, *Orach Chayyim* 444:1.

64   Mishnah, *Pesachim* 1:1.

65   *Sefer Ha-Toda'ah*, vol. 2, 103; *The Book of Our Heritage*, vol. 2, 524. In *The Minhagim: The Customs and Ceremonies of Judaism, Their Origins and Rationale* (New York: Sepher Hermon, 1978), author Rabbi Abraham Chill states his opinion about the wooden spoon. He says we choose that implement because the next morning, during the actual burning of the *hametz*, the spoon (likely bearing traces of *hametz*) can be added to the fire and

easily consumed by the flames. It seems to me, however, that the use of a candle, a feather, and a wooden spoon were simply practical items for cleaning in the dark during the Middle Ages.

66   *Mapa, Orach Chayyim* 432:2.

67   *Mishnah Berurah* 432:2, *sei'f katan* 13. The *Mishnah Berurah* cites Isaac Luria as the origin of the number 10 for the pieces. Luria was one of the foundational influences in the development of Kabbalah.

68   *Ta'amei Ha-Minhagim*, 213.

69   *Tur*/Shulchan Arukh, *Orach Chayyim* 470:1. See also *Beit Yosef* there, which says that firstborn females are also obligated to fast, hearkening to *Midrash Rabbah, Shemot Rabbah* 18:3, which notes that girls were also saved from the 10th plague of killing the firstborn. Taking a different position, Moses Isserles, in both the *Mapa* and *Darkei Moshe*, cites the Maharil's stance that it is not the custom for women to adhere to this fast.

70   *Mishnah Berurah* 470:1, *se'if katan* 10.

71   Maimonides, *Mishneh Torah, Hilkhot Hametz u'Matzah* 3:7; *Tur*/Shulchan Arukh, *Orach Chayyim* 434:2. The *Beit Yosef* there indicates that the actual language used for this formula is not in the B. Talmud, but from the Geonim (heads of the Babylonian academies from the 6th to the 11th centuries). However there is a similar version existent in the J. Talmud, *Pesachim* 5:2.

72   B. Talmud, *Pesachim* 99b; Maimonides, *Mishneh Torah, Hilkhot Hametz u'Matzah* 3:7; *Tur*/Shulchan Arukh, *Orach Chayyim* 434:2–3. Because the Rabbis instituted the starting point for the prohibition against owning *hametz* at midday on Erev Passover (generally understood to be noon, depending upon time zones), they cautioned that we should burn it an hour earlier, at 11:00 A.M.

73   *Tur*/Shulchan Arukh, *Orach Chayyim* 434:1–2, 445:1.

74   *Arukh Ha-Shulchan* 471:1–3.

75   *Mechilta, Bo* on 13:7; B. Talmud, *Pesachim*, 21b, 29a; Maimonides, *Mishneh Torah, Hilkhot Hametz u'Matzah* 1:2–5.

76   Tosefta, *Pesachim* 2:6. See *Tur*/Shulchan Arukh, *Orach Chayyim* 448 for an expansion and development of this scenario, wherein the mention of the ship is omitted to simply say, "If one sells it [hametz] or gives it to a non-Jew outside of one's house."

77   Klein, *A Guide to Religious Jewish Practice*, 112. For a comprehensive discussion on the sale of *hametz* and its development, *see* Zevin, *The Festivals in Halakhah*, vol. 2, 769–80.

78   *The Book of Our Heritage*, vol. 2, ,527.

79   *Tur*/Shulchan Arukh, *Orach Chayyim* 436:1–2.

80   This term was inspired by something written by Noam Zion and David Dishon in *A Different Night: The Family Participation Haggadah* (Jerusalem: Shalom Hartman Institute, 1997), 15.

81   *Tur*/Shulchan Arukh, *Orach Chayyim* 472:2.

82   Mishnah, *Pesachim* 10:1; B. Talmud, *Pesachim* 108a; *Tur*/Shulchan Arukh, *Orach Chayyim* 472:2–3. The Talmud argues about whether one should recline to the right or the left. The codes choose the arguments in favor of reclining to the left because most people will need to eat with their right hand and because the Rabbis believe that people are more likely to choke lying on their backs or reclining to the right side. The *Tur* also records a completely different opinion—that of Avi Ha-Ezri, a 12th-century German authority who argues that it is no longer obligatory to recline. Maimonides claims that one is obligated to recline, but only when eating the matzah and *maror* sandwich during the *korekh* part of the seder and when drinking the four cups of wine (*Mishneh Torah, Hilkhot Hametz u'Matzah* 7:8). The *Arukh Ha-Shulchan* (472:3), aligning himself with Avi Ha-Ezri. says that indeed it is no longer compulsory to recline. He continues to say, however, that it is preferable to recline so that we relive the customs of our ancestors and differentiate this evening from others. Reclining is in the spirit of arousing children to ask questions (reclining is one of the four questions).

83   Dennis E. Smith, "The Greco-Roman Banquet as a Social Institution,"a paper prepared for the Meals in the Greco-Roman World Consultation, AAR/SBL (American Academy of Religion/Society of Biblical Literature) Annual Meeting, Atlanta, Georgia, November 2003.

84   Baruch M. Bokser, *The Origins of the Seder: The Passover Rite and Early Rabbinic Judaism* (Berkeley: University of California Press, 1986); Siegfried Stein, "The Influence of Symposium Literature on the Literary Form of the Pesah Haggadah," *Journal of Jewish Studies* 8 (1957): 13–44; David Golinkin, "The Origins of the Seder," *Insight Israel* 6, no. 8 (April 2006): 76–100.

85   Klein, *Guide to Jewish Religious Practice,* 121.

86   *Turei Zahav, Orach Chayyim* 472:3; *Sefer Toda'ah,* vol. 2, 108.

87   Only five grains are capable of fermentation, and they are the only ones permitted to be used in the unleavened bread we call matzah: wheat, rye, oats, barley, and spelt. These are defined in the Oral Torah. We say *Ha-Motzi* (the blessing over bread) only on bread, leavened or unleavened, made of any of these five grains.

88   Mishnah, *Pesachim* 10:8.

89   B. Talmud, *Pesachim* 119b.

90   *Mishnah Berurah* 478:1; Kitzur Shulchan Arukh 120:11.

91   *Mishnayoth*, vol. 2, *Order Mo'ed*, trans. and ed. Philip Blackman (New York: Judaica Press, 1963), 221, *see* notes to Mishnah 10:8; Baruch M. Bokser, *The Origins of the Seder: The Passover Rite and Early Rabbinic Judaism* (Berkeley: University of California Press, 1986), 65; Golinkin, "The Origins of the Seder," from the Schechter Institute "Faculty Forum," vol. 6, issue no. 8, April 2006, Jerusalem.

92   Klein, *Guide to Jewish Religious Practice*, 124.

93   B. Talmud, *Pesachim* 114b.

94   A portion of this information was supplied by Daniel Cotzin Burg.

95   Maimonides, *Mishneh Torah, Hilkhot Hametz u'Matzah* 7:13; Shulchan Arukh, *Orach Chayyim* 474:1.

96   Mishnah, *Pesachim* 2:8.

97   Isaac Luria, the 16th-century mystic, placed the matzot on the seder plate in this way. The Vilna Ga'on used a three-tiered seder plate based upon Maimonides' rulings. The top level contained *haroset* (left) and *maror* (right); the middle contained two matzot covered with a cloth; and the bottom had the *beitzah* (left) and *zeroa* (right).

98   From a paper by Nanette Stahl, "The Early Printed Passover Haggadah: A Tale of Four Cities: Prague, Mantua, Venice, Amsterdam," presented at the conference of the International Federation of Library Associations and Institutions, August 16–21, 1998.

99   From "A Short History of the Printed, Illustrated Haggadah," Jewish Heritage Online Magazine, www.ifla.org.

100 *Tur*/Shulchan Arukh, *Orach Chayyim* 473:6. English translation from Noam Zion and David Dishon, *A Different Night: The Leader's Guide* to the Family Participation Haggadah (Jerusalem: Shalom Hartman Institute, 1997), 13.

101 For other ideas on an expanded *karpas*, *see* Zion and Dishon, *A Different Night: The Leader's Guide.*

102 *Bayit Hadash, Orach Chayyim* 473:6.

103 A talmudic scholar known as the Bach, an acronymn for his work *Bayit Hadash*, a commentary on the great halakhic work the *Arba'ah Turim.*

104 Tosefta, *Pesachim* 10:3; B. Talmud, *Pesachim* 109a–b. The Talmud quotes Ravina saying that the four cups are for everyone to demonstrate the "conduct of freedom" (*derekh heirut*).

105 B. Talmud, *Pesachim* 108b; *see also* Rashbam there *d'h u'mareh.*

106 The matriarchs are Sarah, Rebecca, Rachel, and Leah. The rivers are the Pishon, the Gihon, the Tigris, and the Euphrates. Besides the two levels used for "Interpretations of Sacred Texts" in this book—*peshat* (simple, literal meaning) and *derash* (historical, Rabbinic inquiry)—the tradition includes *remez* ("hint") and *sod* ("secret"). The four

worlds are *asiyah* ("doing"), *yetzirah* ("feeling"), *beriah* ("thinking"), and *atzilut* ("existing"). The four letters are *yud, hay, vav, hay* (the Tetragrammaton).

107   J. Talmud, *Pesachim* 10; *Midrash Rabbah, Exodus Rabbah* 88.

108   Gen. 40:11–13.

109   J. Talmud, *Pesachim* 10; *Midrash Rabbah, Exodus Rabbah* 88.

110   *Sefer Ha-Toda'ah*, vol. 2, 109. The explanations from the following sources are identified in *Sefer Ha-Toda'ah*. The numbers here correspond to their numbers in the book: (1) the Maharal and *Yalkut Shimoni*, (2) Abarbanel, and (3) *B'nei Yissaschar* and *Ta'amei Ha-Minhagim* (227).

111   Siegfried Stein, "The Influence of Symposium Literature on the Literary Form of the Pesah Haggadah," *Journal of Jewish Studies* 8 (1957): 17. "There is some evidence that four toasts or sacred cups of wine were common at Greek formal dinners and *symposia*. Delight Tolles, a 20th-century Greek scholar, points out that there were two sets of libations common at such events. The first set was three libations to Zeus (god of the sky and ruler of other gods) and the Olympians, the second to the heroes, and the third to Zeus specifically as Soter (Savior). The second set consisted of four libations of sacred drinks to the gods Hygieia (goddess of health), Hermes (guardian of the house), Zeus, and Agathos Daimon (god of good fortune). *See* "Review of *The Banquet-Libations of the Greeks* by Delight Tolles": review author: George W. Elderkin, *The American Journal of Philology* 66:4 (1945): 425–30. This sort of custom seems to be supported by Athenaeus (2nd–3rd centuries) in his *Deipnosophistae* ("The Banquet of the Learned") when he says: "He [the King of Athens] also instituted the custom of taking just a sip of unmixed wine after meat, as a proof of the power of the Good God (Agathos Daimon), but after that he might drink mixed wine, as much as each man chose. They were also to repeat over this cup the name of Zeus Soter (Saviour) as a warning and reminder to drinkers that only when they drank in this fashion would they surely be safe" (*Deipnosophistae* 2.38c–d).

112   Joshua Kulp, "The Origins of the Seder and Haggadah," *Currents in Biblical Research* 4:1 (2005): 118.

113   B. Talmud, *Pesachim* 118b has an alternative version of the text, wherein Rabbi Tarfon, one of the *tannaim* (the sages whose views are recorded in the Mishnah), says that *Hallel* is said over a fifth cup. The standard version of the text says that it is the fourth cup. *See* Beit Yosef, *Orach Chayyim* 481.

114   Malachi 3:23; B. Talmud, *Berakhot* 35b, *Menachot* 45a, *Bekhorot* 24a, *Pesachim* 13a.

115   Zion and Dishon, *A Different Night*, 139.

116   Ibid., 142.

▲   ▲   ▲   ▲   ▲   ▲   ▲   ❧   ▲   ▲   ▲   ▲   ▲   ▲   ▲

117   For some of these ways, *see* Kolot: Center for Jewish Women's & Gender Studies, www.ritualwell.org.

118   B. Talmud, *Pesachim* 13a; J. Talmud, *Pesachim* 3:6.

119   *Mechilta de-Rabbi Yishmael, Pischa* 14.

120   Mishnah, *Sotah* 9:15; B. Talmud, *Sanhedrin* 97a.

121   B. Talmud, *Shabbat* 63a, 30b; *Megillah* 29a. *See also* Maimonides' introduction to the 10th chapter of tractate *Sanhedrin* (*Perek Chelek*).

122   *Mapa, Orach Chayyim* 490:9; *Sefer Abudraham*, 264–65. If Passover begins on the Sabbath, The Song of Songs is chanted on that Shabbat and on the second Shabbat of the holiday. In some cases, people have the custom of reciting The Song of Songs after the seder.

123   The four other scrolls (*megillot*) are chanted as follows: Ecclesiastes on Sukkot (on the Shabbat of the intermediary days), Book of Esther on Purim, Book of Ruth on Shavuot, and Lamentations on Tisha b'Av.

124   Mishnah, *Yadayim* 3:5.

125   *Mechilta* 15:2; *see also* Rashi on The Song of Songs 1:1–2; *see also* Elsie Stern, "The Song of Songs," in *The Jewish Study Bible* (New York: Oxford University Press, 2004), 1565–66.

126   Regarding the day the Temple was built, the Zohar (vol. 2, 143b) states: "The world became fragrant. All the sublime windows opened to shine forth light. There was never such joy in the world. Both the higher and lower realms issued forth in song, singing The Song of Songs."

127   H. L Ginsburg, "Introduction to The Song of Songs," in *The Five Megilloth and Jonah* (Philadelphia: The Jewish Publication Society, 1969), 3.

128   Maimonides, *Mishneh Torah, Hilkhot Yesodei Ha-Torah* 2:2; *Hilkhot Teshuvah* 10:2–3.

129   *Midrash Rabbah* also includes a book on each of the *megillot* (five historical tales that are part of the second section of the Bible called The Writings): The Song of Songs, Ruth, Esther, Ecclesiastes, and Lamentations.

130   Rabbi Nachman ben Rabbi Shmuel ben Nachman.

131   Rabbi Akiva was a renowned 1st-century sage in the Land of Israel.

132   Most likely Rabbi Yehudah bar Ila'ee, who lived in about 120 C.E.

133   A member of the third generation of *amoraim* (Aramaic, "spokesmen"), scholars who interpreted the Midrash between 200 and 500 C.E. in the Land of Israel and Babylonia. Rabbi Yosef died in about 322 C.E.

134   Rabbi Yehudah ben Bateirah is known to have been living in 38 B.C.E.

135   Maimonides, *The Guide of the Perplexed*, vol. 2, trans. Shlomo Pines (Chicago: University of Chicago Press, 1963), 570–71.

136   Abarbanel's commentary on Exod. 2:11ff.

137   Kli Yakar's commentary on Exod. 6:6. *Kli Yakar, Shemos*, vol. I, trans. Elihu Levine (Southfield, Mich.: Targum Press, 2002), 90–92.

138   Nehama Leibowitz, *New Studies in Shemot, vol.1* (Jerusalem: World Zionist Organization, 1986), 71–72.

139   Neil Gillman, *Traces of God* (Woodstock, Vt.: Jewish Lights Publishing, 2006), 89–90.

140   Source: American Jewish Committee, 2006.

141   Quoted from Mishnah, *Pesachim* 10:5.

142   Joseph Campbell, *The Power of Myth* (New York: Doubleday, 1988), 3.

143   Num. 9:1–14.

144   Josh. 5:10–12.

145   2 Chron. 30.

146   2 Kings 23:21–23.

147   Archaeologists have pointed to two primary identifying characteristics of Israelite (vs. Canaan, Egyptian, or Philistine) material culture that correspond to the beginning of the Iron Age in the Levant. These are the "collar-rim" store jar and the so-called four-room house (William Dever, *Who Were the Early Israelites and Where Did They Come From?* [Grand Rapids, Mich.: Wm. B. Eerdmans Publishing Co., 2003], 101–28).

148   The burn layer seems to corroborate the biblical account (Josh. 11:10–13) in which Hazor is "burned in fire." William F. Albright, often called the "Father of Biblical Archaeology," is well known for his support of this "Conquest Theory," citing Yigal Yadin's 1955–1958 excavations at Hazor (W. F. Albright in Louis Finkelstein's *The Biblical Period from Abraham to Ezra* [New York: Harper & Row, 1949], 27–28).

149   In addition to the absence of Late Bronze Age destruction layers at both Jericho and Ai (corroborating with Josh. 6:24 and 8:28), there is internal contradictory evidence within the biblical account. (For a clear summation of the significance of the evidential absence, *see* Dever, *Who Were the Early Israelites?*, 45–47.) If Joshua's account is true and he did vanquish the Canaanites, it is incompatible with the opening verse of the Book of Judges, which states: "After the death of Joshua, the Israelites inquired of the LORD, 'Which of us shall be the first to go up against the Canaanites and attack them?' " (Josh. 1:1). The Peaceful Infiltration Theory is well articulated in a book by Albrecht Alt, *Essays on Old Testament History and Religion* (Oxford: Oxford University Press, 1966) and one by Martin Noth, *The Deuteronomistic History* (Sheffield: JSOT Press, 1981).

150   George Mendenhall, "The Hebrew Conquest of Palestine," *Biblical Archaeologist 25* (1962): 73. See also Norman Gottwald, *The Tribes of Yahweh: A Sociology of the Religion of Liberated Israel, 1250–1050 B.C.E.* (Maryknoll, N.Y.: Orbis, 1979). Both this theory and

the one that follows cite, among other things, greater similarity between Israelite and Canaanite material culture than between that of the Israelites and the Egyptians.

151   Israel Finkelstein and Neil Asher Silberman, *The Bible Unearthed: Archaeology's New Vision of Ancient Israel and the Origin of Its Sacred Texts* (New York: Simon & Schuster, 2001). Finkelstein suggests that the biblical account of the Exodus may have been a later, 7th-century "expansion and elaboration of vague memories of the immigration of Canaanites to Egypt and their expulsion from the delta in the second millennium B.C.E." (ibid., 69). These memories could be shared by the 3rd-century B.C.E. Egyptian historian Manetho, who describes the arrival and eventual departure of the Hyksos, a remarkably similar narrative to the events detailed in the Hebrew Bible.

152   The Merneptah Victory Stele from circa 1210 B.C.E. includes the earliest extra-biblical mention of a people called "Israel."

153   Finkelstein and Silberman. *The Bible Unearthed,* 71.

154   JPS Hebrew-English TANAKH translates *ve-ya'avduni* as "that they may worship me." The root *avad* can be interpreted either as "serve" or "service" (in the sense of prayer or worship).

155   *Midrash Rabbah, Exodus Rabbah* 5:14.

156   Viktor E. Frankl, *Man's Search for Meaning* (New York: Washington Square Books, 1984), 133. Originally published in 1946.

157   In JPS Hebrew-English TANAKH, the transliteration is Abib, although the word is spelled *alef, vet, yud, vet* as opposed to *alef, bet, yud, bet.* Aviv is a more common transliteration.

158   Deut. 14:21, Exod. 23:199, Exod. 34:26, and Deut. 22:10.

159   The Talmud reports a disagreement between these two sages about where to begin the story. According to the Mishnah (*Pesachim* 10:4), the story begins with "disgrace" and ends with "praise." Rav says we should begin with the phrase "in the beginning our ancestors were idol worshippers." Shmuel says it should begin, "We were slaves to Pharaoh in Egypt." B. Talmud, *Pesachim* 116a. Both versions are recorded in the haggadah.

160   Mishnah, *Pesachim* 10:5. The Mishnah represents the Rabbinic oral tradition and was codified in its current form by Rabbi Judah the Prince (Yehudah Ha-Nasi) in approximately 200 C.E.

161   The poem does not have a true title, but is simply referred to by the first two words *Kadesh, Urchatz* ("Sanctify, Wash"). It was written to be sung. People sometimes give it the title *Simanei Ha-Seder* (literally, "Signs of the Seder") or "The Order of the Seder."

162   Nachman Cohen, *The Historical Haggadah* (Yonkers, N.Y.: Torah Lishma Institute, 2002), 6

163   Haviva Ner-David, "Thoughts on Cleaning for Pesach," in *The Women's Passover Companion*, ed. Sharon Cohen Anisfeld, Tara Mohr, and Catherine Spector (Woodstock, Vt.: Jewish Lights Publishing, 2003), 49–53.

164   Judith Lorber, *Night to His Day: The Social Construction of Gender* (New Haven, Conn.: Yale University Press, 1994), 33.

165   Zohar 182a.

166   *The Carlebach Haggadah: Seder Night with Reb Shlomo* (Jerusalem: Urim Publications, 2001), 10.

167   Excerpted from the original on www.jewishfamily.com (accessed February 4, 2008).

168   "The Debate on Machine-Made Matzot" by Philip Goodman in *The Passover Anthology* (Philadelphia: The Jewish Publication Society, 1961), 90–92.

Part 3: The Omer

1   B. Talmud, *Shabbat* 86b; see 86b–88a.

2   Exod. 12:18 ff; B. Talmud, *Shabbat* 87b.

3   Mishnah, *Rosh Hashanah* 1:2; B. Talmud, *Rosh Hashanah* 16b.

4   *Sefer Abudraham*, 271.

5   B. Talmud, *Yevamot* 62b; see also *Midrash Rabbah, Genesis Rabbah* 61:3, where there are variations to the account there.

6   The three other *sefirot* are *keter* ("crown"), *hokhmah* ("wisdom"), and *binah* ("understanding"). These three *sefirot* are the upper, or supernal, *sefirot*, which are understood to form "God's head." According to Kabbalah, these three *sefirot* represent spiritual characteristics that are beyond this world and beyond our human ability to fully access. Therefore, these are not a part of the Omer count, as the intention of the period of the Omer is to ready ourselves within our lower *sefirot* for the giving of the Torah.

7   Lev. 23:15.

8   B. Talmud, *Menachot* 65b–66a.

9   *See* Tosafot, *Menachot* 66a and the Rosh, end of *Pesachim*.

10   Tosafists were sages centered mainly in the Rhineland in the 11th and 12th centuries. They wrote supplementary notes to the commentaries of Rashi on the Talmud.

11   Rabbeinu Tam in Tosafot, *Menachot* 66a.

12   Maimonides, *Mishneh Torah, Hilkhot Temidim u'Musafin* 7:22–23.

13   Shulchan Arukh, *Orach Chayyim* 489:7. This perspective upholds the principle, supported by the Rosh at the end of *Pesachim* (*see* Ran there), which states that if there is a doubt, do not recite the blessing.

14   *Tur*/Shulchan Arukh, *Orach Chayyim* 493:1.

15   Ibid., 493:2.

16   Num. 6:2.

17   Samson, the famous biblical strongman in the Book of Judges (chap. 13–16), was a Nazirite. His hair is described as being the source of his strength; when Delilah deceives him and has it cut off, he loses his power and is captured by the Philistines (Judg. 16:18–21).

18   *Beit Ha-Bechirah* on tractate *Yevamot*, 234.

19   *Sefer Ha-Manhig* 91b; translation in Shlomo Yosef Zevin, *The Festivals in Halakhah*, vol. 2 (New York: Mesorah Publications, 1999), 888.

20   Isaac Klein, *A Guide to Jewish Religious Practice* (New York: Jewish Theological Seminary, 1979), 143–44; Klein cites *Otzar Ha-Geonim, Yevamot* 140.

21   *Mapa, Orach Chayyim* 493:3.

22   Ibid.

23   2 Lev. 19:23.

24   Most were released within three months, on condition that they leave Germany. Of those arrested, between 2,000 and 2,500 died from the brutal conditions inside the camps. Their bodies were cremated, and the ashes were returned to their relatives in packages marked "Postage Due on Arrival."

25   This term was coined by Joseph Goebbels, the Nazi minister of propaganda, who had orchestrated the pogroms.

26   Although November 9 is not an official day of mourning, some organizations hold annual programs to memorialize Kristallnacht.

27   The Nazis also targeted and murdered millions of disabled people, homosexuals, Gypsies, prisoners of war, and ethnic Poles, among others.

28   Within Zionism, a worldwide political movement to establish and support a Jewish homeland, there are various streams, including Labor Zionists, Socialist Zionists, Political Zionists, Revisionist Zionists, and Religious Zionists.

29   Because of the compromise date, some Orthodox rabbis do not endorse participation in Yom Ha-Shoah by their followers.

30   The usual date is the 5th of the Hebrew month of Iyar. If that date falls on a Friday or Saturday, Yom Ha-Atzmaut is celebrated on the preceding Thursday to avoid interfering with the Sabbath.

31   Rabbi Fishman was a signer of the proclamation under the name Hacohen Fishman.

32   Members who were abroad or in Jerusalem made their way later to Tel Aviv to sign the declaration.

33   Avi Hein, "Yom Ha-Zikaron," www.jewishvirtuallibrary.org (accessed February 13, 2008).

34   Translation from www.aish.com (accessed July 15, 2008).

35   A place to which people made pilgrimage over the centuries, when permitted by whomever had conquered the Land of Israel. They wept there over the destruction of the Temple.

36   *The Guide of the Perplexed*, vol. 2, trans. Shlomo Pines (Chicago: University of Chicago Press, 1963), 571.

37   *Sefer Abudraham, Sefirat Ha-Omer* 267, in *The Book of Our Heritage*, vol. 2, trans. Nachman Bulman (New York: Feldheim Publishers, 1997), 682.

38   *Sefat Emet, Emor* 3:173, in *The Language of Truth*, trans. Arthur Green (Philadelphia: The Jewish Publication Society, 1998), 194–95.

39   From the first volume, "Reason in Common Sense," of philosopher George Santayana's five-volume work *The Life in Reason: The Phases of Human Progress* (New York: Charles Scribner's Sons, 1905), 284.

40   David Hartman, *Sinai and the Exodus: Choosing Life in the Midst of Uncertainty* (Jerusalem: Shalom Hartman Institute, 2002), 22–23.

41   Deut. 30:4–5.

42   Mishnah, *Avot* 3:2.

43   Deut. 6:10–12, 7:1–6, 20:10–18; Joshua, chapters 6, 8, and 10.

44   Isa. 11:9, 40:1–31; Dan. 7:13–27.

45   Deut. 7:7, 9:6; Amos 3:2.

46   The idea for such a haggadah was suggested to Rabbi Goren by Rabbi Joseph Lookstein, chairman of the Rabbinical Advisory Committee of the United Jewish Appeal in the United States. Asa Kasher, "The Passover Haggadah and the Haggadah of Yom Ha-Atzmaut," on the website of Oz VeShalom–Netivot Shalom (accessed March 3, 2008).

47   United Jewish Appeal Israel Independence Day Haggadah, 1978.

48   Tevet is the Hebrew month corresponding to December–January.

49   *See* Judith T. Baumel, *Kol-Bikhiot* ("A Voice of Lament") (Hebrew) (Ramat Gan, Israel: Bar Ilan Press, 1992), for a complete history of prayers and religious commemorations of the Holocaust.

50   According to a talmudic story (B. Talmud, *Shabbat* 33b), Shimon bar Yochai composed the Zohar in the middle of the 2nd century C.E. The Zohar seemingly remained a hidden text until the end of the 13th century when Moshe De Leon, a Spanish kabbalist, claimed to have unearthed it. However, most contemporary scholars believe De Leon to be the true author of the Zohar.

51   Vital was born in Tzfat and died in Damascus. He is considered to be the successor to Isaac Luria, who died in 1572. Vital's greatest work is *Etz Chaim* (Tree of Life), He

emphasized that it is a collection of teachings of his master Isaac Luria, who never authored his own book.

52 Each letter of the Hebrew alphabet has a numerical equivalent. *Lamed* is 30 and *gimel* is 3.

53 B. Talmud, *Ketubot* 77b.

54 Arnold M. Eisen, *Taking Hold of Torah: Jewish Community and Commitment in America* (Bloomington: Indiana University Press, 1997), 40–46.

Part 4: Shavuot

1 Theodor Gaster, *Festivals of the Jewish Year* (New York: Morrow Quill, 1952), 60.

2 Tzipporah Heller, "The Commandment of Counting," Aish HaTorah, www.aish.com/omer/omerdefault/The_Commandment_of_Counting.asp (accessed February 3, 2008).

3 Mishnah, *Avot* 5:24.

4 Literally, "two loaves of bread as an elevation offering."

5 Lev. 23:17.

6 2 Kings 22–23. Josiah's reforms were a response to the prophetess's authentication of the curses in a sacred scroll discovered by Hilkiah, the High Priest.

7 Deut. 23:14–17.

8 Mishnah, *Bikkurim* 1:6.

9 "You shall live in booths [sukkot] seven days; all citizens in Israel shall live in booths, in order that future generations may know that I made the Israelite people live in booths when I brought them out of the land of Egypt, I am the LORD your God" (Lev. 23:42–43).

10 B. Talmud, *Menachot* 65–66; Maimonides, *Mishneh Torah, Hilkhot Temidin u'Musafin* 7:11.

11 B. Talmud, *Shabbat* 86–88.

12 The question about which day the Torah was given originates in the verse: "and the LORD said to Moses, 'Go to the people and warn them to stay pure today and tomorrow'" (Exod. 19:10). The Rabbis of the Talmud understand the meaning of "stay pure" as a directive to husbands and wives to temporarily separate from each other and thereby abstain from sex. However, since the verse ambiguously says "stay pure today and tomorrow," we do not know whether the Torah was given two or three days after this separation. There are two ways to deduce an answer. One is by attempting to understand when "today" begins. Does "today" mean starting from the very day in the daylight hours, when the command was given, or starting that evening, when the next "day" begins on the Hebrew calendar. The second way, the one the

Rabbis follow, examines how long it would take for a woman to become completely pure after sexual intercourse. That is, how long does the sperm stay viable in the womb, because so long as the sperm remains viable, its ultimate emission from her body would put the woman in a state of ritual impurity. *See also* Shulchan Arukh, *Yoreh De'ah* 196.

13   Among the most critical analyses of this issue is of the 17th-century Polish scholar Avraham Abele Gombiner, author of a significant halakhic work called *Magen Avraham*. *See* his comments in *Magen Avraham* 494.

14   *Chaye Adam* 131:13. Anthropologist Theodor Gaster also suggests that the floral decorations were based on European Christian customs (which came from pagan customs) of decorating churches during this festival. *See* Theodor Gaster, *Festivals of the Jewish Year: A Modern Interpretation and Guide* (New York: Morrow Quill, 1952), 75–76.

15   Mishnah, *Rosh Hashanah* 1:2; B. Talmud, *Rosh Hashanah* 16b.

16   *Sefer Ha-Toda'ah*, vol. 3, 53.

17   *Mapa, Orach Chayyim* 494:3.

18   Arukh Ha-Shulchan 494:6.

19   Lev. 23:15.

20   *Mishnah Berurah* 494, *se'if katan* 1.

21   Zohar, *Emor* 98a.

22   *Midrash Rabbah, Song of Songs Rabbah* 1:57; *Pirke de-Rabbi Eliezer* 41.

23   The Oral Torah, also called the Oral Law or the Oral Tradition, is a body of commentaries, expositions, and explanations about the Written Torah that was originally passed on to each generation by word of mouth only, to prevent incompleteness and to foster the benefits of intense teacher–student relationships. Once the Second Temple was destroyed and the Jews scattered, fear arose that the transmission of the Oral Torah would falter. The Oral Torah was then written down over a period of time from the 1st to 3rd centuries.

24   *Midrash Rabbah, Exodus Rabbah* 28:6; B. Talmud, *Berakhot* 5a; Mishnah, *Avot* 1:1.

25   *Tanchuma* 58:3; *see also* B. Talmud, *Shabbat* 88a.

26   Zohar, Prologue 8a, *Emor* 98a.

27   The Book of Our Heritage (*Sefer Ha-Toda'ah*) 3:780–81.

28   A translation of Israel Najara's Shavuot *ketubah* can be found in Philip Goodman, *The Shavuot Anthology* (Philadelphia: The Jewish Publication Society, 1992), 99–101.

29   *See* Isaac Klein, *A Guide to Jewish Religious Practice* (New York: Jewish Theological Seminary, 1992), 151.

30   *Mishnah Berurah* 494, *se'if katan* 12.

31	Born in Poland in 1929, Bermant moved at age eight to Scotland, where he became a noted writer and humorist. He died in London in 1998.
32	*Kol Bo* 58.
33	*Mapa, Orach Chayyim* 494:3.
34	The egg on the Passover seder plate is not dairy but parve (neither meat nor milk according to the laws of kashrut). Symbolic contrast exists nonetheless between meat and an egg.
35	In Klein, *Guide*, 151, he cites *Otzar Kol Minhagei Yeshurun* (201) by Abraham Eliezer Hirshowitz as his source for this rationale.
36	Tractate *Soferim* 14:16–18. *Soferim* is written in the style of the Mishnah and is included at the end of tractate *Nezikin* in many editions of the Talmud. Nevertheless, *Soferim* is not considered to be a part of the Talmud, as most scholars date it to the gaonic period, about the 8th century.
37	Rema (Moses Isserles) in *Mapa* and *Darkei Moshe, Orach Chayyim* 490; *Sefer Abudraham* 266.
38	Based on the rulings of the Maharil and Rema. *See* Shlomo Yosef Zevin, *The Festivals in Halakhah*, vol. 2 (New York: Mesorah Publications, 1999), 954–95.
39	There is no consensus in the codes as to whether one should say a blessing before the Book of Ruth is read. See *Mapa, Orach Chayyim* 490:9 and *Mishnah Berurah* there, *se'if katan* 19; *Levush, Orach Chayyim*, 494:2.
40	*Sefer Abudraham* 266.
41	*Yalkut Shimoni* 596; see also *Sefer Abudraham* 266, *Darkei Moshe, Orach Chayyim* 490, and *Levush, Orach Chayyim* 494:2.
42	"True" in the sense that she converts after there is an established nation of Israel with Torah and specific practices. With great awareness, she chooses to be part of a people and its traditions. Earlier—for example during the time of Abraham and around the time of Revelation—people were agreeing to something without such a clear picture of what they were getting into.
43	Ruth 1:15–17.
44	B. Talmud, *Yevamot* 47a.
45	The Book of Ruth ends with a recitation of the line of descent from Perez to David.
46	B. Talmud, *Ketubot* 7b; J. Talmud, *Hagigah* 2:3; *Midrash Rabbah, Ruth Rabbah* 2:3.
47	Deut. 18:18–22.
48	Examples include Exod. 3:1, Deut. 4:10, and 1 Kings 19:8.
49	1 Kings 19:12, translated in JPS Hebrew-English TANAKH as "a soft murmuring sound."
50	B. Talmud, *Bava Batra* 12a.
51	B. Talmud, *Berakhot* 5a; *see also* Mishnah, *Avot* 1:1 and *Midrash Rabbah, Numbers Rabbah* 19:6.

52   J. Talmud, *Pe'ah* 17a.

53   B. Talmud, *Bava Metzia* 59b.

54   Deut. 30:12.

55   B. Talmud, *Rosh Hashanah* 25b. The Talmud clearly affirms that the authority of each present generation is the authority: "Would it enter your mind that a person would go to a judge not living in his own day! See now, you do not need to go to any other judge than that of one's own day. As it says: *Don't say, 'How has it happened that former times were better than these?'* (Eccles. 7:10)."

56   Sa'adia Ga'on was born Sa'adia ben Yosef in Egypt in 882 and later lived in Babylonia, where he was a Jewish philosopher, halakhist, philogist, and composer of liturgical poetry. He served as the *ga'on* (literally, "genius"), or head of the academy at Sura and transformed it into a leading institution. He died in 942. Yehuda Ha-Levi was an important and influential Jewish poet and philosopher who was a physician by profession. He was born in Spain in 1075 and died there in 1141. Maimonides (Rabbi Moses ben Maimon) was also a physician and philosopher. He is the author of the first written Jewish legal code, the *Mishneh Torah*, and of the famous commentary, *Guide of the Perplexed*. He was born in 1135 in Spain and died in 1204 in Egypt.

57   Throughout his philosophical writings, Maimonides continues to assert the importance of reason and philosophy. He argues continuously that the laws of the Torah are rational and intended to guide us in a healthy and balanced life. He suggests that while the stories and even words of the Torah help us to know God according to our intellectual capacity, we must use reason, intellect, and philosophy to uncover the true meaning of the Torah and its precepts. Maimonides is unequivocally a rationalist who deeply values philosophy, but concedes that one can never really define or absolutely comprehend God. *See* his *Guide of the Perplexed*, particularly the introduction, 1:1, 2, and 5, and 3:26ff, as well as his *Shemoneh Perakim* (literally, "Eight Chapters").

58   Based on a passage in the Babylonian Talmud (*Gittin* 60a), some also believe that the Torah was handed down little by little over the course of the 40 years of wandering in the desert. In either case, the traditional view of Revelation is that the Torah is a direct quote from God.

59   Scribe as an honorific title used for other biblical figures, such as Moses, Enoch, and David.

60   The four authors are known by their initials J, E, P, and D. The J author, or Jawhist (pronounced Yah-wist), is identified by the use of God's name in the four-letter Tetragrammaton *yud, heh, vav, heh*; the E author, or Elohist, is identified by the use of

God's name as *Elohim;* the P author, or Priestly author, is credited for composing most of the Book of Leviticus and other sections concerned with the priesthood; and the D author, or Deuteronomist, is credited for composing the Book of Deuteronomy. (The D author is also credited with writing six Books of the Prophets: Joshua, Judges, 1 and 2 Samuel, and 1 and 2 Kings, found in Nevi'im, the second part of the Bible.) The theory further suggests that these four documents were gathered, combined, and edited by the R source, or Redactor.

61   The most popular and accessible books on the Documentary Hypothesis are by Professor Richard Elliot Friedman. Of particular interest are *Who Wrote the Bible* (San Francisco: HarperCollins Publishers, 1997) and *The Bible with Sources Revealed* (San Francisco: HarperCollins Publishers, 2003).

62   Norman Lamm, *The Condition of Jewish Belief: A Symposium Compiled by the Editors of Commentary* (New York: The Macmillan Company, 1966), 124–25.

63   *See* Joel Roth, *The Halakhic Process: A Systemic Analysis* (New York: Jewish Theological Seminary of America, 1986).

64   For other scholars, *see* Robert Gordis and Max Gelb, *Understanding Conservative Judaism* (New York: Rabbinical Assembly, 1978) and *The Dynamics of Judaism: A Study in Jewish Law* (Bloomington: Indiana University Press, 1990); Elliot Dorff, *Conservative Judaism: Our Ancestors to Our Descendants* (New York: United Synagogue of Conservative Judaism, 1996).

65   *See* Abraham Joshua Heschel, *God in Search of Man: A Philosophy of Judaism* (New York: Farrar, Straus and Giroux, 1955), 185.

66   *Sifrei,* Deuteronomy 41, translated by Barry Holtz in *Finding Our Way: Jewish Texts and Lives We Live Today* (Philadelphia: The Jewish Publication Society, 2005), 36–7.

67   Rabbi Simlai was a talmudic sage from the 3rd century. He lived in Israel. and Babylonia. The calculation of 613 mitzvot is attributed to him.

68   This rabbi is likely Levi bar Sisi, a talmudist who lived in 3rd-century Israel and Babylonia.

69   Yehuda bar Yechezkel, a prominent 3rd-century *amora* (literally, "explainer").

70   A famous talmudist who lived in the 2nd and 3rd centuries.

71   JPS Hebrew-English TANAKH translates the verse as, "You have but to inquire about bygone ages that came before you, ever since God created man on earth, from one end of heaven to the other: has anything as grand as this ever happened, or has its like ever been known?"

72   JPS Hebrew-English TANAKH translates the phrase as, "for God has come only in order to test you, ..."

73   Translation from Isadore Twersky, *A Maimonides Reader* (West Orange, N.J.: Behrman House, 1972), 446–47.

74   An oft-quoted sage in the Talmud who lived in the Land of Israel during the 2nd century.

75   *Tanchuma Buber,* Deuteronomy 1a, translated by Elliot Dorff in *The Unfolding Tradition: Jewish Law After Sinai* (New York: Aviv Press, 2005), 38.

76   *God in Search of Man* is a companion volume to Heschel's *Man Is Not Alone: A Philosophy of Religion* (New York: Farrar, Straus and Young, 1951).

77   Heschel, *God in Search of Man,* 184–5.

78   Emmanuel Levinas, "Revelation in the Jewish Tradition," in *Beyond the Verse: Talmudic Readings and Lectures,* trans. Gary D. Mole (Bloomington: Indiana University Press, 1994), 129–50.

79   There are two versions of the Talmud: the Jerusalem Talmud (completed in the 5th century in northern Israel) and the more extensive Babylonian Talmud (completed in the 6th century in Babylonia). The compilers were Rabbinic scholars whose families had escaped from the terroristic reign of the Romans.

80   *Sifrei* 343; B. Talmud, *Avodah Zarah* 2b.

81   *Gur Aryeh,* Shemot 17:19.

82   B. Talmud, *Shabbat* 88a, and Rashi.

83   *Midrash Rabbbah, Exodus Rabbah* 29:9.

84   This blessing covers all Torah study for that day. However, we have the option of saying the blessing again before any additional study sessions, in which case, we usually say only the first ending.

85   Daniel Gordis, *God Was Not in the Fire: The Search for a Spiritual Judaism* (New York: Scribner, 1995), 94.

86   Franz Rosenzweig, *On Jewish Learnning,* ed. Nahum N. Glatzer (New York: Schocken Books, 1955), 98.

87   The phrase *Aseret Ha-Devarim* appears elsewhere in the Torah; *see* Exod. 34:28 and Deut. 4:13 and 10:4. An alternative version of the term, *Aseret Ha-Dibrot,* is also found in Rabbinic literature.

88   Exod. 24:12, 25:16, and 32:15

89   B. Talmud, *Shabbat* 104a.

90   Mishnah, *Tamid* 5:1.

91   B. Talmud, *Makkot* 23b–24a.

92   J. Talmud, *Berakhot* 3c; B. Talmud, *Berakhot* 12a.

93   The Bible does not set up laws in terms of crime and punishment. That system was

established by the Talmud and later Jewish legal codes, and, of course, the legal codes of nations are written that way.

94   Any additional days that some people now observe were added in the early stages of the Diaspora.

95   June 15, 1967.

96   Translation by Arthur Green.

97   Translation from JPS Hebrew-English TANAKH: 2nd ed. (Philadelphia: The Jewish Publication Society, 1999).

98   Deut. 11:18.

99   This is Yitzhak Meir Alter of Ger (1799–1866, Poland), founder of the Ger hasidic dynasty. All his 13 sons died during his lifetime, and he was succeeded in 1870 by his young grandson, Rabbi Yehuda Leib Alter of Ger, known as the Sefat Emet.

100   Rabbi Cohen was born in the Bronx section of New York City in 1924. He served as chancellor of the Jewish Theological Seminary from 1972 to 1986, during which time he ordained the first female Conservative rabbi and established the first Conservative rabbinical program in Jerusalem. He died in 1991.

101   Irving Greenberg, *The Jewish Way: Living the Holidays* (New York: Simon & Schuster, 1993), 73–75.

102   My [Greenberg] translation. *Pirkei Avot* (Ethics of the Fathers), a collection of rabbinic wisdom and ethics, has also been translated by Judah Goldin in *The Living Talmud* (New York: New American Library, 1957).

103   Joseph B. Soloveitchik, "The Lonely Man of Faith," in *Tradition: A Journal of Orthodox Jewish Thought*, vol. 7, no. 21 (Summer 1965), pp. 5–67, especially p. 29.

104   Ibid., pp. 28–29.

Part 5: Tisha b'Av

1   Milton Steinberg, *The Making of the Modern Jew: From the Second Temple to the State of Israel* (New York: Behrman House, 1964), 63.

2   For more on this messianic transformation of the fast days, *see* Maimonides, *Mishneh Torah, Hilkhot Ta'aniyot* 5:19.

3   In relation to Shabbat or a holy day, a "day" lasts about 25 hours rather than the 24 we measure out on an everyday basis. According to Jewish law, a day begins at sunset. To be certain that a complete day is observed, we light the ritual candles at least 18 minutes before sunset. To further ensure complete observance, we do not conclude Shabbat or a holy day until at least three stars are visible in the night sky. Because the stars may be obscured, various formulas exist to determine the end of Shabbat or a

holy day, the most stringent being 24 hours plus 72 minutes after the official candlelighting time of the preceding evening. A major fast lasts about 25 hours on the same basis.

4   *See* 2 Kings 25:1; Jer. 52:4; and Ezek. 24:2.

5   *Mapa, Orach Chayyim* 551:2.

6   The three *Haftarot* of Admonition are (1) Jer. 1:1–2:3 (Parashat Mattot); (2) Jer. 2:4–28, to which Askenazim add verse 3:4 and Sephardim add verses 4:1–2 (Parashat Mase'ei) ; and (3) Isa. 1:1–27 (Parashat Devarim).

7   *Midrash Rabbah, Lamentations Rabbah* 1.

8   Mishnah, *Ta'anit* 4:6; *Tur/Shulchan Arukh, Orach Chayyim* 551:1–4.

9   Shuchan Arukh, *Orach Chayyim,* 551:7.

10   Num. 13–15.

11   Except for Caleb, whom God recognized as being the only spy to say conquest was surely possible. Num. 13:30,14:30.

12   B. Talmud, *Ta'anit* 29b.

13   Monday, July 18, 1994, the 10th of Av.

14   Shulchan Arukh, *Orach Chayyim* 554:1.

15   Arukh Ha-Shulchan, *Orach Chayyim* 554.

16   Shulchan Arukh, *Orach Chayyim* 554:1. The acceptable parts of Rabbinic literature to study, traditionally speaking, are tractates *Mo'ed Katan* (chapter 3, laws of mourning and excommunication) and *Gittin* (55–56, passages about the destruction of the Temple and Jerusalem) of the Talmud, and the Midrash and commentaries on the books of Lamentations and Job.

17   Shulchan Arukh, *Orach Chayyim* 552.

18   *Mapa, Orach Chayyim* 559:2.

19   Shulchan Arukh, *Orach Chayyim* 559:3.

20   *Sefer Ha-Toda'ah,* vol. 2, 379.

21   Shulchan Arukh, *Orach Chayyim* 555:1.

22   The identity of the Messiah is not revealed at birth as it is in Christianity.

23   J. Talmud, *Berakhot* 2:4; *Pesikta Rabbati* 28:3; *Sefer Ha-Toda'ah,* vol. 2, 379.

24   Shulchan Arukh, *Orach Chayyim* 555:1. See also *Mishnah Berurah* there, *se'if katan* 3.

25   The seven *Haftarot* of Consolation are (1) Isa. 40:1–26 (Parashat Va-'Ethannan), (2) Isa. 49:14–51:3 (Parashat 'Ekev), (3) Isa. 54:11–55:5 (Parashat Re'eh), (4) Isa. 51:12–52:12 (Parashat Shofetim), (5) Isa. 54:1–10 (Parashat Ki Tetse'), (6) Isa. 60:1–22 (Parashat Ki Tavo'), and (7) Isa. 61:10–63:9 (Parashat Nitsavim).

26   *Tosefta, Ta'anit* 2:10.

27   *See* Jer. 2:18, 5:7-9, 9:1-5, 11–13 and 37:5–10 for examples.

28   *See* Lam. 3:43, 5:7, and 4:17 for examples.

29   Num. 13 and 14.

30   J. Talmud, *Ta'anit* 4:10, 69c. Translated by William G. Braude in *The Book of Legends: Sefer Ha-Aggadah*, eds. Hayyim Nahman Bialik and Yehoshua Hana Ravnitzky (New York: Schocken Press, 1992), 99.

31   *Avot de-Rabbi Natan* B 48. Translation by Reuven Hammer in *Or Hadash* (New York: The Rabbinical Assembly, 2003), 6.

32   Translation by Braude in *Book of Legends*, 391.

33   The Satan in Judaism is part of God's angelic court, serving as the proscecuting attorney. This Satan is not the same as Satan—the devil—as described in other religious traditions.

34   Zohar, *Vayishlach* 170b.

35   Steinberg, *Making of the Modern Jew,* 31, 50–51.

36   B. Talmud, *Sukkah* 51b.

37   B. Talmud, *Yoma* 9b.

38   *Bava Metzia* is part of larger section of the Talmud called *Nezikin*, which deals with the laws of civil damage.

39   This Camp Ramah in Connecticut, which began in 1953, was one of the precursors of today's Camp Ramah in New England, located in Palmer, Massachusetts.

40   The first phase of the "1948" war actually begins on November 29, 1947, with the passage of the United Nations Partition Plan.

41   B. Talmud, *Makkot* 24b.

42   A ravine in Kiev where the Nazis murdered more than 33,000 of the city's Jews on September 29 and 30, 1941.

43   The most common acronymn for Isserles is Rema.

44   *Hasidic Tales of the Holocaust* published in New York by Oxford University Press. Yaffa Eliach derived the stories from interviews and oral histories.

45   This character is based on the real Miles Lerman who served as the founding chairman of the U.S. Holocaust Memorial Museum in Washington, D.C. He died at age 88 in January 2008.

46   Mishnah, *Ta'anit* 4:8; B. Talmud, *Ta'anit* 31a.

47   *See* Rashi there, *d"h she'ulin.*

48   B. Talmud, *Ta'anit* 30b–31a.

49   *Midrash Rabbah, Lamentations Rabbah* 33; J. Talmud, *Ta'anit* 4:10, 69c.

50   Males from 20 to 50 years of age.

51   Num. 36:8–9, which discuss laws about inheritance, and Judg. 21:1, which discusses a ban against marrying specifically into the tribe of Benjamin.

52   B. Talmud, *Bava Batra* 121b.

53   According to Jewish law, weddings are prohibited on Shabbat, as well as Rosh Hashanah, Yom Kippur, Sukkot (principal days only), Passover, and Shavuot because of the restrictions on travel and work. Weddings are also prohibited on Tisha b'Av and the minor fast days because on these days, the mood is meant to be mournful. Weddings are also traditionally prohibited during the seven weeks of the Omer, but authorities from different streams of Judaism differ about whether this applies to the entire seven weeks. Weddings are permitted on Purim, Hanukkah, and the intermediate days of Sukkot.

54   Nogah Hareuveni, *Nature in Our Biblical Heritage* (Kiryat Ono, Israel: Neot Kedumim, The Biblical Landscape Reserve in Israel, 1980), 91–100.

55   Ibid., 95.

56   Rabban is a title given only to patriarchs and to presidents of the Sanhedrin (Jewish supreme court).

57   Alan Lew, *This Is Real and You Are Completely Unprepared: The Days of Awe as a Journey of Transformation* (New York: Little, Brown & Company, 2003), 52–63.

Part 6: Guidance along the Way

1   B. Talmud, *Eruvin* 63b; *Shabbat* 30a; *Menachot* 100a.

2   B. Talmud, *Avodah Zarah* 3b; *Hagigah* 5b.

3   J. Talmud, *Berakhot* 9a; B. Talmud, *Berakhot* 22a; *Shabbat* 83b.

4   Mishnah, *Avot* 1:4, 2:17, 19, 3:3–4, 7, 10, 21, 4:11; Maimonides, *Mishneh Torah, Hilkhot Talmud Torah* 4:19; *Tur, Orach Chayyim* 153:1.

5   B. Talmud, *Shabbat* 127a.

6   Known in biblical times as Yabniel, Yavneh is west of Jerusalem and south of Tel Aviv.

7   Mishnah, *Avot* 2:9.

8   Rabbi Meir, also known as Reb Meir Baal Ha-Nes (1st century C.E., Israel) lived in the time of the Mishnah and is considered one of the greatest of the *taanim* of the second generation.

9   Mishnah, Avot 6:1.

10   *Pesikta Rabbati: Homiletical Discourses for Festal Days and Special Sabbaths 1 & 2.* Yale University Press, 1968, as part of the Yale Judaica Series.

11   The school was "free" because it required no entrance examinations or testimonials,

offered no degrees, and encouraged free inquiry. It was open to Jews and non-Jews and was connected to Judaism as a whole, rather than to any particular stream of Judaism. In contrast to traditional academies of learning, instruction was highly interdisciplinary. The school was called a "house" partly because of the name of the tradtional Jewish *beit ha-midrash* ("house of study"). And yet it did not occupy a permanent building; the lectures and seminars were conducted in rented halls and private homes.

12   *The Language of Truth: The Torah Commentary of the Sefat Emet, Rabbi Yehudah Leib Alter of Ger.* Translated and interpreted by Arthur Green (Philadelphia: The Jewish Publication Society, 1998).

13   Translated by Nachman Bulman. Revised and adapted by Dovid Landesman and Joyce Bennett (Jerusalem and New York: Feldheim Publishers, 1997).

14   The Talmud refers to the work as *Sifra de-be Rav.*

Glossary

Aggadah
The nonlegal portions of Rabbinic literature, including moral lessons, prayers, legends, and folklore. Their analysis and explication of the Bible are primarily homiletic.

Akdamut (literally, "Introduction")
A poetic introduction to the Ten Commandments that is read on Shavuot. Written in Aramaic, the poem, which praises God, was composed by Rabbi Meir ben Yitzchak Nehorai in 11th-century Germany.

aliyah (literally, "ascension"); pl. aliyot
A division within a given Torah reading. The number of *aliyot* varies by day: a minimum of three *aliyot* at a weekday Torah reading, four on Rosh Hodesh, five on a festival day, six on Yom Kippur, and seven on Shabbat. *Aliyah* is also the term for the honor of reciting the blessings before and after the reading.

Amidah (literally, "Standing")
The central Jewish prayer that is said silently while standing. It is also referred to as *Ha-Tefillah* (The Prayer) and as the *Shemoneh Esrei* (Eighteen Blessings).

amora; pl. amoraim
A Rabbinic sage of the 2nd–5th centuries who explained the teachings of the Oral Law. The word comes from the Aramaic *amar* ("to say or to speak"), and by extension *amoraim* are "interpreters." The *amoraim* who lived in Israel have, in general, the title "rabbi" and those who lived Babylonia have the title "rav" or "mar." Their legal discussions and debates were eventually codified in the Gemara. In contrast, the *tannaim* were earlier Rabbinic sages who directly transmitted the uncodified Oral Law.

Aramaic
An ancient Semitic language closely related to Hebrew. Jews are understood to have adopted Aramaic during the Babylonian exile, thus leading to the use of Aramaic in parts of the TANAKH (e.g., Daniel) and all of the Talmud and the Zohar. The *Kol Nidrei* prayer on the evening of Yom Kippur and the *Kaddish* are in Aramaic.

Aseret Ha-Dibrot or *Aseret Ha-Devarim* (literally, "The Ten Statements" or "The Ten Words") The Ten Commandments.

Ashkenazim

Jews with long-ago ancestors from Germany or France. Throughout the medieval period of persecution, many Ashkenazim migrated to other parts of Europe, especially Poland and Russia.

Atzeret

The Rabbinic term for Shavuot. The exact translation is uncertain, although it is generally translated as "conclusion" or "gathering."

Av

The 11th month on the Hebrew calendar. It corresponds to July–August. Although the meaning is uncertain, the name comes from *Abu*, possibly related to "father,"

bikkurim (literally "first fruits")

The first fruits, including the first grains to ripen each season, which were brought as offerings to the Temple in Jerusalem, starting on Shavuot and continuing to Sukkot and, under certain circumstances, until Hanukkah. They include any of the "seven species" (*shivat minim*)—the staple foods of the biblical Land of Israel: olives, grapes, wheat, barley, figs, dates, and pomegranates.

derash (literally, "inquiry")

A figurative interpretation of a text in contrast to *peshat,* which is the plain meaning of a text.

Diaspora (from the Greek for "dispersion")

The Jewish communities outside of the Land of Israel. The concept and term originated in the 6th century B.C.E. when the Second Temple was destroyed by the conquering Babylonians, who forced the Israelites to leave their country and settle in new places. The Hebrew equivalent for Diaspora is *galut* (literally, "exile").

Eikhah (literally, "Alas")

Hebrew name for the Book of Lamentations, which is found in Kethuvim (The Writings), the third part of the TANKAH.

▲ ▲ ▲ ▲ ▲ ▲ ▲ ▲ ▲ ▲ ▲ ▲ ▲ ▲ ▲

Exodus (literally, "Going Out")

The Israelites' entire flight from slavery in Egypt to freedom. Also the Greek title of the second of the Five Books of Moses, which in the original Hebrew is called Shemot ("Names"), taken from the first verse, "These are the names of the sons of Israel who came to Egypt with Jacob ... ." It includes the Israelites' being given the Ten Commandments at Mount Sinai and ends with the building of the *mishkan* (Tabernacle) in the wilderness.

Feast of Weeks See Shavuot.

First Fruits See *bikkurim*.

Four Children

Traditionally known as the "Four Sons" (Hebrew, *arba banim*), a section of the Passover haggadah that describes the wise child, the wicked child, the simple child, and the one who does not know how to ask. The questions have been interpreted variously as metaphors for ourselves, our children, and the nation of Israel. They are seen as a model of how to transmit and interpret the story of the Exodus and the Jews' entire heritage to succeeding generations. This famous passage is based on four places in the Torah that speak about the dialogue between parents and children (Exod. 12:25–26,13:8,14; Deut. 6:20–21).

Four Questions

The famous paragraph in the Passover haggadah chanted by the youngest child. The central question is *"Mah nishtanah ha-lailah ha-zeh?"* with specific inquiries about four things: matzah, bitter herbs, the dipping of food, and the practice of reclining. The subsequent comments on the questions are framed in the personalities of the Four Children (see above). The text originated about 2,000 years ago, as far back as the Mishnah, likely in the form of words used in Second Temple times.

ga'on (literally, "genius"); pl. **ge'onim**

A title of honor bestowed on the spiritual heads of the Babylonian academies between the 6th and 11th centuries. The ge'onim compiled the Babylonian Talmud, answered questions from Jews in the Diaspora about religious law, and presided over the courts of law that arbitrated disputes between Jews, In 18th-century Lithuania, the title was also given to Rabbi Elijah ben Shlomo Zalman, the Ga'on of Vilna, in recognition of his mathematical genius and great talmudic and kabbalistic scholarship.

goad
A pointed rod used to make an animal move.

haftarah; pl. *haftarot*
A selected portion from the biblical Book of Prophets that is read following the Torah reading (*parashah*) on Shabbat and most holidays.

hag (literally, "celebration" or "holiday"); pl. *hagim*
A holiday for which there are traditional observances and customs. *Hag* also refers to the principal days of the festivals of Passover and Sukkot. See *hol ha-mo'ed.*

Hag Ha-Bikkurim (literally, "The Festival of First Fruits")
One of the biblical names for Shavuot.

Hag Ha-Katzir (literally, "The Festival of the Harvest")
One of the biblical names for Shavuot.

halakhah (literally, "the way"); pl. *halakhot*
Jewish law, including the rules, observances, and requirements of Jewish life, which originated in the Torah. The Rabbis organized the laws into the Mishnah and Talmud. The term is derived from the three-letter Hebrew root *heh.lamed.khaf.*, or *lalekhet*, meaning "to go" or "to walk."

Hallel (literally, "Praise")
Psalms 113 to 118 recited on festivals and on Rosh Hodesh as a display of joy and gratitude.

Hasidism (from the Hebrew word *hasid*, "pious one")
A Jewish religious movement that began in 18th-century Eastern Europe. Rabbi Yisrael ben Eliezer (b. 1698–d. 1760, Ukraine) is understood to be the founder. He became known as the Baal Shem Tov (Master of the Good Name). His teachings, based on Kabbalah, emphasize the spiritual through joy in living, the holiness of the common man, and the power and transcendence of prayer.

ḥol ha-mo'ed (literally, "the mundane of the festival")

The intermediary, less restrictive days between the most sacred days (*ḥagim*) of both the festival of Passover and the festival of Sukkot. In the Diaspora, these are the third through sixth days; in Israel, the second through sixth days.

Ineffable Name

The ancient name of God that no one knows today or that we are not able to use in speech. It is represented in writing by the four Hebrew consonants *yud, heh, vav, heh*, called the Tetragrammaton (Greek for "four letters"). We do not know the corresponding vowels, and so Jews speak the word *Adonai*, meaning "my LORD," in place of the Ineffable Name.

Iyar

The eighth month on the Hebrew calendar. Called *Ziv* in the Bible, Iyar corresponds to April–May. The name comes from *ayaru*, meaning "light and brightness of blossoming flowers" (related to the Hebrew word for light, "*or*").

Kabbalah (literally, "Reception")

The tradition of Jewish mysticism, which maintains that there are hidden truths within the Torah. The primary resource for Kabbalah is the Zohar. According to Kabbalah there are four worlds or spheres of creation through which 10 different emanation of God flow: *atzilut* ("emanation"), *beriyah* ("creation"), *yetzirah* ("formation"), and *assiyah* ("action"). Hasidism bases many of its teachings upon Kabbalah.

kashrut (literally, "fit" or "proper")

The body of Jewish dietary laws dealing with foods, combinations of foods, and how these foods are to be prepared and eaten. The term in English is "kosher," which is also used to describe objects that are made in accordance with Jewish law and are fit for ritual use.

Kiddush (literally, "Sanctification")

The blessing recited over wine. It is said every Sabbath, on Jewish holidays, and before celebratory meals to sanctify these occasions.

kitel (literally, "a gown")

A man's white robe, usually of linen. It is part of the clothing in which the dead are buried. It is also worn on certain special occasions and holidays: Rosh Hashanah; Yom Kippur; during the recitation of *Musaf* on the eighth day of Sukkot (for *Tefillat Geshem*); during the recitation of *Musaf* of the eighth day of Passover (for *Tefillat Tal*) and at the seder; and on one's wedding day. The wearing of a *kitel* is primarily an Ashkenazic custom.

Kohen; pl. *Kohanim*

A member of the Jewish priesthood. Priestly status is inherited, as all *Kohanim* are to be descendants of the patriarch Aaron (brother of Moses), who was the first priest and a member of the tribe of Levi. The *Kohanim* performed the sacred rituals during the era of the Temple in Jerusalem.

Lag ba-Omer (literally, "33rd [day] of the Omer")

A spring holiday that falls 33 days from the second day of Passover, during the counting of the Omer. Its origins are obscure; today people celebrate with dancing, singing, bonfires, and picnics. The Hebrew calendar date is the 18th of Iyar. See Omer.

machzor; pl. *machzorim*

A specialized prayer book for holy days and festivals. The most prevalent *machzorim* are for the High Holy Days of Rosh Hashanah and Yom Kippur. *Machzorim* also are published for Sukkot, Passover, and Shavuot.

Maggid (literally, "Telling")

The narrative portion of the haggadah. It retells of the story of the Exodus from Egypt and the first Passover. It begins with the youngest person asking The Four Questions, designed to provoke participation in the evening. It ends with the second cup of wine. *Maggid* is also the term for a popular preacher, especially in Hasidic circles.

Mattan Torah (literally, "Giving of the Torah")

Hebrew expression for the Revelation at Mount Sinai.

megillot (literally, "scrolls")

A term for five books—the *hamesh megillot*—found in Kethuvim (The Writings), the last part of the TANAKH (Bible). Each of the *megillot* is assigned to be read on a different holiday: The Song of Songs on Passover, the Book of Ruth on Shavuot, the Book of Lamentations on Tisha b'Av, the Book of Ecclesiastes on Sukkot, and the Book of Esther on Purim. The singular form of this word is "megillah."

midrash (literally, "elucidation" or "exposition"); pl. **midrashim**
A story about laws, customs, or rituals of Jewish life mentioned in the Torah. Some midrashim are detailed discussions, some are similar to fables, and others are like sermons with a moral. Scholars continued to produce collections of midrashim as late as the 12th century, in places such as Greece, Italy, and France. Even today, works are being created in the midrashic style.

minhag (literally, "custom"); pl. *minhagim*
A custom observed and transmitted by the Jewish people. *Minhagim* often reflect the time and place of the Jews who first kept them. For many people, adherence to Jewish customs is as strictly maintained as adherence to Jewish law (*halakhah*).

mishkan (literally, "place of dwelling")
The Tabernacle, a portable sanctuary built by the ancient Israelites as a dwelling place for the Divine Presence. It was used from the time right after the Exodus until King Solomon constructed the Temple in Jerusalem. Elements of the *mishkan*, the Israelites' center for the performance of rituals and sacrifices, were incorporated into the Temple.

mitzvah (literally, "commandment"); pl. **mitzvot**
One of the religious obligations detailed in the Torah, the majority of which fall into the positive category of religious, ethical, or moral obligations. The Torah also contains negative mitzvot, which are prohibitions.

Mount Sinai
The biblical place at which Moses and the Israelites received the Torah. Its geographical location is an ongoing subject of study and speculation.

Musaf (literally, "Additional")
The additional *Amidah* prayer recited on Shabbat, Rosh Hodesh, and holidays. It represents the additional temple sacrifice that was given on such days.

New Month or **New Moon** See Rosh Hodesh.

Nisan

The seventh month in the Hebrew calendar. Called *Aviv* in the Bible, Nisan corresponds to March–April. The name comes from *nisanu*, meaning "first produce."

Omer (literally, "Sheaf")

A grain offering that was made at the Temple in Jerusalem on the second day of Passover. It signaled the start of the harvest season. Today, in lieu of the offering, Jews "count the Omer" by saying a blessing on each of the 50 days from the second day of Passover until the start of the holiday of Shavuot.

"One Only Kid" (Hebrew, *Chad Gadya*)

A beloved Passover song, disarming in its simplicity, which teaches of the eternal Jewish hope that at the end of days, God will vanquish the angel of death and inaugurate a world of peace. Generations of children have added their voices to this song.

parashah (literally, "portion"); pl. *parshiyot*

The weekly Torah portion, also called *sidrah*. The Torah is divided into 54 of these portions—one section for each week of a leap year on the Hebrew lunar calendar. In non-leap years some of the portions are combined to create double *parshiyot* that compensate for the reduced number of weeks.

Passover

The spring pilgrimage festival commemorating the Israelites' Exodus from Egypt. It is also known as the Feast of Freedom or the Feast of Matzot. The Hebrew name is Pesach. Its Hebrew calendar date is the 15th of Nisan, a day that falls in late March or early April.

Pentecost (literally, "50th")

The Greek term, often used in Christian biblical literature, for the Jewish holiday of Shavuot.

peshat (literally, "simple")

The plain meaning of a text in context as opposed to *derash*, which is the homiletical meaning.

▲　▲　▲　▲　▲　▲　▲　　　▲　▲　▲　▲　▲　▲　▲

Pharisees (in Hebrew, *Perushim*)

A sect of Rabbinic sages during the Second Temple period. Their school of thought developed the practical implications of the Mishhah (the Oral Law), and in so doing, clarified and expanded the laws of the Bible. The Pharisees separated themselves from non-Jews and from Jews who did not follow *halakhah* (Jewish law). They were opposed by a sect called the Sadducees, who did not accept the entire Oral Law. After the destruction of the Temple, the Pharisees were the only sect to remain in existence. Their views became normative for the entire Jewish people.

Pietist

A member of an influential Christian movement that combined the Lutheran emphasis on biblical doctrine with the Calvinist, and especially Puritan, emphasis on individual piety.

Purim (literally, "Lots")

A highly festive holiday that falls in the middle of the Hebrew month of Adar (corresponding to February–March). During Purim, Jews gather to read the entire Megillah (literally, "Scroll") of Esther. In that biblical story, the evil Haman, adviser to the king of Persia, casts "lots" to determine a date for destroying all the Jews. Purim commemorates the Persian Jews' deliverance from this attempted extermination.

Rabbinic era

The time of greatest Rabbinic development, when Rabbinic Judaism evolved to become normative Judaism. The first division of this era was that of the sages. They were called *tannaim*, a word that comes from the Aramaic word for "repeat." In Aramaic (a language written in Hebrew characters), the root for that word is *tav.nun.alef.*, equivalent to the Hebrew root *shin.nun.heh.*, which is also the basis for the word "Mishnah" (the foundational text of the Oral Law). Thus the *tannaim* were "Mishnah teachers" who repeated and passed down the Oral Torah. Most of the *tannaim* lived in the period between the destruction of the Second Temple (70 C.E.) and the Bar Kochba Revolt (135 C.E.). The second division of the Rabbinic era is that of the *amoraim*, a word that comes from the Aramaic for "speaker." The *amoraim* continued to interpret and transmit Jewish law, thought, and practice, as they expanded upon the foundations laid by the *tannaim*. This work occurred at academies in Israel (Tiberias, Caesarea, and Tzippori) and in Babylonia (Nehardea, Pumpeditha, and Sura). The Talmud, which was primarily compiled about 400 C.E. in Israel and about 500 C.E. in Babylonia, provides the fullest expression of the *amoraim.*

responsa
The body of literature comprising responsa—authoritative answers to questions of Jewish law posed to rabbis and religious scholars. Thousands of rulings have been produced and recorded, from ancient through modern times.

Rosh Hashanah (literally, "Head of the Year")
The Jewish New Year. It falls on the first and second days of Tishrei, the seventh Hebrew month (in September or October). Rosh Hashanah always falls on the Rosh Hodesh (new moon) that is closest to the autumnal equinox.

Rosh Hodesh (literally, "Head of the Month")
The new moon and the beginning of each Hebrew month. While it is marked today as a special occasion with distinctive liturgy, in biblical times Rosh Hodesh was celebrated more elaborately, as an outright festival. Before the advent of a fixed calendar, the Israelites depended upon the official declaration of Rosh Hodesh to determine when the holidays would occur.

Sadducees (in Hebrew, *Tzeudukim*)
A Jewish sect that existed during the time of the Second Temple. Its precise character is not clear, but the Sadducees apparently rejected anything not openly written in the Bible, including such ideas as belief in an afterlife and resurrection of the dead. Allied with the wealthy and prominent classes of Jerusalem, the Sadducees had close ties to the foreign rulers of Judea, and they looked with favor upon Greek culture. But the destruction of the Second Temple in 70 C.E. ended the existence of all contemporary Jewish sects and factions except for one—the Sadducees' principal rival, the Pharisees, whose belief system was reestablished as Rabbinic Judaism.

sages
A descriptive term to indicate those rabbis who contributed the greatest insights and developments in Jewish thought and practice. Most occurrences of the term refer to Rabbis of the Rabbinic era, but sometimes the term is used for rabbis from the medieval period (for example, Nachmanides).

Sanhedrin

The highest court of the Land of Israel from mid-2nd century B.C.E. to 425 C.E. At its height, the Sanhedrin did more than make judicial rulings on civil, criminal, and ritual matters; it also functioned to a large extent as a legislature, involved in the major communal issues of the day. The name comes from the Greek term for "Council of Elders" (*Synedrion*).

sefirah (literally, "portion"); pl. *sefirot*

One of the 10 emanations, or varying aspects, of God in the universe. The *sefirot* play a central role throughout kabbalistic doctrine and teachings. Each *sefirah* embodies a divine quality and, according to Kabbalah, the *sefirot* are the underlying forces in the world and in the Torah.

Sefirat Ha-Omer (literally, "The Counting of the Omer")

The seven weeks beginning on the second day of Passover and ending on Shavuot. Each of the 49 days is counted with a special blessing. "The Sefirah" or "the Omer," as the period is more commonly called, is largely a somber time when certain mourning customs are observed.

Sephardim

Jews who trace their ancestry back to Spain before their expulsion in 1492. (*Sepharad* is the Hebrew word for Spain.) Sephardic holiday customs, cuisine, liturgy, and even Hebrew differ in some ways from those of the Ashkenazim, the name of the group of Jews who trace their family history back to France and Germany. (*Ashkenaz* is the Hebrew word for Germany).

Shabbat; pl. *Shabbatot*

The Sabbath, or day of rest. It begins at sunset on Friday night and ends about 25 hours later, after sunset on Saturday night. (The extra hour ensures that the full 24-hour period is observed.)

Shabbat Ha-Gadol (literally, "The Great Sabbath")

The Sabbath immediately preceding Passover. After the Torah portions, a special haftarah (Malachi 3:4–24) is read. Traditionally, rabbis deliver a lengthy discourse about the laws of Passover. In Ashkenazic communities, part of the Passover haggadah is read during the afternoon service.

Shalosh Regalim (literally, "Three Pilgrimages")
A term for the three major festivals of Passover, Shavuot, and Sukkot. On these occasions during biblical times, Jews went on pilgrimages to Jerusalem to make special offerings at the Temple.

Shavuot (literally, "Weeks")
One of the three pilgrimage festivals. Also known as the Feast of Weeks and as the Harvest Festival, it commemorates the giving of the Torah at Mount Sinai and celebrates the first harvest of the fruits and grains of spring. The seven-week period that falls between Shavuot and Passover is called the Omer (short for "The Counting of the Omer" or for *Sefirat Ha-Omer*). The Hebrew calendar date for Shavuot, which usually falls in May or June, is the sixth of Sivan.

Shekhinah (literally, "Dwelling")
One of the names for God, and explicitly the presence of God, commonly described as a light or radiance that illuminates the world. The word *Shekhinah* has the same root as *lishkon*, which is *shin.kaf.nun.*, meaning "to dwell." It is often associated with the *mishkan* and with the Temple in Jerusalem.

Shemini Atzeret
The eighth day of Sukkot, which holds special significance as its own holiday. Jews thank God for the harvest and ask for winter rain to prepare the ground for spring planting.

siddur; pl. *siddurim*
A book that sets forth Hebrew prayers in a very specific order based on times and seasons: time of day, time of week, whether an ordinary day (*yom hol*) or a sacred day (*yom tov*), whether an ordinary season or a festival season, and whether a life-cycle event is taking place. The word siddur comes from the Hebrew root *samekh.dalet.resh.*, meaning "to order." Dozens of different *siddurim* are published, varying by stream of Judaism and by country, yet all share a similar underlying structure. See also *machzor.*

Song of Songs, The
One of the five *megillot* in Kethuvim (The Writings), the third part of the TANAKH (Bible). Traditionally attributed to King Solomon, it is chanted on the Shabbat that occurs during Passover and consists of a series of love poems. The Talmud and medieval Jewish sources interpret The Song of Songs (in Hebrew, *Shir Ha-Shirim*) as

a metaphor for the love between God and the Jewish people. Some modern scholars see it as a collection of love poems for a bride and groom; others consider the book to contain the love drama between a shepherd and a maiden who is also desired by a king. Various Hasidic and kabbalistic practices, such as going to forests and fields for prayers and meditation, are directly related to imagery found in The Song of Songs.

Sukkot (literally, "Booths")

One of the three pilgrimage festivals. Also known as the Feast of Booths or Feast of Tabernacles, it occurs on the 15th of Tishrei in late September or early October. Sukkot marks the fall harvest and commemorates the Exodus from Egypt. The Torah says that the Israelites dwelled in *sukkot* (temporary huts or booths) during their desert journey.

tanna, pl. *tannaim*

A teacher of the Oral Law, in particular one of the sages of the Mishnah. The name is derived from the Aramaic *teni* or *tena* (to teach). The period of the *tannaim*, which lasted about 210 years (10–220 C.E.), is generally divided by Jewish scholars into five or six sections or generations. The purpose of the division is to show which teachers developed their principal activities contemporaneously. The teachings of the *tannaim* were interpreted by the *amoraim*.

Temple

The most holy place of worship and sacrifice in ancient Israel. Located in Jerusalem, it was the successor to the *mishkan* (portable sanctuary). King Solomon built the First Temple in the late 10th century B.C.E., but it was destroyed by the Babylonians in 586 B.C.E. About 50 years later, the Jews began construction of the Second Temple, completed in 515 B.C.E. on the ruins of the First Temple. More than 500 years later, in 70 C.E., it, too, was destroyed, this time by the Roman general Titus, in response to the Jews' unsuccessful "Great Revolt." The Western Wall in Jerusalem is revered today because it is a remnant of the "mount" (or base) of the Second Temple.

teshuvah (literally, "return")

A term referring to the "return to God," often translated as "repentance." It is one of the most significant themes and spiritual components of the High Holy Days.

Tikun Leil Shavuot (literally, "Set Order of Study for the Night of Shavuot")
The Ashkenazic name for the custom of staying up all night to study on Shavuot. *Tikun Leil Shavuot* is also the name of the selection of literature used that night, including biblical, mishnaic, talmudic, and kabbalistic writings. In Sephardic communities, the night is called *Mishmarah* (literally, "Nightwatch") and is celebrated by reading special *piyyutim* (religious poems).

Tisha b'Av (literally, "the Ninth of Av")
A day of mourning and fasting that marks the dates of destruction of both the First and Second Temples.

Tishrei

The seventh Hebrew month on the Hebrew calendar. Called *Ethanim* in the Bible, Tishrei corresponds to September–October. The name comes from *tashritu*, meaning "beginning." Rosh Hashanah, Yom Kippur, and Sukkot all occur in Tishrei.

tithe (Hebrew, *ma'aser*)
During the time of the Temple, the $1/10$ portion of agricultural produce or livestock that Jews were required to set aside for the pilgrimage festivals. The tithe was used for three biblically designated purposes: as a donation to the Levites, as a donation the poor, or as food to be consumed by the farmer and his family once they reached Jerusalem. The tithe was considered proof of trust in God and God's ability to provide sustenance.

Tu b'Av (literally, "the 15th of Av")
A joyous and romantic holiday celebrated during the summer in Israel. In ancient times, it marked the beginning of the wine harvest.

Yom Ha-Atzmaut (literally, "The Day of Independence")
Israel's independence day, which commemorates the founding of the State of Israel on May 14, 1948. Its Hebrew calendar date is the 5th of Iyar, the day after Yom Ha-Zikaron (Day of Remembrance).

Yom Ha-Shoah (literally, "The Day of Calamity or Destruction")
Holocaust remembrance day. The day set aside by the Israeli Knesset for remembering the 6 million Jews murdered by the Nazis. It corresponds to the day in 1943 when the Jews began an uprising in the Warsaw Ghetto. The Hebrew calendar date is the 27th of Nisan, a week after the seventh day of Passover.

Yom Ha-Zikaron (literally, "The Day of Remembrance")
(1) A solemn Israeli holiday that honors the memory of soldiers and others killed defending the State of Israel. Its Hebrew calendar date is the 4th of Iyar, which usually falls in September. (2) One of the alternate names for the holiday of Rosh Hashanah.

Yom Kippur ("Day of Atonement")
The most holy and solemn day of the Jewish calendar, filled with pleas for forgiveness and with acts of self-denial, including fasting. It falls on the 10th day of the Hebrew month of Tishrei, which is usually in late September or early October.

z'man heiruteinu (literally, "the time of our freedom")
An expression often used in the prayer book and other sacred literature when referring to the days of Passover.

z'man mattan Torateinu (literally, "the time of the giving of our Torah")
An expression often used in the prayer book and other sacred literature when referring to Shavuot.

Contributing Authors

Alan Abrams is a teacher and chaplain at Reading Hospital and Medical Center in Reading, Pennsylvania. He was ordained by the Ziegler School of Rabbinic Studies at American Jewish University and holds master's degrees in Talmud from the Jewish Theological Seminary and in public policy from Columbia University.

Bradley Shavit Artson is vice president of American Jewish University and dean of its Ziegler School of Rabbinic Studies. A doctoral candidate in Contemporary Jewish Theology at Hebrew Union College–Jewish Institute of Religion, Rabbi Artson is the author of many articles and several books, including *The Bedside Torah: Wisdom, Dreams, & Vision* and *Gift of Soul, Gift of Wisdom: A Spiritual Resource for Mentoring and Leadership*.

Michael Berenbaum is the director of the Sigi Ziering Center for the Study of the Holocaust and Ethics at American Jewish University, where he is also a professor of Jewish studies. Beginning in 1987, he oversaw the development of the Holocaust Memorial Museum in Washington, D.C., as project director and then served as the first director of its research institute. Later he became president and CEO of The Survivors of the Shoah Visual History Foundation. He was the executive producer, writer, and historian for the documentary *Desperate Hours* about Turkey and the Holocaust, among many other films on which he has worked. He is the executive editor of the *New Encyclopaedia Judaica* and the author of numerous books including *After Tragedy and Triumph: Modern Jewish Thought and the American Experience; The World Must Know: The History of the Holocaust;* and *Not Your Father's Antisemitism*.

Daniel Cotzin Burg holds master's degrees in both rabbinic studies and Jewish education from American Jewish Universtiy and was ordained by its Ziegler School of Rabbinic Studies. He is on the staff of Anshe Emet Synagogue in Chicago.

Arnold M. Eisen is chancellor of the Jewish Theological Seminary. He received his doctorate in the history of Jewish thought from Hebrew University and has taught at Tel Aviv University, Columbia University, and Stanford University. His publications include *Taking Hold of Torah: Jewish Commitment and Community in America; Rethinking Modern Judaism: Ritual, Commandment, Community;* and *The Jew Within: Self, Family and Community in America*, coauthored with sociologist Steven M. Cohen.

Pinchas Giller was ordained by Yeshiva University and received his doctorate in Jewish thought from the Graduate Theological Union at the University of California, Berkeley. He is an associate professor of Jewish thought at the Ziegler School of Rabbinic Studies at American Jewish University and the author of *The Enlightened Will Shine: Symbolism and Theurgy in the Later Strata of the Zohar* and *Reading the Zohar: The Sacred Text of the Kabbalah.*

Philip Goodman was born in New York in 1911 and studied at Yeshiva University and the College of the City of New York. He was ordained in Israel at the yeshiva headed by Chief Rabbi Abraham I. Kook and became a congregational rabbi in New York for nine years. In 1942, he joined the staff of the National Jewish Welfare Board (JWB). During World War II he wrote and co-edited a number of publications for the use of the Jewish members of the armed forces. Upon his retirement from JWB in 1976, the Jewish Book Council granted him a "Special Award for Jewish Anthology," in recognition of his cumulative efforts as the anthologist of eight volumes published by The Jewish Publication Society: seven holiday books and one on marriage (the last co-authored with his wife, Hanna). That same year, Rabbi Goodman and his family settled permanently in Israel, where he became an officer of Israel Endowment Funds, a position he retained until his death in 2006.

Arthur Green is affiliated with Hebrew College in Newton Centre, Massachusetts, where he is the rector of The Rabbinical School and also the Irving Brudnick Professor of Philosophy and Religion. He was ordained by the Jewish Theological Seminary and received his doctorate from Brandeis University, serving there as a professor in the Philip W. Lown School of Near Eastern and Judaic Studies. From 1987 to 1993, Rabbi Green was president and dean of the Reconstructionist Rabbinical College. Among the books he has written are *Seek My Face: A Jewish Mystical Theology; Ehyeh: A Kabbalah for Tomorrow;* and *These Are the Words: A Vocabulary of Jewish Spiritual Life.*

Irving Greenberg is the president of The Steinhardt Foundation for Jewish Life. Previously he served as rabbi of the Riverdale Jewish Center in New York City, as an associate professor of history at Yeshiva University, and as founder and chairman of the department of Jewish studies at City College of the City University of New York. Rabbi Greenberg was the co-founding president in 1974 of the National Center for Learning and Leadership (CLAL).

Reuven Hammer served as president of the International Rabbinical Assembly from 2002 to 2004 and was the first Israeli to be elected to that position. He received his rabbinic ordination and doctorate in theology from the Jewish Theological Seminary and a doctorate in special education from Northwestern University. He is the editor of *The Jerusalem Anthology: A Literary Guide* and the author of *Entering the High Holidays: A Complete Guide to the History, Prayers, and Themes,* winner of the National Jewish Book Award. Both books were published by The Jewish Publication Society.

Alan Lew is rabbi emeritus of Congregation Beth Sholom in San Francisco and the cofounder and current director of the Makor Or Jewish Meditation Center. Rabbi Lew teaches at the Jewish Theological Seminary, where he was ordained, and at the Graduate Theological Union of the University of California, Berkeley. He is the author of *One God Clapping: The Spiritual Path of a Zen Rabbi,* which won the PEN Josephine Miles Award for Literary Excellence; *Be Still and Get Going: A Jewish Meditation Practice for Real Life;* and several books of poetry.

Adam Naftalin-Kelman is the director of Hillel at the University of Colorado, Boulder. After working as a certified public accountant, he pursued and received rabbinical ordination from the Ziegler School of Rabbinic Studies at American Jewish University, where he also served as director of development.

Haviva Ner-David is a religious feminist and scholar living in Israel. An active member of Women of the Wall and Mavoi Satum, she is the author of *Life on the Fringes: A Feminist Journey Toward Traditional Rabbinic Ordination* and has written articles on women's issues and Jewish law.

Mark I. Rosen is a research scientist who teaches in Brandeis University's Hornstein Jewish Professional Leadership Program and is associated with the university's Cohen Center for Modern Jewish Studies. Dr. Rosen received his doctorate in organizational behavior from the University of Wisconsin, Madison, and was formerly a management professor at Bentley College. Dr. Rosen is the author of *Thank You for Being Such a Pain: Spiritual Guidance for Dealing with Difficult People.*

Marc Soloway is the spiritual leader of Congregation Bonai Shalom in Boulder, Colorado. His rabbinical training began in his native London at the Leo Baeck

College, followed by studies at the Conservative Yeshiva in Jerusalem and the Ziegler School of Rabbinic Studies at American Jewish University, from which he received his ordination.

David Wolpe is the rabbi of Sinai Temple in Los Angeles. He was ordained by the Jewish Theological Seminary, where he later taught and where he served as assistant to the chancellor. He has also taught at American Jewish University and at Hunter College. A frequent contributor to magazines and newspapers on Jewish topics and subjects of general religious interest, he is also a frequent guest and commentator on national television. He is the author of several books, including *The Healer of Shattered Hearts: A Jewish View of God*; *Teaching Your Children about God*; *Why Be Jewish?* and *Floating Takes Faith: Ancient Wisdom for a Modern World.*

Index

n

O

p

About the Author and the Editor

Paul Steinberg is a rabbi and educator at Congregation Valley Beth Shalom in Encino, California. He holds master's degrees in both education and rabbinic studies and was ordained by the Ziegler School of Rabbinic Studies at American Jewish University. He is the author of the *Study Guide to Jewish Ethics* (JPS, 2003) and several articles on the Hebrew Bible and on Jewish education. Throughout his career, Rabbi Steinberg has stressed Judaism's emphasis on the transformational power of study, as well as its approach to living a moral life.

Janet Greenstein Potter is a freelance writer and editor based in Philadelphia. Among the JPS publications she has edited are the National Jewish Book Award runner-up *Wise and Not So Wise: 10 Tales from the Rabbis* (2004); *Praise Her Works: Conversations with Biblical Women* (2005); *Zayda Was a Cowboy* (2005); and *Sarah's Journey* (2005). She was the editor and project manager for *The Kids' Catalog of Animals and the Earth* (JPS, 2006), a book about the environment and the Jewish tradition.